International
Fish Dishes

NINA FROUD
and
TAMARA LO

PELHAM BOOKS

First published in Great Britain by
PELHAM BOOKS LTD
52 Bedford Square
London, WC1B 3EF
1974

ISBN 0 7207 0692 0

Set and printed in Great Britain by
Tonbridge Printers Ltd, Peach Hall Works, Tonbridge, Kent
in Baskerville ten on eleven point, on paper supplied by
P. F. Bingham Ltd, and bound by Dorstel Press
Harlow

Also by Nina Froud and Tamara Lo

THE WORLD BOOK OF SWEETS AND DESSERTS
INTERNATIONAL MEAT DISHES

International
Fish Dishes

CONTENTS

To Anne
who loves everything
that comes from the sea

ACKNOWLEDGEMENTS

We owe a debt of gratitude to so many people throughout the world, restaurant chefs, cookery experts and other talented men and women, for sharing their recipes with us, that it would be impossible to list them all.

In particular we want to thank the following: Marina Pereyra de Aznar, Elizabeth Gili for the Spanish recipes from their family collections, Grete Grumme for her Danish herring recipes, Caroline Jury for the splendid gravad lax, Jacqueline Poux for her Jersey ormers recipe, Marianne de Barde for sending us the recipe for Renken, Starnberg Style.

Our thanks as usual to Kathleen Tranmar and Monica Wilkins for their untiring help with the preparation of the manuscript.

Last, but by no means least, we wish to thank Mr J. F. Blagden and his staff, for their unfailing kindness to us not only in supplying us with whatever fish or shell fish we need, but also in providing us with much useful information.

LIST OF ABBREVIATIONS

oz – ounce
lb – pound
gr – grams
kg – kilogram
dcl – decilitre (1/10 litre)
ml – millilitre

MEASUREMENTS

Metric, Imperial and American weights and measures are given in the recipes. These are not always straight conversions, but suitable adjustments.

Amounts of all ingredients have been proportionally scaled up or down, to ensure that the results are in no way impaired. The cups, tablespoons and teaspoons are American Standard.

Oven temperatures are given in all recipes in °C, °F and Gas Marks. Allowances, however, have to be made for variations of settings on different models of cookers and manufacturers' temperature charts should be consulted.

OVEN TEMPERATURES

	Electricity		Gas
	°C	°F	
Cool	107 to 121	225 to 250	0 to ½
Very Slow	121 to 135	250 to 275	½ to 1
Slow	135 to 149	275 to 300	1 to 2
Very Moderate	149 to 177	300 to 350	2 to 3
Moderate	190	375	4
Moderately Hot	204	400	5
Hot	218 to 233	425 to 450	6 to 7
Very Hot	246 to 260	475 to 500	8 to 9

Introduction

All sea and fresh water fish, crustaceans and molluscs can easily be made into delicious and attractive dishes. We hope that our readers will find this collection of recipes interesting, varied and tempting enough to make fish feature more frequently on their family and party menus. Fish, in addition to being delicious to eat, is an excellent food rich in phosphorous and vitamins. For body building, its protein content is every bit as good as meat.

FRESH FISH

All white fish (cod, haddock, whiting) is easily digested and doctors often recommend it for invalids and children. Its flesh has low fat content and this makes it important in slimming diets. The fat in white fish is mainly concentrated in the liver.

In oily fish, such as herring, mackerel and salmon, the fat is in the flesh. They are richer in vitamins A and D and have much more flavour than white fish.

The price and availability of various kinds of fish are subject to many influences, not least the weather. There is no way of guaranteeing what catch the fishermen may bring back. Their being successful or unlucky results in overabundance or scarcity of some types of fish. It is best therefore not to start out with a rigid shopping list, but to see what is available, looks good and suits your taste and pocket.

We are lucky to have an excellent fishmonger who is always willing to give honest advice on the 'best buy' of the day. You may be surprised that at times it is the cheaper varieties of fish which are recommended.

CHOOSING FISH

Make sure the fish you buy is absolutely fresh. Reject a fish which

9

looks flabby, has dull eyes or pale gills. The flesh should be firm, the eyes bright, the skin should have a gloss and there must be no smell of staleness.

FROZEN FISH

This is available in many forms, including kippers in butter sauce, fillets coated with egg and breadcrumbs and ready for cooking, and of course the fish fingers of which all children seem to be fond. There are also cod and haddock fillets, salmon steaks and whole trout.

Fish, if it is deep-frozen as soon as it is landed and if it is correctly handled, preserves its freshness until used. With frozen fish there is no waste, no scaling and cleaning, and the cooking smells are not nearly so strong as with fish from the slab.

The general rules about choosing frozen foods are most important when buying frozen fish. Never take a damaged packet or one that is not absolutely rock-hard. Check manufacturers' instructions about storing frozen fish in the freezing compartment. Make sure your freezing compartment is not too full—there must be space in it for the cold air to circulate.

Follow directions for thawing and cooking. Frozen fish can be cooked unthawed, but it has to be cooked at a lower temperature and longer than fresh fish. Allow frozen prawns and other shellfish to thaw thoroughly before using, otherwise they'll taste like pencil rubbers.

GENERAL NOTES ON THE COOKING OF FISH

Always try to cook the fish the day you buy it. Although carefully wrapped it will keep in a refrigerator for a day or so, its flavour will inevitably deteriorate with its loss of freshness.

To scale fish, scrape on both sides with the back of a knife, holding the fish by the tail and scraping towards the head. Put under cold running water to rinse off scales.

To clean round fish, slit the belly, remove entrails, rub off any black tissues with a litle salt and rinse in cold water.

To clean flat fish, cut off fins, remove gills, slit the belly on the underside, remove entrails and rinse. Among the flat fish the back and belly are represented by the flattened sides and the eyes are both on the same, coloured side. Flat fish is classified into right- and left-sided species, depending on whether the eyes are on the right or the left of the head. Plaice and most species of sole are right-sided, brill and turbot are left-sided.

To skin fish, wet it, and starting at the tail cut the skin to loosen, press with the right thumb to hold flesh down and gently pull off the skin with the left hand—or the other way around, if you are left-handed!

To fillet flat fish, cut the flesh from head to tail down the backbone, insert the knife in the slit and lift the flesh from the bone. Turn the fish around, and proceed in the same way to lift the fillet from the other side. Turn the fish over and cut off the rest of the fillets, obtaining two fillets from each side.

To fillet round fish, which only gives one fillet on each side, slit down the centre back to the bone, starting at the head cut along the belly, press the knife against the bones and slice the fillet off in a clean movement. Repeat the same for the other side.

You can ask your fishmonger to clean, skin and fillet the fish for you. But, whether you do it yourself or have it done for you, always keep the bones, skin and trimmings for making court-bouillon in which to cook the fish and for incorporating in the sauce.

Fish is too often ruined by overcooking. Cooking time is indicated in the recipes, but you can test whether it is done. If a light pressure on the thickest part of the fish shows that the flesh comes away from the bones, it is ready.

For boiling or poaching, the type of liquid required is indicated in all recipes and instruction for various court-bouillons are given in the book. Whether you are using court-bouillon or salt water, simmer the fish gently, with the water barely shivering. Don't use too much liquid, keep the fish just covered——this is to preserve both the soluble nutrients and the flavour.

For frying, make sure the fish is dry—that is why recipes stipulate that fish should be wiped with a cloth after washing.

For deep frying, make sure your fat is hot and do not lower the temperature too drastically, by putting in too many pieces at one time. If you use a basket, put it in the deep fat pan and drop the fish into it, using the basket to lift the cooked fish. This is particularly important if the fish is coated with batter or breadcrumbs, as all such dressings tend to stick to the bottom of the frying basket.

To grill fish, dry thoroughly, brush with melted butter or oil (in the case of whole fish, score the surface to facilitate penetration of heat) put on a greased, heated grill and cook as indicated in recipes.

Instructions for steaming, stewing and baking fish are given in the recipes.

USE OF INDEX

Whenever standard ingredients are mentioned—such as mayonnaise, sauces, fumets etc.—please check in the index for the page reference of the actual recipe.

Basic Preparations:

COURT-BOUILLON

Court-bouillon is an aromatised liquid for cooking fish and shellfish.

SALT WATER COURT-BOUILLON

Allow 1½ teaspoons salt to 1 litre (1 quart or 4 cups) of water. Use for poaching various fish: cod, perch, whitefish, haddock, salmon, etc. To preserve whiteness of fish, add 1 tablespoon vinegar (or lemon juice) per litre (quart) of water. For lobster and other crustaceans court-bouillon is generally made of salt water, as above, flavoured with thyme and a bay leaf, though sometimes thinly sliced onions, carrots, parsley and peppercorns are added.

COURT-BOUILLON AU BLEU

For river trout, carp, pike. This is made of salt water (see above) with the addition of vinegar, carrots, and onions, parsley, thyme, bay leaf and peppercorns. For another variation, see the recipe for Mackerel, Flemish style. See also Truite au Bleu.

WHITE WINE COURT-BOUILLON Á LA MIREPOIX

Mirepoix is a mixture of diced, sliced or shredded vegetables, cooked in butter or other fat and added to soups sauces, etc. This court-bouillon is used for poaching or braising fish.

2½ dcl (½ pint or 1 cup) finely sliced mixed vegetables: carrot, leek, onion, celery
1½ tablespoons butter
small sprig thyme
crushed fragment bay leaf
2½ dcl (½ pint or 1 cup) dry white wine
2½ dcl (½ pint or 1 cup) fish stock or fumet (p 14)

Cook the vegetables gently on very low heat in butter until soft. Do not allow to brown. Transfer to small saucepan, add thyme, bayleaf and wine. Bring to the boil, then simmer to reduce by half.

Add good strong fish stock, simmer for 6–7 minutes and use as required.

RED WINE COURT-BOUILLON À LA MIREPOIX

Follow recipe for White Wine Court-Bouillon à la Mirepoix, using red wine instead of white.

FISH STOCK

1 kg (2 lb) bones, head and trimmings of various fish (whiting, sole, haddock, plaice, etc.)
1 chopped onion
60 gr (2 oz or ¼ cup) mushroom parings (stalks etc.)

2 sprigs parsley
1 sprig thyme
¼ bay leaf
½ teaspoon lemon juice
pinch salt
½ litre (1 pint or 2 cups) water
2 dcl (⅓ pint or 1 cup) dry white wine

Put onion, mushroom parings, parsley, thyme and bay leaf in a stock pot. Cover with fish bones and trimmings, add lemon juice, season with salt, moisten with wine and water, bring to the boil, skim, then simmer gently for 30 minutes. Strain through a muslin bag.

For fish stock made with red wine, use equal amounts of wine and water.

FISH FUMET

Fumet is concentrated fish stock, used for enriching and giving body to sauces. To make fumet, boil down strained fish stock to reduce and give it a thicker consistency.

SIMPLE FISH STOCK

To make 1 litre (1 quart) stock:

1–2 fish heads
fish bones and trimmings
1 chopped onion
1 sliced carrot

pinch salt
bouquet garni
1½ litre (1½ quarts or 6 cups) water

Put all ingredients in a pan, cover with water, bring to the boil. Reduce heat, cover, simmer for 30 minutes and strain.

DASHI

The Japanese use dashi as the basis for stocks, soups, sauces and dressings. It is very easy to make and the ingredients are available in shops specialising in Oriental produce. The two vital ingredients are konbu seaweed and katsuobushi (bonito fillets) cut into shavings. In an emergency a light strained fish stock may be used.

7½ gr (¼ oz or 3 teaspoons) konbu seaweed	35 gr (1¼ oz or 5 tablespoons) katsuobushi shavings
1 litre (1 quart or 4 cups) water	¼ teaspoon Aji-no-Moto (monosodium glutamate)

Put konbu seaweed in a pan with water, heat and remove from heat as soon as boiling is established. Add katsuobushi, reheat, and remove from heat at first sign of boiling. Season with Aji-no-Moto, allow to stand for 10 minutes, strain and use as required.

ASPIC JELLY FOR FISH

1 litre (2 pints or 4 cups) fish stock	2 egg whites and shells
	1 glass sherry
25 gr (1 oz or 2 tablespoons) gelatine	4 tablespoons vinegar

Cool and strain the fish stock. If it was cooked with a bouquet garni and vinegar or lemon juice, it will not need any further spicing. If you have only cooked fish heads, bones, skin and trimmings in salted water, then cool and skim all fat off the stock, use a little of it to dilute the gelatine and put stock, gelatine, bouquet garni (sprig of thyme, parsley and a bay leaf) and a stick of celery into a saucepan.

Beat the whites, wash the egg shells and add both to the fish stock to clarify it. Start heating, whisking all the time. As soon as boiling is established, add sherry (and vinegar or lemon juice, if the stock was not acidulated during original cooking).

Simmer for 10 minutes, strain and use as directed in individual recipes.

QUICK ASPIC JELLY

½ litre (1 pint or 2 cups) fish stock	½ bay leaf
1 teaspoon chopped tarragon	30 gr (1 oz or ¼ cup) gelatine
2–3 sprigs parsley	3 tablespoons sherry (or Madeira)
juice of 1 lemon	salt
10 peppercorns	1 egg white and shell
1 chopped shallot (or ½ onion)	

15

Boil the stock with tarragon, parsley, lemon juice, peppercorns, shallot and bay leaf for 10 minutes. Dissolve the gelatine in 2 tablespoons of cold water and add to the stock. Simmer for 5 minutes, add sherry and salt to taste, and strain. To clarify the jelly, bring the stock to the boil. Beat the egg white and crush the shell and add both to the stock. Simmer for 5 minutes, strain once again and use as directed.

TOMATO ASPIC

15 gr ($\frac{1}{2}$ oz or 1 tablespoon) gelatine

2 tablespoons water

2$\frac{1}{2}$ dcl ($\frac{1}{2}$ pint or 1 cup) tomato pulp

120 ml (4 oz or $\frac{1}{4}$ cup) fish stock (or water)

salt

cayenne pepper

Soak gelatine in water, put it into a saucepan with tomato pulp and stock. Season with salt and a pinch of cayenne pepper, heat, stirring until the first sign of boiling, remove and strain through a cloth.

Cold Hors-d'oeuvre

ENGLISH POTTED SHRIMPS

8–10 Servings

1 kilo (1 quart) fresh shrimps
125 gr (4 oz or ½ cup) fresh
  butter
¼ teaspoon mace

¼ teaspoon nutmeg
½ teaspoon salt
¼ teaspoon cayene pepper
clarified butter

Boil the shrimps, shell and de-vein. Melt butter in a saucepan, season with mace, nutmeg, salt and cayenne pepper, stir. Add shrimps, simmer on very low heat for 15 minutes. Remove from heat, decant into small pots, pour over enough clarified butter to cover shrimps and leave to cool. When cold, cover with a circle of waxed paper and top with a metal or cardboard cap, or a piece of cellophane secured with a rubber band. Keep in a refrigerator.

POTTED SALMON

8–10 Servings

1 kg (2 lb) salmon
white wine court-bouillon

500 gr (1 lb) clarified butter

Clean, wash and dry the salmon and poach in court-bouillon for 15 minutes. Allow to cool, remove skin and bones and slice the fish. Put in an ovenproof dish, baste with plenty of butter, cover and bake in the oven for 15 minutes 205°C (400°F or Gas Mark 5).

Remove from oven, allow to cool completely. Decant into jars, pour in the rest of the clarified butter so that the fish is completely covered with it. Seal and store in a refrigerator.

Salmon potted in this way is delicious and will keep for 2 weeks. Serve with a salad.

POTTED TROUT

Follow recipe for Potted Salmon (p. 17).

AVOCADO WITH PRAWN OR CRAYFISH MOUSSE

6 Servings

3 ripe avocado pears
lemon juice
6 tablespoons peeled, cooked
  prawns or crayfish tails

6 tablespoons cream
4 tablespoons mayonnaise
salt and cayenne pepper

Cut the avocados in half, remove stone, sprinkle with lemon juice to prevent discoloration. Combine prawns or crayfish with cream and mayonnaise in a blender. Season with salt. Switch on and blend until smooth. Taste for seasoning, add a dash of lemon juice, blend for another 20 seconds.

Pile the cream on the avocado pears, sprinkle with cayenne pepper.

KIPPER MOUSSE

8 Servings

2¼ dcl (½ pint or 1 cup) liquid
  aspic
a few stuffed olives
500 gr (1 lb) smoked kippers
2¼ dcl (½ pint or 1 cup) milk
a pinch of mixed herbs
30 gr (1 oz or 2 tablespoons)
  butter

30 gr (1 oz or 4 tablespoons)
  flour
1 beaten egg
125 ml (¼ pint or ½ cup) cream
lemon juice
freshly ground black pepper

Line individual moulds or one large mould with cold liquid aspic jelly. Decorate the bottom with slices of olives, secure with a little more of the aspic jelly. Leave the moulds in the refrigerator until ready to use.

Cook the kippers in the milk with a pinch of mixed herbs for 5 minutes. Strain off the milk and keep for sauce. Remove any skin and bones from the fish and flake finely. Make a white sauce with butter and flour and the milk in which the fish was cooked. Cool, add remaining aspic, fish, beaten egg, cream, lemon juice and pepper.

Fill the moulds with this mixture and leave to set. Turn out before serving.

AVOCADO MOUSSE WITH PRAWNS

8–10 Servings

This is a most rewarding party dish since it is easy to make, can be made well in advance—except for the final filling and decorating—looks beautiful on a buffet table and makes a delicious first course. The quantities given are calculated for up to 10 servings and you need a 1½–litre 3–pint or 6–cups) ring mould. You can also use any leftover cooked fish, shellfish, as filling.

1 tablespoon unflavoured gelatine	120 ml (4 oz or ½ cup) sour cream
4 tablespoons cold water	salt and pepper
240 ml (½ pint or 1 cup) boiling water	½ litre (1 pint or 2 cups) tomato aspic
1 teaspoon castor sugar	250 gr (½ lb) peeled prawns
1–2 avocado pears	1 tablespoon sherry
1 tablespoon lime or lemon juice	120 ml (4 oz or ½ cup) double cream
120 ml (4 oz or ½ cup) mayonnaise	120 ml (4 oz or ½ cup) tomato pink mayonnaise

Mix gelatine with cold water, add boiling water, stir to dissolve completely, add sugar and leave until it sets to a syrupy consistency.

Mash the avocado pears (reserving half a pear for final garnishing), sprinkle with lime juice to prevent discoloration, blend in mayonnaise and sour cream, season to taste, stir in half set jelly, mix well, pour into a rinsed mould and chill. When the avocado aspic is set, pour over it the next layer which is tomato aspic, with a few prawns stirred into it. Chill until set. Sprinkle prawns with sherry, dress with a mixture of cream and tomato mayonnaise.

Unmould on to a chilled serving dish, fill the middle with the prawns in their pink mayonnaise, garnish with thin slices of avocado and serve.

ASPARAGUS WITH SHRIMPS

4 Servings

1 small bundle green asparagus	2½ dcl (½ pint or 1 cup) mayonnaise
250 gr (½ pint or 1½ cups) peeled shrimps	4 hard-boiled eggs seasoning

Snap off tough lower ends of asparagus, scrape, wash in running water, tie into bundles. Cook in salted water until just tender, drain carefully and cool. Cut into bite-sized chunks. Arrange with shrimps in a serving dish, mix with mayonnaise, garnish with quartered, hard-boiled eggs and serve.

TARAMASALATA

This Mediterranean cod roe pâté is delicious. Serve it with hot Arab bread.

4 Servings

120 gr (4 oz) pressed salt cod roe
2 slices white bread
1 tablespoon grated onion
1 clove crushed garlic (optional)

180 ml (6 oz or ¾ cup) olive oil
juice of 1 lemon
1 tablespoon finely chopped parsley
black olives for garnish

Soak the roe in cold water for a few minutes to remove excess salt. Cut crusts off bread slices and soak bread in water. Squeeze out surplus water from roe and bread and put together into a mortar. Pound into a paste. Add onion and garlic and continue to pound until the paste is smooth, or pass the mixture through a blender. Gradually, as for mayonnaise, stir in alternately little amounts of oil and lemon juice. Stir until the pâté is smooth, light and well blended.

Spoon into an hors-d'oeuvre dish, sprinkle with parsley, garnish with olives and serve.

KIPPERS WITH EGG AND ONION MAYONNAISE IN HOT PITA

6 Servings

2–3 hard-boiled eggs
1½ tablespoons finely chopped onion
1 teaspoon finely chopped chives or spring onions

salt and freshly ground black pepper
mayonnaise
1–2 pita loaves
2 plump smoked kippers, boned
butter

Chop the hard-boiled eggs, combine with onion and chives, season with salt and pepper and add enough mayonnaise to bind the mixture. Put pita to heat in the oven. Slice the kippers as thinly as smoked salmon, and serve with pita and egg and onion mayonnaise.

Each diner can butter his or her piece of hot pita, put a generous helping of egg and onion mayonnaise on or in it, top with a slice of kipper and eat until all is gone.

STUFFED EGGS

Cut hard-boiled eggs in half. Take out the yolks and mix with whatever you like to use as stuffing. Or cut off a little at both ends of the eggs to give them stability, carefully remove yolks and stuff the eggs to taste. Various salads and salpicons can be used as stuffings for eggs. Decorate the stuffed eggs, glaze over with jelly, arrange on a dish, garnish with parsley.

Suggestions for filling for stuffed eggs :

Skinned, boned and mashed sardines, or tunny in oil, pounded with a little butter, seasoned with salt, pepper, grating of nutmeg and a dash of lemon juice.

Crabmeat, peeled prawns or shrimps, dressed with mayonnaise or another suitable sauce.

Anchovies, blended with some béchamel or thick béchamel sauce flavoured with anchovy essence and sprinkled with grated cheese.

Smoked salmon, added to the yolks mixed with equal amount of butter and garnished with small sprigs of parsley. Or, for super special occasions—caviar, with a few drops of lemon juice.

PRAWN PÂTÉ

4–5 Servings

500 gr (1 lb) prawns
court bouillon
3 tablespoons lemon juice
grated rind of 1 lemon

3 sprigs fresh dill (or parsley)
pepper and salt
4–5 tablespoons olive oil
clarified butter

Poach prawns in court-bouillon until they turn bright pink. Shell, de-vein and put them through a mincer. Blend in lemon juice, lemon rind, dill and pepper and salt to taste. Beat in gradually enough olive oil to obtain a smooth paste, and continue beating the mixture until it is creamy.

Pack the pâté into small jars, cover with clarified butter and seal. Chill and serve with hot toast.

ANCHOVY ROLLS À LA NICOISE

Dress de-salted anchovy fillets with tarragon butter and roll up. Remove pulp from tomatoes (the smallest you can find), and put in anchovy rolls. If you happen to have any small amount of cooked fish, blend it with a little mayonnaise and use it as a foundation for the anchovies. Sprinkle with chopped parsley and a trickle of olive oil.

ANCHOVY SALAD NORMANDY

Marinate anchovy fillets, as described in recipe for Anchovies, Greek Style (p. 22). Drain, cut slantwise into small strips, mix with a thin ring of beetroot cut into minute dice and sprinkled with olive oil. There is a Russian variation for similarly diced anchovies, apples and potatoes, dressed with oil, and garnished with chopped chives and grated horseradish.

ANCHOVIES, GREEK STYLE

Arrange anchovies in a terrine, sprinkle with chopped thyme, a tiny pinch of crushed bay leaf and a few peppercorns. Cover with boiling fish court-bouillon and leave to marinate for 24 hours. Put anchovies in a small serving dish, spoon over a little of the marinade, decorate with slices of peeled lemon, and sprinkle with fresh chopped fennel.

LOBSTER COCKTAIL

4 Servings

1 crisp lettuce heart
2 small cooked lobsters
1 large tomato
125 ml (4 oz or ¼ cup) mayonnaise
2–3 tablespoons cream or coconut milk
salt
lemon
2 tablespoons whipped cream
cayenne pepper

Wash and shake out the lettuce until absolutely dry. Tear into small pieces and arrange in glass goblets. Slice the lobster meat. Peel the tomato, and rub through a sieve or purée in a blender. Mix with mayonnaise and cream or coconut milk. Season, put in lobster slices, fold in whipped cream. Mix well and spoon the lobster on to the lettuce foundation. Add a tiny pinch of cayenne pepper, garnish with lobster claws, decorate with a wedge of lemon and chill before serving.

PRAWN COCKTAIL

Follow recipe of Lobster Cocktail above, allowing 60 gr (2 oz) shelled prawns per person.

CALIFORNIAN PRAWN COCKTAIL IN GRAPEFRUIT CUPS

4 Servings

2 grapefruit
250 gr (8 oz) cooked prawns
4 tablespoons shredded lettuce
2 tablespoons peeled diced cucumber
2 tablespoons shredded celery mayonnaise

Cut the grapefruit in half, remove segments, discarding seeds and membranes. Keep the grapefruit shells. Leave 4 prawns for

22

decoration, peel the rest. Put a portion of lettuce in each grape-fruit shell. Mix prawns, grapefruit segments, cucumber, celery and mayonnaise.

Spoon into grapefruit cups, decorate with whole prawns and serve cold.

SMELTS IN MARINADE

4 Servings

12 Smelts
flour
oil for frying
salt and pepper
2 sliced onions

pinch thyme
1 crumbled bay leaf
12 peppercorns
2–3 cloves
vinegar

Clean and dry the smelts carefully. Dip in flour and fry quickly in boiling oil to brown on both sides. Drain the smelts, season, arrange in a deep dish. Scald the onion with boiling water and drain. Put rounds of blanched onion on smelts, sprinkle with thyme and bay leaf, add a few peppercorns and cloves. Cover with cold vinegar and leave for 12 hours in this marinade.

SHRIMPS COOKED IN BEER, WITH DILL

4 Servings

500 gr (1 lb or 3 cups) peeled
  shrimps
beer

125 ml (4 oz or ½ cup)
  mayonnaise
1 tablespoon chopped dill
crisp, shell-shaped lettuce leaves

Cook shrimps in enough boiling beer to cover, until they turn pink. Cool in the beer, drain and chop coarsely. Dress shrimps with mayonnaise, sprinkle with dill and chill. Serve in lettuce 'cups'.

JELLIED EELS

6 Servings

1½ kg (3 lb) eels cut in 5 cm
  (2 inch) pieces
water

1½ teaspoons salt
1 bay leaf
juice of 1 lemon

Wash the eels, put into a saucepan, cover with water, add salt, bay leaf and lemon juice, bring to the boil, skim the surface, reduce the heat and simmer for 45 minutes. Remove from heat, turn out into a deep serving dish or into small individual bowls and leave in a cool place to set.

23

GREEN PEPPERS STUFFED WITH HADDOCK AND ANCHOVIES

8 Servings

250 gr (8 oz or 1 cup) flaked, cooked smoked haddock

125 gr (4 oz or ½ cup) minced anchovies

360 gr (12 oz or 1½ cups) peeled, seeded and chopped tomatoes

16 stoned black olives

4 cloves garlic

4 tablespoons dry breadcrumbs

4 tablespoons olive oil

4 green peppers

3 tablespoons butter

In a bowl, mix haddock, anchovies and tomatoes. Finely chop or mince olives and garlic together and add to haddock. Add breadcrumbs and olive oil. Mix well.

Quarter peppers lengthwise and remove seeds and any inner membranes. Fill resulting 'boats' with haddock mixture and place on a buttered baking tray. Dot with remaining butter and bake for 30 minutes at 190°C (375°F or Gas Mark 4).

Place stuffed peppers on a serving dish and allow to cool. Serve cold.

SALTED HERRINGS

This is the most popular cold hors-d'oeuvre in many parts of Europe, but it is important to get the right type of herring. It is definitely not pickled or marinated, but salted herring which is recommended. Most good delicatessen shops keep it.

If the herring is unfilleted, soak it in strained cold tea or milk for 5 to 6 hours before use. Then rinse, remove skin and bones. Cut in thin slices diagonally. Arrange on a dish in the shape of a herring. Garnish and dress with alternate rows of sliced hard-boiled eggs, potato, fresh or pickled cucumber, and thin onion rings. The garnishes must be arranged neatly and decoratively. Or surround with pickled mushrooms and sprinkle with chopped onion and parsley.

When the garnishing is complete prepare one of the following dressings and pour over the herring :

(1) Mix 2 tablespoons of olive oil with 1 tablespoon of capers and a little chopped onion.

(2) 2 or 3 tablespoons vinegar mixed with a little salt and pepper, 1 teaspoon of sugar and 2 tablespoons olive oil.

(3) Blend an egg yolk with 1 teaspoon of made mustard, 1 teaspoon sugar, 1 tablespoon oil, 1½ tablespoons vinegar or lemon juice, a little salt to taste. Mix well.

All the above dressings are much improved by the addition of a spoonful of sour cream.

PICKLED HERRINGS

3–4 Servings

1–2 filleted pickled herrings
1 slice white bread
cold milk
1 teaspoon French mustard
1 teaspoon wine vinegar

1 tablespoon freshly grated
  horseradish
1 teaspoon sugar
125 ml (¼ pint or ½ cup) cream

Soak the fillets in cold water for several hours. Cut the crusts off the bread, soak it in milk, squeeze out, mix with the mustard, vinegar, horseradish and sugar. Whip cream lightly, add to mixture, pour over the herrings.

SPICY SALT HERRING IN WHITE WINE

4 Servings

2 salt herrings
strained cold tea
thin slices of onion and lemon
pinch crushed rosemary
½ bay leaf, crushed

freshly ground pepper
125 ml (4 oz or ½ cup) dry
  white wine
3 tablespoons olive oil

Split the herrings, remove the bones and let the herrings and their roes steep in cold tea for 12 hours. Clean the fillets, cut into narrow strips and place in a bowl, alternating with slices of hard and soft roes, onion and lemon. Sprinkle with rosemary, bay leaf and pepper. Shake wine and oil together to mix thoroughly, pour over the herring and leave for a couple of hours to allow the herring to be permeated by the wine.

HERRINGS WITH SOFT ROE SAUCE

Skin the fillets, soak, trim, slice, arrange attractively, and cover with soft roe sauce (p. 211).

SHERRY HERRING

3–4 Servings

1–2 pickled herrings
watercress
1 tablespoon dry sherry

½ teaspoon rose paprika
1 small onion

Drain the herrings, cut into bite-size pieces and arrange on a mound of watercress. Sprinkle with sherry and paprika and garnish with thin onion rings.

HERRING WITH MUSTARD SAUCE

2–4 Servings

2 plump filleted salt herrings
milk
1 small sliced leek
1 small sliced carrot
1 stalk celery, shredded
1 tablespoon French mustard
2 teaspoons sugar

½ teaspoon salt
1 tablespoon vinegar
1 tablespoon oil
125 ml (4 oz or ½ cup) double cream

Soak the herring fillets in milk (or strained, strong tea) over-night. Drain, cut into pieces, put in a dish and cover with leek, carrot and celery. Mix mustard with sugar, salt, vinegar and oil. Whip in the cream, pour the sauce over the fillets, and allow to stand 2–3 hours before serving.

SALT HERRING WITH CREAM CHEESE AND CHIVES

3–4 Servings

2 filleted salt herrings
milk
pepper
dried dill
chopped onion
2 tablespoons sugar
125 ml (4 oz or ½ cup) vinegar

2 grated cooking apples
90 gr (3 oz or 6 tablespoons) cream cheese
125 ml (4 oz or ½ cup) cream
1 tablespoon lemon juice
1 tablespoon chopped chives

Soak the herring fillets in milk overnight. Remove from milk and rinse. Grate the pepper coarsely, mix with dill, onion, sugar and vinegar. Pour this mixture over the herrings, and leave for 5–6 hours. Drain the fillets and put in a dish on a foundation of coarsely grated apples.

Blend cream cheese, cream and lemon juice, pour this dressing over the herrings and sprinkle with chives.

ROLLMOPS

Use marinated and strongly spiced fillets of herring. Stuff with a gherkin, roll up and secure with a cocktail stick. Serve in an hors-d'oeuvre dish decorated with thin onion rings.

CHOPPED HERRING, JEWISH STYLE

4 Servings

2 salt herrings, soaked in water
    for 2 hours
1 slice crustless white bread
2 tablespoons vinegar
1 tablespoon finely chopped
    onion

1 large grated apple
pinch freshly grated black pepper
2 tablespoons oil
small pinch sugar (optional)
6 lettuce shells
2 hard-boiled chopped eggs

Rinse herring, bone and chop. Soak bread in vinegar, mash with a fork and mix with herring. Add onion, apple, pepper, oil and sugar. Mix well. arrange on lettuce shells, sprinkle with chopped egg and serve cold.

SASHIMI (RAW FISH)

This is a great Japanese speciality, one which is considered an exquisite delicacy yet one which has probably inspired more prejudice than any other dish. People who swallow raw oysters, cockles and mussels with relish, are reluctant to experiment with raw fish. In the majority of cases, they are afraid of its 'fishy' smell or taste. Once they overcome this reluctance and try sashimi, they'll be agreeably surprised to discover that it has neither. The taste is delicate and the only definable quality in the smell is its supreme freshness.

Sashimi consists mainly of slices of raw fish, lobster, crayfish, cuttlefish, etc., but chicken can also be used. To render it more easily digestible, and for added flavour, it is usually served with grated horseradish (wasabi) and soya sauce.

The most suitable varieties of fish to serve as sashimi are salmon, sea bream, tunny, cuttlefish—all crustaceans—lobster, prawns, crayfish, shrimps. The first essential is absolute freshness.

To prepare : Scale the fish, remove head, tail and fins, clean out and discard entrails. Wash thoroughly and leave to soak in cold water. Bone the fish and skin the fillets. Cut the fillets with a very sharp knife, at an angle of 30°, into slices $3\frac{3}{4}$ cm ($1\frac{1}{2}$ in.) wide and $1\frac{1}{4}$ cm ($\frac{1}{2}$ in.) thick. Alternatively, firm fleshed fish can be cut into $2\frac{1}{2}$ cm (1 in.) dice. Thin fleshed fish is normally shaved off in the thinnest possible slanting or uniform slices.

SALMON OR SEA BREAM SASHIMI

4 Servings

250 gr (8 oz) salmon or sea
    bream
1 bunch watercress

2 teaspoons grated horseradish
4 tablespoons shoyu

Prepare and slice the fish as described in the introduction note. Arrange on a dish in the shape of a salmon or bream. Decorate with watercress. Mix horseradish with shoyu and serve separately. This is used for a dip for the sashimi slices.

SMOKED SALMON

Smoked salmon, ideally, should be freshly cut, from a nice thick, juicy-looking side. If served as an independent first course, allow 60 gr (2 oz) per portion and keep wrapped in a cool place (not the refrigerator) until ready to serve.

We like it not too thinly cut, served straight on the plate—without any lettuce bedding—garnished with crisp bouquets of parsley and lemon wedges, with a pepper-mill filled with good black peppercorns and a plate of thin brown bread and butter beside it.

SMOKED SALMON IN CUCUMBER CANOES

Choose small ridge cucumbers. Peel, cut in half lengthwise, scoop out the pulp, dice it and toss in French dressing. Cut the salmon into thin strips, mix with diced cucumber, pile into cucumber canoes, garnish with watercress and serve.

SMOKED SALMON WITH CAVIAR À LA RUSSE

For a really extravagant gala occasion manipulate a small slice of smoked salmon into a cornucopia and fill with a tiny spoonful of caviar.

SMOKED SALMON WITH POTTED SHRIMPS

A few narrow ribbons of smoked salmon, twisted into a curl, and served on crisp lettuce leaves, with a spoonful of potted shrimps (p. 17) makes a delightful mixture.

SMOKED SALMON WITH EGG AND HORSERADISH CREAM

Roll each slice of smoked salmon into a cone, fill with horseradish cream, put a quarter of a hard-boiled egg into each cone and serve on really crisp lettuce leaves.

I first met this combination in Denmark, but it is quite popular throughout Scandinavia.

SMOKED SALMON BOSTON STYLE

4 Servings

125 gr (4 oz) smoked salmon
125 gr (4 oz or ½ cup) cooked
  mushrooms
1 peeled green pepper
1 peeled red pepper

mayonnaise
Tabasco sauce
2 hard-boiled eggs
parsley

Cut smoked salmon into very thin short strips. Add mushrooms and peppers, cut to match. Season with mayonnaise mixed with a few drops of Tabasco sauce. Arrange on an hors-d'oeuvre dish, surround with the chopped yolks and whites of hard-boiled eggs and sprigs of parsley. Sprinkle with chopped parsley and serve.

HAWAIIAN SCALLOPS IN LIME JUICE

4 Servings

500 gr (1 lb) scallops
1 thinly sliced onion
1 tablespoon white vinegar
salt and freshly grated pepper

cayenne pepper
125 ml (4 oz or ½ cup) fresh
  lime juice

Wash the scallops, dry, leave whole. Put in a dish, cover with onion, sprinkle with vinegar. Season to taste with salt, pepper and cayenne pepper. Add lime juice, toss the scallops well. Chill for 7–8 hours. Serve with hot toast.

If fresh lime juice is not available, use lemon juice. On no account use bottled lime juice.

SMOKED EEL

Skin the eel and cut the flesh into long thin strips. Arrange on serving plates, garnish with lemon wedges and serve with brown bread and butter, or freshly made toast and horseradish and walnut sauce (p. 208).

ANCHOVIES

Whatever use is made of anchovies it is advisable to de-salt them. Just rinse in cold water, dry, then cut and treat as required. To serve plain, arrange anchovy fillets in a pleasing pattern in an hors-d'oeuvre dish, cover with olive oil and leave until needed. If tinned anchovies are used, take them out of the tin, arrange on lettuce leaves or in an individual dish.

They can be garnished with chopped parsley, chives, cayenne pepper, hard-boiled egg, etc., so long as the essential flavour of the anchovies is not smothered.

Allow three or four fillets per portion.

ANCHOVIES WITH HARD-BOILED EGGS

Cut the anchovy fillets into small dice, season with oil, lemon juice, salt and pepper. Garnish with separately chopped yolks and whites of egg, sprinkle with capers and chives or chopped parsley. Anchovies can be laid on a foundation of lettuce and garnished with olives, slices of beetroot, spring onions, slices of lemon, strips of red or green pepper, and the thinnest of onion rings.

CAVIAR

Caviar—the roe of the sturgeon—is the queen of hors-d'oeuvre. As the quantities which one can afford are rather minute, it is just as well to make the best of its presentation. Whether pressed or soft, caviar should be served cold, garnished with parsley and lemon cut in sections. Serve butter separately.

There are people who maintain that the only way to eat caviar is with a spoon, and a distinguished slimming conscious Russian Poet started a fashion in Moscow of eating caviar on cucumber slices.

Traditionally, blini are considered the best foundation for serving caviar.

RED CAVIAR

This is best served on thin slices of rye bread. Serve butter and finely chopped spring onions separately.

AVOCADO WITH PRAWN COCKTAIL

4 Servings

2 avocado pears	4 tablespoons French dressing
250 gr ($\frac{1}{2}$ pint or $1\frac{1}{2}$ cups) shelled prawns	lettuce
	lemon

Halve the pears and remove stone. If necessary enlarge the cavity slightly. Toss the prawns in French dressing, pile into avocado pears. Arrange on crisp lettuce leaves, garnish with lemon wedges, chill and serve.

HALIBUT, PACIFIC ISLANDS

The treatment here is akin to the Japanese sashimi (p. 27), but the lime juice and rum dressing make a delightful variation.

4 Servings

500 gr (1 lb) halibut	1 teaspoon salt
2½ dcl (½ pint or 1 cup) boiling water	juice of 3 limes
	1 teaspoon white rum

Wash the halibut, cut into uniform bite-size pieces and put in a dish. Dilute salt in water, pour over the fish and leave for one hour. Drain, rinse and drain thoroughly again.

Arrange in a serving dish, pour lime juice over the halibut, sprinkle with rum and serve with salad.

TUNNY IN OIL

Arrange tinned tunny on an hors-d'oeuvre dish, dress with oil and garnish with capers or fresh parsley.

TUNNY À LA NANTAISE

Cut tunny in oil into slices, cover with a thin coating of horse-radish butter, sandwich two by two and arrange in a circle on a dish, alternating with rounds of cooked beetroot. Garnish the centre of the plate with a salad of mussels and potatoes. Sprinkle with chives and chopped tarragon.

SPRATS

Take the heads and tails off the fish and skin them. Arrange on a plate and sprinkle with chopped shallots and parsley, moisten with oil and vinegar, leave in this marinade for several hours before serving. Arrange on a horse-d'oeuvre dish and garnish with fresh parsley.

SMOKED TROUT

Buy smoked trout the day you wish to serve it and make sure it is soft to the touch. Remove head, skin and bones and arrange fillets on a serving dish. Sprinkle with lemon juice. Serve with horseradish and walnut sauce. Hand thin brown bread and butter separately.

SARDINES IN OIL

Arrange on an hors-d'oeuvre dish, dress with oil, garnish with capers and fresh parsley.

PARSLEYED SARDINES

Arrange sardines on individual chilled plates. Chop one large bunch parsley finely and mix with 3 tablespoons finely chopped shallots and 2 tablespoons French dressing (p. 207). Sprinkle each serving thickly with the parsley mixture and serve very cold.

SARDINES IN LEMONS, LISBON STYLE

4 Servings

4 good sized lemons	2 hard-boiled eggs
large tin Portuguese sardines	1 teaspoon chopped parsley
4 tablespoons oil and lemon	salt and pepper
dressing	bunch watercress

Wash the lemons, cut off ends to give them stability, cut in half, squeeze out the juice. Remove all pith and discard. Lift the sardines out of the tin, drain well, remove tails and bones and mash them. Season with salt and pepper, sprinkle with oil and lemon dressing.

Shell the eggs, chop the whites and sieve the yolks separately. Add the whites and parsley to the sardine purée and stuff the lemon cups with the mixture. Sprinkle the tops with sieved yolk. Arrange on a dish, garnish with little bunches of watercress and serve.

This treatment can also be applied to any leftovers of cooked fish, which can be flaked, bound with a little mayonnaise and put in lemon cups.

Hot Hors-d'oeuvre

WHITEBAIT

6 Servings

1¼–1½ kg (2½–3 lb) whitebait	salt
deep fat for frying	cayenne pepper
flour	lemon

Keep the whitebait on ice until ready to cook. Heat fat to correct temperature. (See note on Deep Frying.) Dry the whitebait on a cloth, dredge lightly with flour. Put a small portion of whitebait in a wire basket, shake off surplus flour and plunge into hot fat for 3–4 minutes, shaking the basket frequently.

Lift the basket, shake to drain off fat, turn whitebait on to absorbent kitchen paper and keep warm. Continue to fry the rest of the fish. Season with fine dry salt and cayenne pepper and serve with lemon cut into wedges.

WHITEBAIT ANTIBOISE

6 Servings

4–8 tablespoons (1–1¼ lb) whitebait	1 crushed clove garlic
butter	4–8 eggs
1–1½ tablespoons Gruyère cheese	salt and pepper
	chopped parsley

Taking a tablespoon of whitebait at a time, roll in flour and fry in butter in a sauté pan. Cut cheese into very small dice and add to whitebait together with garlic. Break eggs into the same pan. Season to taste and bake in the oven until the eggs set. Sprinkle with parsley and serve.

WHITEBAIT, ILMEN STYLE

6 Servings

1¼–1½ kg (2½–3 lb) whitebait
salt
½ teaspoon pepper
4 tablespoons flour
2 tablespoons olive oil
2½ dcl (½ pint or ½ cup) sour cream

2 beaten egg whites
fat for deep frying
parsley
lemon
salted cucumbers
pickled beetroot salad

Wash and gently pat the whitebait dry, sprinkle with salt and pepper. Mix flour with oil, add a pinch of salt, stir in sour cream, and egg whites and blend well. Dip whitebait into this batter one by one, and plunge into deep fat for about a minute. The fat should be as hot as possible and only a few of the fish at a time should be fried to prevent their sticking together. As soon as they are crisp, drain, arrange in a heap on a napkin-covered dish.

Decorate with sprigs of parsley and wedges of lemon, and serve with salted cucumbers and pickled beetroot salad.

CROQUE POISSON (sort of French fish rarebit)

4 Servings

500 gr (1 lb) fresh or frozen cod (haddock, etc. or four cod steaks)
30 gr (1 oz or 2 tablespoons) melted butter
4 rashers of streaky bacon

60 gr (2 oz or 4 tablespoons) grated cheese (whatever you want to use up)
4 slices white bread
2 teaspoons Dijon mustard

If using frozen fish, follow instructions on the packet for thawing. (See p. 10).

Brush fish with melted butter and grill for 4 minutes. Turn and repeat on the other side. During the latter 4 minutes, lightly grill the bacon on both sides, and drain on kitchen paper. Cover fish with grated cheese and while that is melting and going bubbly, toast the bread. Spread the toast with mustard. Place a portion of fish on each slice of toast, top with bacon and pop under the grill for a final 30 seconds.

COD'S ROE IN SCALLOP SHELLS

4 Servings

500–625 gr (1–1¼ lb) cod's roe
salted water
vinegar
butter

4 scallop shells
2½ dcl (½ pint or 1 cup) Mornay sauce
toasted breadcrumbs

34

Poach the cod's roe for 10 minutes in enough salted water to cover, with a little vinegar added to it. Drain and cut into uniform small pieces. Butter 4 scallop shells, distribute the roes among them, coat with hot Mornay sauce, sprinkle with breadcrumbs, dot with a few small pieces of butter, put under the grill to brown the top and serve.

MUSHROOM STUFFED WITH SNAILS

4–6 Servings

2 dozen large mushrooms
2 tablespoons butter
1 teaspoon chopped parsley
1 teaspoon chopped shallots
salt and pepper
cayenne pepper

olive oil
2 dozen prepared (or tinned) snails (p. 177)
breadcrumbs
lemon
watercress

Chop the mushroom stems finely. Melt butter, add the stems, parsley, shallots, salt, pepper and cayenne to taste, and sauté for 1 minute. Dip the mushroom caps in olive oil seasoned with salt and pepper to taste, and grill until tender.

Spread the stem mixture in the cups, imbed a snail in each, sprinkle with breadcrumbs, dot with escargot butter (p. 201) and grill until the top is browned.

Serve on a heated dish, garnished with lemon wedges and watercress.

MUSHROOMS STUFFED WITH PRAWNS

4 Servings

8 large field mushrooms
125 gr (4 oz or ¾ cup) peeled prawns
1 tablespoon butter
4 tablespoons fresh minced pork
1 tablespoon finely chopped celery

¼ teaspoon ginger
salt and pepper
2 tablespoons oil
1 teaspoon soya sauce

Remove stems from mushrooms and wipe caps. Chop prawns. coarsely, toss in butter to warm through, then mix with pork, celery and ginger, season with salt and pepper to taste and fill mushrooms with mixture. Heat oil in pan, put in mushrooms carefully, stuffed side up, sprinkle with soya sauce, cover and simmer for 10 minutes.

FRESH SALMON WITH OKRA (LADIES' FINGERS), CANADIAN STYLE

4 Servings

500 gr (1 lb) fresh salmon
2 tablespoons oil
salt and paprika pepper
500 gr (1 lb) cooked okra
  (ladies' fingers or bindi)

120 gr (4 oz) white wine
2 tablespoons lemon juice
1 diced red sweet pepper
1 diced green sweet pepper

Cut fresh salmon into square pieces and sauté in oil. Season with salt and paprika. Add poached okra pods (ladies' fingers), moisten with white wine and lemon juice. Cover with a lid and simmer for a few seconds. Leave to cool. Arrange in an hors-d'oeuvre dish. Garnish with peeled, diced red and green peppers and sprinkle with olive oil.

Canapé Hors-d'oeuvre

DANISH HERRING AND SALMON CANAPÉS

Slice a dark rye loaf, spread with horseradish butter, garnish with thin strips of smoked salmon, alternating with fillets of herring. Separate each piece of fish with a little fresh caviar and surround with a border of chopped chives.

CANAPÉS NANTAISE

Slice sandwich bread thinly and trim the slices into long oval shapes, spread with sardine butter. Garnish with skinned, boned fillets of sardines in oil; finish off with sardine butter to make the canapés look like fish.

SMOKED EEL CANAPÉS

Slice a sandwich loaf, spread with mustard butter or with horseradish butter. Garnish with thin slices of smoked eel and surround with yolk of hard-boiled eggs and chives, chopped separately.

PRAWN OR SHRIMP CANAPÉS

Cut a sandwich loaf into round slices, spread with prawn or shrimp butter, and garnish with prawn or shrimp tails arranged in a rosette. Surround with a border of prawn or shrimp butter or with chopped parsley.

LOBSTER CANAPÉS

Follow the recipe for prawn canapés, substituting lobster butter and lobster for prawn butter and prawns.

HOLLANDAISE CANAPÉ (SOFT HERRING ROE AND HERRING FILLETS)

Slice a sandwich loaf. Spread the slices with a purée of soft herring roes, garnish with fillets of herring arranged in a criss-cross pattern. Fill each opening with chopped yolks of hard-boiled eggs and surround with a border of chopped parsley.

HERRING AND HORSERADISH BUTTER CANAPÉ

Slice a dark rye leaf, spread the slices with horseradish butter. Garnish with slivers of herring fillets, alternating with thin ribbons of good tart apples. Brush lightly with oil and surround with a border of chopped chives.

CAVIAR BUTTER CANAPÉ

Cut a sandwich loaf, brown loaf, or unsweetened brioche into round slices. Spread with caviar butter or with fresh butter. Surround with a border of caviar butter. Garnish the centre with fresh caviar, and sprinkle with a pinch of chives.

AURORA CANAPÉS

Use a round-shaped unsweetened brioche loaf. Spread with butter, garnish with a thin slice of smoked salmon, put a round of beetroot in the middle, sprinkle with a pinch of minced yolk of hard-boiled egg and surround with a piped border of butter.

ANCHOVY CANAPÉS

Use long slices of bread with the crusts cut off. Spread lightly with maître d'hôtel butter. Cut anchovy fillets into small pieces and arrange on bread slices. Make demarcation lines between pieces of anchovy, using yolks and whites of hard-boiled eggs, chopped separately, and chopped parsley. Decorate with small bouquets of curly parsley.

Pastry Hors-d'oeuvre

ANCHOVY STRAWS

Roll out puff pastry to a thickness of $\frac{1}{2}$ cm ($\frac{1}{8}$th in.) and cut into pieces about 7–8 cm (3 in.) wide. Spread with chopped anchovy and hard-boiled egg blended with anchovy butter. Garnish with a de-salted anchovy fillet. Bake in the oven pre-heated to 220°C (425°F or gas Mark 6) for 20 minutes.

CREAMED HADDOCK STRAWS

Spread with creamed haddock, seasoned to taste, blended with Béchamel sauce. Prepare as above.

NORWEGIAN STRAWS

Spread the straws with chopped hard-boiled eggs bound with a little béchamel sauce. Bake, allow to cool and garnish with a Norwegian anchovy fillet (kilki).

DUTCH EEL STRAWS

Bake the straws, spread with a little anchovy butter, top with a thin slice of smoked eel, seasoned with a little lemon juice and cut to fit the straw.

STRAWS MUSCOVITE

Prepare pastry as described, cover with a thin layer of fish forcemeat, cool and cover with black or red caviar before serving.

DARTOIS

Dartois are similar to straws, except that their garnish is sandwiched between two ribbons of puff pastry, and they are cut after cooking.

Roll out the puff pastry as for straws, cut into strips and put on a moistened baking tray. Spread the middle of the strip of pastry with the garnish of your choice, leaving 1¼ cm (½ in.) clear on each side, and making sure the garnish is cold. Cover with another strip of pastry of the same size but slightly thicker than the foundation. Moisten the edges with water and press down the top strip gently but firmly. Make a few light cuts along the edges, brush with egg and score the surface lightly.

Bake in a hot over 220°C (425°F or Gas Mark 6) for 20–25 minutes. Cut into rectangles about 2½ cm (1 in.) long.

All preparations and forcemeats given in the recipes for straws can be used for dartois.

ANCHOVY DARTOIS

Garnish with fish forcemeat. Decorate with de-salted anchovy fillets; cover with a layer of puff pastry, and finish off as described.

SARDINE DARTOIS

Made like anchovy dartois, using well-trimmed fillets of sardines in oil.

TUNNY DARTOIS

Made like sardine dartois, using thin slices of tunny in oil.

SALMON QUICHE

4 Servings

pastry case (p. 41)
60 gr (2 oz) bread
360 gr (12 oz or 1½ cups)
   cooked or tinned salmon

2 eggs
2½ dcl (½ pint or 1 cup) warm
   milk
salt and pepper

Prepare the pastry case and bake 'blind' as described in recipe for buckling or kipper flan (p. 41). Grate the bread or put it through a blender to make fine crumbs. Spread breadcrumbs on a sheet and bake in the oven until crisp. Break up fish into pieces —do not mash. Put fish and breadcrumbs into pastry case. Put eggs and milk into blender, blend to mix milk. Pour into pastry case and bake until set.

Serve hot or cold.

MUSSEL AND SHRIMP FLAN À LA NORMANDE

4 Servings

1 flan case baked 'blind'
1 litre (1 qt) mussels poached
  in court-bouillon
Normandy sauce
8 oysters

4 eggs
salt and pepper
4 tablespoons peeled shrimps or
  prawns
croutons fried in butter

Bake the pastry case as described below.

Poach the mussels, discard shells. Dress mussels with sauce and put into flan case. Keep warm. Poach oysters in their own juice, de-beard.

Break the eggs, season, scramble lightly and pile on top of mussels. Cover with shrimps, spoon over some sauce. Garnish the top with oysters, pour the remainder of sauce around them.

Surround with crôutons and serve.

BUCKLING OR KIPPER FLAN

4 Servings

125 gr (4 oz or 1 cup) flour
salt
120 gr (4 oz or 8 tablespoons)
  butter or vegetable margarine
iced water
2–3 skinned, boned bucklings
120 gr (4 oz or 2/3 cup) stoned
  black olives

1 small chopped onion,
  softened in butter or vegetable
  margarine
2 beaten eggs
pepper
milk (or water)
few tablespoons dried beans
  (or rice)

Mix flour with a pinch of salt, cut in butter with a knife and add enough iced water to blend the pastry, sprinkling the water in a tablespoon at a time, anl blending it in evenly. Roll out the pastry, line a 20 cm (8 in.) flan tin, press down gently, to make it fit and prevent formation of bubbles underneath, and crimp edges. Prick the bottom of the flan all over with a fork, cover with a circle of greaseproof paper, cut to fit the bottom, and fill with dried beans or rice.

Bake in a hot over 204°C (400°F or Gas Mark 5) for about 30 minutes or until the flan case becomes lightly browned. Remove beans which can be used again for a similar operation. Discard paper. This is called baking a case 'blind'.

Flake the bucklings, put in the flan case with olives and onion. Season the eggs, add a little milk (or water)—bearing in mind that this mixture is to form the custard over the bucklings; it should come up to the rim of the flan case but not spill over. Bake in the oven 190°C (375°F. or Gas Mark 4) until the flan sets.

Serve hot or cold. Excellent with a green salad.

SARDINE VOL-AU-VENT

This is a splendid standby for buffet meals and has the advantage of being good served hot or cold. The important rules to remember are: for cold vol-au-vent both the pastry case and the filling must be cold before the filling is put in. If they are to be served hot, heat them separately and fill just before serving.

Instead of making one large vol-au-vent you can make small bouchées, prepared in exactly the same way but much smaller in size. Cut out circles of required size, put on damp baking sheet, mark out top with a smaller pastry cutter and proceed as above. The fillings can also be presented in little puff pastry cornets. (p. 44).

4 Servings

puff pastry
1 beaten egg
1 tin sardines
1 tablespoon tomato sauce

salt and pepper
dash lemon juice
1 tablespoon grated cheese

Roll out puff pastry to a thickness of 2 cm (¾ in.). To make a perfect round shape, put a dish on top of the pastry and trace out the shape with the point of a knife. Cut out, leaving the edges clean, without dragging the pastry. Place on a wet baking sheet, mark the inner ring and cut down to about half the thickness of the pastry. Brush the marked top with beaten egg. Mark slanting cuts outwards from the inner ring, to facilitate lifting the baked 'lid' put in a very hot oven 246°–260°C (475°–500°F or Gas Mark 8–9) for 10 minutes, then reduce heat to 205°C (400°F or Gas Mark 5).

When baked, remove inner ring, carefully scoop out the soft inside, return to oven for a moment to seal the scooped out surface and your case is ready.

Drain the sardines, remove tails and bones, then mash and mix with tomato sauce. Season, add lemon juice and grated cheese, blend well and fill the vol-au-vent case, when required.

Variations:
Vol-au-vent with flaked fish or lobster in lobster sauce.
Vol-au-vent with anchovy twists and scrambled eggs.

Vol-au-vent with mussels and prawns in white wine sauce.

Vol-au-Vent with crayfish in velouté sauce flavoured with anchovy essence.

Vol-au-vent with poached oysters in Normandy sauce.

BUGEY PRAWN TURNOVERS

Bugey has the reputation of having the best cuisine in France. Brillat-Savarin was born in Belley, one time chef lieu of the department, famous in the annals of gastronomy. These prawn turnovers, also called chaussons à la Nantua, are often served as a hot hors-d'oeuvre or lunch dish on Sundays.

12–15 turnovers

puff pastry	Nantua sauce
4 dozen prawns	prawn butter
white wine court-bouillon with	beaten egg
vegetables (p. 13)	butter

Prepare puff pastry paste and leave in refrigerator. Cook the prawns in court-bouillon, drain and shell. Leave to cool. Make Nantua sauce, incorporating the liquid in which the prawns were cooked, and leave to cool. Stir in prawn butter.

Roll out the pastry. Cut into rectangular pieces $\frac{3}{4}$ cm ($\frac{1}{4}$ in.) thick, 10 cm (4 in.) long and $6\frac{1}{2}$ cm ($2\frac{1}{2}$ in.) wide. Put several prawns (3 or 4, depending on size) and a tablespoon of sauce on one end of the pieces of pastry. Turn them over to enclose the filling. Press the edges to seal. Brush with egg, put on lightly buttered baking sheets and bake in a moderately hot oven 205°C 400°F or Gas Mark 5) for 15 minutes.

If there is any sauce left over, heat it gently and serve with the turnovers, for your guests to pour a spoonful inside each chausson.

NANTUA EGG TARTLETS

3–6 Servings

6 tartlet cases baked blind	6 lightly poached eggs
6 tablespoons cooked peeled	Nantua sauce
prawns	

Divide the prawns between the 6 tartlet cases. Put a poached egg into each, cover with Nantua sauce.

CAVIAR AND OYSTER TARTLETS

Prepare little boat-shaped tartlets (called barquettes). Fill each with a spoonful of fresh caviar, press it gently in the centre to make a foundation for the freshest de-bearded oyster and serve.

Serve small wedges of lime (or lemon) separately.

CAVIAR BARQUETTES

Garnish the barquettes with caviar cream, decorate the top with a design traced out in little pearly caviar grains.

SMOKED SALMON BARQUETTES

Fill the barquettes with smoked salmon cream and top with a tiny slice of smoked salmon.

SMOKED SALMON WITH SPINACH BARQUETTES

Smoked salmon cut in thin slices, garnished with small barquettes filled with creamed spinach.

CAVIAR ECLAIRS

Using choux paste, (p. 216) bake very small eclairs, leave until quite cold, fill with caviar cream, brush with a little cold melted aspic to give them an attractive gloss, and serve iced.

SMOKED SALMON ECLAIRS

Follow the recipe for caviar eclairs (above), fill with a purée of smoked salmon and butter, glaze with a brushing of aspic, and serve chilled.

DUCHESSES

Make choux paste. Pipe it in the shape of little balls on to a baking sheet, using a plain, round nozzle 1¼ cm (½ in.) in diameter. Place these about 8 cm (3 in.) apart. Brush with beaten egg, bake in a moderately hot oven 205°C (400°F or Gas Mark 5) for 15 minutes, then reduce heat to 150°C (300°F or Gas Mark 2) and bake until the walls of the little puffs are rigid. Remove from heat and leave until quite cold.

Then slit along one side and pipe or spoon in desired filling.

PUFF PASTRY CORNETS

Cornet-shaped moulds are available only in shops specialising in kitchen equipment. We have, on occasions when our kitchen did not rise to such gadgets, used carrots !

Prepare the puff pastry as described (p. 216). Roll out to a thickness of 3–4 cm ($\frac{1}{8}$ in.) Cut into strips about 2$\frac{1}{2}$ cm (1 in.) wide and 25 cm (10 in.) long. Roll these strips around cornet-shaped moulds. Put the cornets on a moistened baking sheet, brush with egg and bake in a hot oven for 12–15 minutes.

Leave to cool, then fill with the desired filling and serve.

ANCHOVY BOUCHÉES

Bake small patty cases of puff pastry. Spread anchovy fillets with a mixture of anchovy and tarragon butters. Fill patties two-thirds with flaked tunny fish blended with mayonnaise. Top each one with an anchovy roll. Blend a mashed, hard-boiled egg yolk with butter and pipe a dollop of this mixture over the truffle.

Arrange on a dish, garnish with fresh parsley and serve.

Fish Soups

BOUILLABAISSE

Bouillabaisse, properly made, is one of the most exquisite fish soups in existence. But, alas, as authentic reproduction is impossible outside the Mediterranean area, because one vital ingredient, rascasse—an otherwise dull fish, which by some chemical magic lends to the bouillabaisse its characteristic mouthwatering flavour —is not found anywhere else.

Bouillabaisse as a party dish should have as many varieties of fish and crustaceans (not molluscs) as possible. It provides a substantial meal—the soup and the fish being served together.

Obviously a dish of such excellent virtues could not go unsung in a country justly conscious of her gastronomical achievements. Among many other French writers and poets, Méry esteemed it worthy of taking time off from his satirical writing to dedicate an ode to its glory, and has left us a record of the essential ingredients for a succulent bouillabaisse, 'a real Marseilles ragoût, and not a lying dish'. Of rascasse, he says :

> 'Tis true, a very common fish.
> But in a bouillabaisse it does exude
> A marvellous aroma.

8–10 Servings

250 gr (½ lb) turbot
250 gr (½ lb) rock salmon
250 gr (½ lb) conger eel
2 dozen Dublin Bay prawns
250 gr (½ lb) whiting
250 gr (½ lb) bass
250–375 grs (½–¾ lb) red mullet
4 pounded cloves garlic
2 chopped onions
shredded white of 2 leeks
250 gr (½ lb or 1 cup) peeled, sliced tomatoes

pinch thyme
½ bay leaf
2 tablespoons roughly chopped parsley
1 tablespoon chopped fennel
a piece of orange peel
1 dcl (4 oz or ½ cup) olive oil
boiling water
salt and pepper
½ teaspoon saffron
6–8 slices of bread

46

Clean the fish, bone and cut into uniform pieces; halve the prawns lengthwise. Put garlic, onions, leeks, tomatoes, thyme, bay leaf, 1 tablespoon parsley, fennel, and orange peel into a saucepan. Place the firm-fleshed fish (turbot, rock salmon, eel) and the prawns on top of this vegetable foundation. Pour oil over the whole.

From this moment, for a successful bouillabaisse, timing is vital. Do not proceed further if you are not going to be ready to serve it within a quarter of an hour. If you are ready to go on, heat to boiling point, pour over enough boiling water just to cover the ingredients and boil very fast for 7 minutes, adding salt, pepper and saffron. Add the rest of the fish—the more delicate whiting, bass and mullet (which would disintegrate if put in to cook earlier), and continue to boil very fast for another 7 minutes.

Put a piece of bread, home-made, if possible (not toast) into each deep soup plate, or into a soup tureen, pour the liquid on it and serve at once. Arrange the fish and the prawns on a separate platter, sprinkle with chopped parsley and serve at the same time.

SALMON AND CHAMPAGNE UKHA

Ukha is a Russian fish soup. This is a particularly luxurious recipe for special occasions. Any dry white wine may be substituted for champagne. Ukha served with fish coulibiac (p. 136) makes a splendid main course.

4 Servings

1 litre (1 quart of 4 cups) stock	$\frac{1}{2}$ kg (1 lb) salmon, cut into
2 eggs whites	portions
1 tablespoon chopped tarragon and chervil	1$\frac{1}{2}$ tablespoons chopped dill or spring onions
salt and pepper	$\frac{1}{2}$ bottle champagne
	1 peeled thinly sliced lemon

Slightly warm the stock, preferably good court-bouillon for fish strengthened with fumet, or a light chicken stock. The stock should be barely tepid.

Put egg whites in a pan, add tarragon and chervil and whisk to mix. Pour on stock and bring to the boil, whisking all the time. As soon as boiling is established, turn down heat and simmer very gently for 30 minutes. Season to taste. Strain through napkin rinsed out in water and thoroughly wrung out.

Twenty minutes before serving, bring stock to the boil, put in salmon portions and poach on simmering heat for 15 minutes. Carefully take out the fish, put in a heated soup tureen, sprinkle with chopped dill or spring onions and keep warm.

47

In a separate saucepan, heat champagne to boiling point and add to soup. Pour soup over salmon and serve at once. Put one lemon slice in each plate.

HOT AND SOUR SOUP WITH FISH, PEKIN STYLE

6 Servings

6 dried Chinese mushrooms
1 fish, 1½–1¾ kg (3–3½ lb)
   (mullet, bream or sea trout)
1¼ litre (2½ pints or 5 cups)
   water
salt

6 peppercorns
1¼ dcl (¼ pint or ½ cup)
   vinegar
1 onion, sliced
2 cloves garlic
2–3 dried chillis
1 tablespoon soya sauce

Soak the mushrooms in enough lukewarm water to cover, for 20 minutes. Drain and remove stalks.

Scale, clean and wash the fish, but leave head and tail on. Put it in a pan or fish kettle, with water, salt, peppercorns, vinegar and onion. Bring to the boil, skim, reduce heat and simmer for 15 minutes.

Crush garlic with chillis, dilute with soya sauce, blend well and add to fish soup. Add mushroom caps, simmer for 5 minutes.

Take care not to overcook or break the fish. Place it whole on a heated serving dish. Serve soup and fish at the same time in separate bowls.

ZUPPA DI PESCE (ITALIAN FISH SOUP)

8 Servings

2½–3 kgs (5–6 lbs) mixed fish
   (cod, haddock, mullet, eel,
   carp, mackerel, whiting)
2–3 small squid
100 ml (3½ oz or 7 tablespoons)
   olive oil
30 gr (1 oz or 2 tablespoons)
   butter
2 medium-sized, thinly sliced
   onions

1–2 crushed cloves garlic
1 kg (2 lb or 6 cups) peeled,
   chopped tomatoes
2–3 tablespoons chopped
   parsley
1 tablespoon tomato paste
boiling water, fish stock and/or
   180 ml (6 oz or ¾ cup) dry
   white wine
2 tablespoons vinegar
salt and pepper

A good Italian fish soup requires a variety of fish, it is best to plan it therefore for 8–10 people.

Wash and cut the fish into portions. Use heads and trimmings to make fish stock and strain. It will not be very strong, but will certainly have more body and flavour than plain water.

While the fish stock is cooking, prepare the sauce which makes the foundation of the zuppa di pesce. Heat oil and butter in a big saucepan. Fry onion until it becomes soft. Add garlic, cook together for 2–3 minutes. Add tomatoes and parsley and simmer for 5 minutes, stirring from time to time. Dilute tomato paste with a cupful of the fish stock and pour into saucepan. Simmer uncovered for 2 minutes.

Put in fish, add remaining fish stock. You must have enough liquid to cover the fish. If there is not enough fish stock, make up with boiling water. Bring to the boil, add wine and vinegar, simmer gently for 15 minutes. Season with salt and freshly ground pepper.

RUSSIAN WHITEBAIT SOUP

6 Servings

480 gr (1 lb) whitebait
1½ litres quarts) vegetable
  court-bouillon
90 gr (3 oz or ½ cup)
  buckwheat (kasha)

1½ tablespoons butter
salt and pepper
1 tablespoon lemon juice
120 ml (4 oz or ½ cup) cream

Wash the whitebait and remove heads if you object to them. Drain, sprinkle with one teaspoon of salt, and leave in a colander for 30 minutes.

Strain court-bouillon, bring to the boil and add buckwheat. Add butter, stir and simmer until buckwheat is soft. Put in whitebait, boil, remove scum off the top, simmer for one minute, add lemon juice, season to taste with salt and freshly ground pepper and remove from heat. Add cream and serve.

PALAMOS SOUP

6 Servings

300 gr (10 oz) monk-fish
300 gr (10 oz) hake
1¾ litres (1¾ quarts) water
1 sliced onion
2 teaspoons salt
240 gr (1 lb) tomatoes

60 gr (2 oz or 6 tablespoons)
  potato flour
3 raw egg yolks
2 tablespoons milk
60 gr (2 oz or 4 tablespoons)
  butter

Wash the fish but do not cut. Put in a pan with water, onion and salt. Bring to the boil. Drop in tomatoes and let them cook until soft. Remove tomatoes with a perforated spoon, then rub through a sieve into the pan with the fish soup. Cook for 30 minutes. Remove fish and strain soup.

In a clean saucepan, mix potato flour with a cupful of cooked fish stock. Gradually add the rest of the fish stock, stirring. Mash hake, add to soup and simmer for 15 minutes, stirring frequently. Dice the monk-fish.

Dilute yolks with milk in a soup tureen. Blend in butter, adding it in small pieces. Put in diced monk-fish. Pour in hot soup, stir and serve.

PORTUGUESE FISH SOUP

This is one of those substantial soups to be served as a main course.

6 Servings

1 medium-sized onion
2–3 tablespoons olive oil
375 gr (12 oz) cod or haddock
1½ litres (3 pints or 6 cups) water
180 gr (6 oz or ¼ cup) peeled prawns
3 tablespoons chopped parsley
salt and pepper
1 teaspoon chopped basil
3 hard-boiled eggs
6 slices toast
2 tablespoons roasted slivered almonds

Chop the onion finely and fry lightly in oil, using a saucepan large enough to take all ingredients. Cut fish into portions and lay on top of onions. Add water, prawns and parsley. Bring to the boil, season to taste and add basil. Cover and simmer for 8–10 minutes.

Chop the hard-boiled eggs. Put some hard-boiled egg and a slice of toasted bread in each plate, pour soup over them, sprinkle with almonds and serve piping hot.

ST. LAWRENCE RIVER FISH CHOWDER

From—*River Guide at the Thousand Islands*, 1904.

Place in a deep kettle (an old-fashioned one is best) one layer each of salt pork, sliced potatoes, fish (whatever one happens to have cooked; any river fish is suitable), pilot crackers, and sliced onions. Season with red and black pepper, juice of one lemon, and salt to taste. Pour in milk enough to cover it all: then add a tablespoon of butter, and cook very slowly.

SPANISH LENT SOUP

6 Servings

2 carrots
2 leeks
3 tomatoes
2 sprigs parsley
butter
several heads of hake (or pieces of any other fish)
2 litres (2 quarts) water
½ litre (1 pint or 2 cups) mussels
1 tablespoon oil
6 tablespoons rice
3 fillets of sole (or plaice)
salt and pepper

Clean, peel and slice the carrots, the leeks and the tomatoes and chop the parsley, fry lightly in 2 tablespoons of butter in a saucepan. Add the heads of hake and all other fish except the sole. Brown very lightly and add water. Cook for 90 minutes, strain. Wash the mussels. Heat oil, drop the mussels in, loosen and discard the mussel shells and add to the soup.

Wash the rice in several waters and put in the soup. Cook for 15 minutes. Wash the sole fillets, cut them in half longways and add to the soup. Season well. Simmer for 10 minutes and serve.

FRENCH MUSSEL SOUP
4 Servings

2 litres (2 quarts) mussels
120 ml (4 oz or ½ cup) dry
   white wine
2 teaspoons chopped parsley
salt
small bouquet garni
butter
2 finely chopped onions
1 crushed clove garlic

½ litre (1 pint or 2 cups)
   boiling water
120 ml (4 oz or ½ cup)
   scalded milk
pepper and salt
8 slices French bread
2 raw yolks
120 ml (4 oz or ½ cup) cream
juice of 1 lemon

Scrape and wash mussels thoroughly. Put in a pan with white wine, parsley, ½ teaspoon salt and bouquet garni. Boil for 4–5 minutes until the mussels open. Keep warm but do not allow to cook any longer, otherwise you will make the mussels rubbery.

Strain the pan juices through double muslin and keep. In a large saucepan heat 60 grs (2 oz or 4 tablespoons) butter and gently fry onions and garlic until pale golden. Add strained mussel liquor, boiling water and milk. Bring to the boil, then simmer for 15 minutes. Taste, add salt, if necessary, and season with pepper.

Take mussels out of their shells and add to soup.

Fry slices of bread in butter and keep hot. Beat yolk and cream in a soup tureen, stir in lemon juice, pour hot soup over the mixture. Serve with fried bread.

PORTUGUESE PRAWN SOUP
4 Servings

2–3 tablespoons olive oil
1 large sliced onion
1 sliced carrot
2 large peeled and chopped
   tomatoes
120 ml (4oz or ½ cup) dry
   white wine

2 tablespoons port
½ kg (1 lb or 2½ cups) prawns in
   their shells
1 litre (1 quart or 4 cups)
   water
100 gr (3½ oz or ½ cup) rice
salt and pepper
1 tablespoon butter

Heat oil in a saucepan and fry onion and carrot for 5 minutes. Add tomatoes, fry for a further 5 minutes. Pour in wine and port, reduce heat to simmering.

Wash prawns and add to saucepan. Cook until they turn bright pink. Add water, bring to the boil and with a perforated spoon take out prawns. Add rice to the pan, season with salt and pepper.

Shell and de-vein prawns, keep a few for garnish, pound the rest in a mortar to paste and add to pan. Simmer until the rice is done. Rub through a sieve or purée the soup in a blender. Reheat, stir in butter adding it in small pieces and serve.

COSTA BRAVA MACARONI AND MUSSEL SOUP

6 Servings

½ litre (1 pint or 2 cups) mussels (small ones)	240 gr (8 oz or 2 cups) cut macaroni
1 tablespoon butter or oil	2 tablespoons tomato paste
1½ litres (1½ quarts) stock	salt and pepper

Rinse the mussels thoroughly. Heat butter or oil in a saucepan and drop the mussels into the hot fat to open them. Remove the shells, leaving the mussels in the saucepan. Add stock, bring to the boil and put in macaroni and tomato paste. Season to taste, cook for 25 minutes and serve.

RUSSIAN CRAYFISH AND RICE SOUP

Large freshwater crayfish are usually used for this soup in Russia. Dublin Bay or Pacific prawns are recommended.

6 Servings

12–18 large prawns	1½ tablespoons butter
1½ litres (3 pints or 6 cups) water	1 tablespoon flour
salt	6 tablespoons cooked rice
2 sprigs dill (or parsley)	120 ml (4 oz or ½ cup) sour cream
1 chopped onion	1 tablespoon chopped dill or parsley

Wash prawns, put in saucepan, cover with water, add a teaspoon of salt, dill and onion. Bring to the boil and simmer gently until they change colour. Strain and keep the liquid in which the prawns were cooked. Remove flesh from tails and claws, if using Dublin Bay prawns, put in a clean saucepan, add enough of the liquid in which the prawns were cooked to cover and reserve.

Pound the rest of the prawns, i.e., legs and shells, in mortar and fry in butter stirring until the mixture acquires a dark red colour. Sprinkle in flour, blend well and fry together for 2–3 minutes. Little by little add 2½ dcl (½ pint or 1 cup) of the liquid in which the prawns were cooked. Bring to the boil, strain through muslin and add to remaining prawn liquid. Add prawn tails and claws with their liquid and the rice. Season to taste with salt and freshly ground pepper.

Heat sour cream without boiling, add to soup. Reheat soup without allowing it to boil, sprinkle with chopped dill and serve.

CANARY ISLANDS OCTOPUS SOUP

6 Servings

1 medium-sized onion	2 tablespoons chopped parsley
2–3 tomatoes	1½ litres (1½ quarts) water
oil	salt and pepper
1 octopus (or cuttle fish)	bread slices

Peel and wash the onion and the tomatoes, slice them and fry in 2 tablespoons of oil in a saucepan. Clean and cut the octopus into small pieces and add to the onion and tomatoes. Fry together for 10 to 15 minutes, add parsley and water. Simmer for 2 to 3 hours. Season to taste. Fry several slices of bread per person, drop them into the soup, cook for another 15 minutes and serve.

SHARKS' FIN SOUP

6–8 Servings

375 gr (12 oz) sharks' fins	6 tablespoons bamboo shoots
1 knob 2½ cm (1 inch) fresh ginger	½ litre (5 pints or 10 cups) hot chicken stock
1 clove crushed garlic	2 tablespoons Shao Shing or sherry
cold water	soya sauce
1 leg of chicken	1 teaspoon sesame oil
120 gr (4 oz or ½ cup) raw breast of chicken	vinegar
60 gr (2 oz or ¼ cup) Chinese (or smoked) ham	salt

Soak the sharks' fins in water for 24 hours. Boil them slowly for 4 hours with ginger and garlic in double the amount of water required to cover them. Drain and remove any flesh on the fins. Put it in a basin, place the chicken leg on top and steam slowly for 2 hours. Remove the chicken leg and any water which may have dropped on the fins. Shred chicken breast, ham and bamboo shoots into fine strips. Put sharks' fins into saucepan, pour in enough stock to cover and boil for 5 minutes. Add chicken, ham, bamboo shoots and wine, and simmer for another 5 minutes.

Add a few drops of soya sauce, sesame oil, vinegar and salt to taste and serve.

BALEARIC FISH SOUP

6 Servings

butter or oil
1 onion
480 gr (1 lb) hake
480 gr (1 lb) fish (cod or
  haddock)

1 litre (2 pints or 4 cups) well
  scrubbed mussels
1½ litre (1½ quarts) water
10–12 slices bread
salt and pepper

Melt 2 tablespoons of butter in a saucepan. Chop the onion, cut the fish into biggish portions, leaving the bones in for the time being, fry lightly with the onion, turning the fish carefully so as not to break it. Take off the fire while you heat some oil in another saucepan and drop in the washed mussels to loosen their shells. Carefully bone the fish and replace in the saucepan, add mussels and their oil. Pour in water. Cook for a few minutes while you prepare some fried bread (the quantity will depend on how thick you want the soup—say a couple of pieces per person).

Season well—add 2–3 teaspoons of salt and a generous pinch of pepper—then float the fried bread on top, simmer for half an hour and serve.

DUBLIN COCKLE AND MUSSEL SOUP

6 Servings

2 litres (2 quarts) mussels
1 litre (1 quart) cockles
1 small onion
1 clove garlic
60 gr (2 oz or 4 tablespoons)
  butter
120 ml (4 oz or ½ cup) dry

white wine
1½ litres (3 pints or 6 cups)
  fish stock or milk
3–4 tablespoons kneaded butter
250 ml (½ pint or 1 cup) cream
2–3 tablespoons sherry
salt and pepper

Scrub and debeard the mussels and wash them and the cockles in cold running water thoroughly. Chop the onion and garlic finely and cook gently for a few minutes in 2 tablespoons of the butter in a large saucepan. Add the cockles and mussels, white wine, 250 ml (1 pint or 2 cups) boiling water. Cover and cook briskly for 5 minutes until the shells have opened.

Take the cockles and mussels out of the stock, cool, remove from shells. Put in a saucepan with a little of the cooking liquid and remaining butter to keep warm. Put the empty shells back into the rest of the cooking liquid, add fish stock or milk and boil for about 25 minutes to concentrate.

Strain into a clean saucepan and stir in the keaded butter in small pieces. Simmer until sauce thickens slightly. Add cream and sherry, season with salt and pepper. Reheat and, at the last minute, add the cockles and mussels. Serve in bowls with toasted brown bread.

AMERICAN OYSTER SOUP

6 Servings

1 litre (1 quart) oysters and
  their liquor
¾ litre (1½ pints or 3 cups) milk

salt and black pepper
2 tablespoons butter
120 ml (4 oz or ½ cup) cream
paprika

Remove shells and strain oyster juice through double muslin into large saucepan. Rinse oysters and add to their juices. Gently heat, simmer for 4–5 minutes on low heat. Add milk, heat almost to boiling point, season to taste with salt and freshly ground pepper. Stir in butter, adding it in small pieces.

Add cream, stir and remove from heat. Check seasoning, sprinkle with paprika and serve at once.

JAPANESE LOBSTER SOUP

4 Servings

½ kg (1 lb) lobster
salt
2 sliced leeks
125 gr (4 oz or 1/3 cup)
  shredded cabbage

sprig chopped parsley
1 litre (2 pints) dashi
shoyu

Cut off lobster's head and chop body into portions. Boil lobster and vegetables separately in salted water. Heat the dashi. Drain the cooked lobster chunks and vegetables, season with shoyu to taste, divide among four bowls, add piping hot dashi, and serve. An equivalent quantity of prawns may be substituted for lobster.

CARIBBEAN CRAB GUMBO

4–6 Servings

2–3 cooked crabs or 360 gr
  (12 oz or 1½ cups) crab meat
2 tablespoons butter
2 tablespoons olive oil
1 large chopped onion
1 seeded, shredded green pepper
½ seeded, shredded red pepper
½ tablespoon chopped chives

240 gr (8 oz) okra
  clove crushed garlic
3 large peeled, chopped
  tomatoes
bouquet garni
water
salt
120 ml (4 oz of ½ cup) cream

Extract crab meat, make sure there are no small pieces of shell, and flake the meat.

Heat 1 tablespoon each of butter and oil and lightly fry onion until soft. Add green and red pepper, fry together for 3–4 minutes and transfer to a large saucepan. In remaining butter and oil lightly fry crab meat, sprinkle with chives, stir and add to onion and peppers.

Slice okra. Add okra, garlic, tomatoes and bouquet garni to

saucepan. Add enough water to cover, bring to the boil and season to taste with salt. Cover and simmer for 1 hour. Remove from heat, stir in cream and serve.

The gumbo is a thick soup; thick enough to serve as a stew, and can be eaten with rice.

LOUISIANA OYSTER GUMBO

4–6 Servings

1½ dozen oysters
75 gr (2½ oz or 5 tablespoons) batter
1½ tablespoons flour
1 litre (1 quart) clear fish stock (p. 14) or water
1 chopped onion

2 tablespoons chopped spring onions
spring thyme
½ crushed bay leaf
salt and pepper
1 tablespoon chopped parsley

Drain liquid from oysters, strain and keep. Wash oysters to make sure there is no grit left in them.

Heat butter, add flour, cook until the roux acquires a pale golden colour. Dilute with stock or water. Add liquid from the oysters, onion, spring onions, thyme, bay leaf and seasoning to taste. Bring to the boil, cover, simmer for 15 minutes. Add oysters, cook for 5 minutes. Sprinkle with parsley and serve with plain boiled rice.

CRAB AND SWEET CORN SOUP

This delicious Chinese soup can be made in less than 10 minutes, using ingredients from the store cupboard. The actual cooking time is only 3 minutes.

6 Servings

150 gr (5 oz) fresh cooked or canned crab meat
1 beaten egg white
1 litre (1 quart) chicken stock (or water with a bouillon cube)
1–2 slices fresh ginger, shredded
1 large can sweet corn

pinch salt
pinch Ve-Tsin (optional)
1–2 tablespoons dry sherry
½ teaspoon sesame oil
1 heaped teaspoon cornflour
2 tablespoons cold water
½ tablespoons chopped fresh chives or spring onions

Finely shred crab meat. Mix with beaten egg white. Bring stock to the boil. (If using a stock cube watch out for its salt content and reduce seasoning proportionately.) Add ginger and sweet corn and allow to come to the boil again. Add salt, Ve-Tsin, sherry and sesame oil. Stir in cornflour diluted with water. Cook, stirring for 1 minute.

Add crab meat, and bring to the boil, cook for 15 seconds. Sprinkle with chives or spring onions and serve.

CRAYFISH BISQUE

6 Servings

150 gr (5 oz or 11½ tablespoons)
  rice
2¼ litres (2¼ quarts or 9 cups)
  light stock
2 carrots
1 onion
1 parsnip
150 gr (5 oz or 10 tablespoons)
  butter

1 sprig thyme
1 small bay leaf
12–18 crayfish
salt and pepper
6 tablespoons brandy
2½ dcl (½ pint or 1 cup) dry
  white wine
120 ml (4 oz or ½ cup) cream
pinch cayenne pepper

Wash rice carefully and cook it in 2½ cups of the stock. Meanwhile cut carrots in half, remove core, and chop finely. Chop onion and parsnip and sauté gently with carrot in 1 tablespoon butter. Add thyme and bay leaf. Increase heat and add crayfish, salt and pepper. Sauté briskly. Pour in brandy, light it, and put out the flame by pouring on white wine. Simmer for 8 minutes. Remove from heat.

Take out half the crayfish, extract flesh from tails, and set aside in a little stock. To the other half add the hot rice, and pound until the mixture acquires a creamy consistency. Rub through a sieve, pressing it through with a wooden spoon. Put the purée into a saucepan and dilute with the rest of the stock. Add cream, blend, and remove from heat. Incorporate butter, and flavour with a small pinch of cayenne pepper.

Serve garnished with the remaining crayfish tails, cut into pieces. This soup should be the colour of cooked crayfish.

LOBSTER BISQUE

Follow recipe for Crayfish Bisque, substituting equivalent amount of lobster for crayfish.

FLORIDA SEA-FOOD BISQUE

6 Servings

240 ml (½ pint or 1 cup) light
  chicken stock
120 ml (4 oz or ½ cup) milk
1 tablespoon butter
12 fresh oysters
a few drops Tabasco
120 gr (4 oz or ½ cup) flaked
  fresh crab meat

120 gr (4 oz or 1 cup) roughly
  chopped peeled prawns
2 tablespoons sherry
salt and pepper
pinch nutmeg
120 ml (4 oz or ½ cup) double
  cream
½ teaspoon paprika

In a saucepan heat stock and milk, add butter and stir to dissolve. Pour into the saucepan any liquid from the oysters, straining it carefully. Cut the oysters into bite-sized pieces.

Add oysters, Tabasco, crab meat and prawns to pan. Simmer for 10 minutes. Add sherry, season with salt and pepper, sprinkle in nutmeg. Keeping on very low heat, so that the bisque does not boil, blend in cream. Remove from heat, decant into soup bowls, sprinkle with paprika and serve piping hot.

Cold Fish Dishes

GRAVAD LAX

Traditional Swedish Midsummer Feast Salmon. Caroline Jury brought this recipe back from Sweden where this dish was prepared for her by her friend Meta Borch-Johnsen. Caroline said the taste was so beautiful she started to cry! The dill pickling process takes up to 30 hours, so the dish can be made well in advance.

4–6 Servings

1 kg (2 lb) middle cut fresh salmon
lots and lots of dill
5 tablespoons sugar
5 tablespoons sea salt
1 teaspoon roughly milled white pepper

To garnish:
more dill
lemon slices
new boiled potatoes
black pepper

Pat the salmon dry with a cloth or piece of kitchen paper. Cut salmon lengthwise and remove all the bones. Liberally rub both pieces of salmon with a mixture of sugar, salt and white pepper. Place a layer of dill in a basin as a foundation for half the fish, skin down. Cover with dill and put the second half of the salmon on this, skin side up, so that the thick end of the top piece goes over the thin end of the lower.

Cover with dill and add any remaining sugar, salt and pepper mixture. Cover with plate and put a weight on top—any old iron will do. Leave in the refrigerator for 15–30 hours.

Serve the salmon cut in thick slices with fresh dill, lemon slices, fresh new boiled potatoes and ground black pepper and a sauce made of :

1 tablespoon 'sweet' mustard (available from delicatessen shops)
1 teaspoon French mustard
1 tablespoon sugar

1 tablespoon white wine vinegar
10–15 tablespoons oil
and yet more chopped dill

59

Mix mustards, sugar and vinegar in a bowl. Add the oil, a drop at a time (as for making mayonnaise) until the sauce is thick and smooth. Add the dill.

CEVICHE (MACKEREL MEXICAN STYLE)

6–8 Servings

1 kg (2 lb) mackerel (or other firm fleshed fish)
lemon juice
120 ml (4 oz or ½ cup) olive oil
1 medium-sized chopped onion
2 ripe, large, peeled chopped tomatoes
12–16 chopped green olives

4 tablespoons chopped fresh coriander (or watercress)
1 finely chopped green chilli
salt
vinegar
2 medium-sized avocado pears

Skin and bone the fish and cut into uniform 1¼ cm (½ in.) cubes. Put in a deep dish, add enough lemon juice to cover the fish. Allow to stand for a couple of hours to macerate. This lemon treatment is all the cooking the fish needs. Pour off surplus liquid. Add oil, onion, tomatoes, olives, coriander and chilli. Season with salt and vinegar to taste. Mix carefully.

Peel avocado, slice and dip immediately in lemon juice to prevent discoloration. Garnish the fish with avocado slices, chill and serve.

POTTED CHAR

This recipe comes, originally, from Norway.

8–10 Servings

1 kg (2 lb) char
white wine court-bouillon

500 grs (1 lb) clarified butter

Clean, wash and dry the char and poach in court-bouillon, for 15 minutes. Allow to cool, remove skin and bones and slice the fish. Put it in an ovenproof dish, baste with plenty of butter, cover and bake in the oven for 15 minutes at 190°C (375°F or Gas Mark 5). Remove from oven, allow to cool completely, decant into jars, pour in the rest of the clarified butter so that the fish is completely covered with it, seal and store in a refrigerator.

Char potted in this way will keep for 2 weeks. Very useful if you come by more than you need for the day and wish to preserve it for a week or more.

Serve with a salad.

CARP, ISRAELI STYLE

4 Servings

1 medium carp
1 small chopped onion
4 chopped shallots
3 dcl (12 oz or 1½ cups) oil
2 tablespoons flour
2 dcl (½ pint or 1 cup) white wine
salt

cayenne pepper
2 crushed cloves garlic
pinch thyme
¼ bay leaf
pinch saffron
30 gr (1 oz or 2 tablespoons) blanched, chopped almonds
1 tablespoon chopped parsley

Skin the carp, cut into uniform slices. Heat 3 tablespoons oil and gently cook onion and shallots, without browning. Add carp, sprinkle with flour, stir gently, cover with wine, season with salt and pepper, add garlic, thyme and bay leaf, sprinkle with a few tablespoons oil, bring to the boil, then simmer on a low heat for 20 minutes.

Drain the carp slices and re-form in the original shape on a long dish. Boil down the liquid in which the fish was cooked by two-thirds. Away from direct heat, whisk in the rest of the oil, add saffron and almonds, pour over the carp and leave to cool. Sprinkle with parsley and serve.

COLD RED MULLET À LA NIÇOISE

4 Servings

4 small mullets
salt and pepper
3 tablespoons olive oil
3 chopped shallots
1 crushed clove garlic

500 gr (1 lb or 3 cups) peeled, chopped tomatoes
12 anchovy fillets
60 gr (2 oz or ½ cup) stoned olives

Scale the fish, cut off fins, clean out, but leave the livers. Wash and gently dab with a cloth to dry. Season on the inside with salt and pepper. Rub with a little olive oil and grill until done and both sides are uniformly browned.

While the fish is grilling prepare the sauce. Heat the rest of the oil and gently fry shallots with garlic for 2–3 minutes. Add tomatoes and increase heat to cook down the sauce to a thick consistency. Season to taste.

Arrange the fish in a serving dish, pour the sauce over it and leave until cold. Decorate the top with anchovies in a criss-cross pattern, stud with olives and serve.

GEFILTE FISH

The name 'gefilte' means 'stuffed' and originally the preparation described in this recipe was intended as stuffing either for carp or pike.

6 Servings

1¼ kg (2½ lbs) assorted fish—
haddock, bream, cod, hake
¾ litre (1½ pints or 5 cups)
    water
salt
white pepper
1 finely chopped onion

3 chopped celery stalks
2 tablespoons medium matzo
    meal or equivalent amount of
    white bread
2 eggs
2 sliced onions
1–2 sliced carrots

Trim and fillet the fish. Use bones, heads and skins for making fish stock, well seasoned with salt and pepper. Put the fish, chopped onion, celery and matzo meal through a mincer. Season, stir in eggs. Shape the mixture into balls.

Line a fish kettle with sliced onions. Strain fish stock into it. Add carrots and gently put in fish balls. Slowly bring to the boil and simmer for 2 hours. Lift the fish out with a slotted spoon, put on a serving dish, decorate each piece with a slice of carrot. Cook down the stock to reduce and concentrate it, taste for seasoning, spoon a little over the gefilte fish, leave to set and serve cold.

FILLETS OF SOLE WITH TEHINA

Either sole, lemon sole, or plaice fillets can be used for this dish. If it is intended as an hors-d'oeuvre, the ingredients indicated will suffice. If you wish to serve it as a main course—and it makes an attractive summer meal—double the quantities.

4 Servings

4 fillets of sole
salt and pepper
2–3 tablespoons cod's roe pâté
    (see Taramasalata p. 20)
1 chopped hard-boiled egg

1 tablespoon lemon juice
tehina (p. 221)
1 tablespoon chopped parsley
black olives for garnish

Wash, dry and skin the fillets. Cut them across into strips about 5 cm (2 in.) wide, season with salt and pepper. Pre-heat oven to 190°C (375°F or Gas Mark 4).

Mix cod's roe pâté with chopped hard-boiled egg. Spread pieces of fish with roe and egg mixture, roll up and secure with cocktail sticks. Put in an ovenproof dish, add lemon juice, cover and bake for 20 minutes. Remove, allow to cool. Coat with tehina, sprinkle with parsley, garnish with black olives and serve cold.

ESCABECHE (PERUVIAN SOUSED FISH)

4–6 Servings

750 gr–1 kg (1½–2 lb) sea bass
2 medium-sized onions
2 cloves garlic
2½ cm (1 inch) piece fresh
   ginger
6 tablespoons olive oil
salt and pepper

120 gr (4 oz or 2 cups)
   mushrooms
1 green pepper
2½ dcl (½ pint or 1 cup) good
   vinegar
120 ml (¼ pint or ½ cup) water
1½ tablespoons sugar

Use the fish whole, with the head removed. Wash and dry fish. Cut onions into rings, slice garlic and ginger finely. Heat half the oil, brown the fish on both sides, sprinkle with salt and pepper and remove from pan.

Add remaining oil to pan, fry onions and garlic for 5 minutes. Add ginger, cook for 1 minute. Slice mushrooms. Seed and shred green pepper. Add mushrooms and pepper to the onion mixture. Stir and fry for 2 minutes. Add vinegar, water and sugar, bring to the boil, then reduce heat to very low and simmer for 2–3 minutes.

Add fish to pan, spoon the hot marinade over it, simmer for 5 minutes and remove from heat. Allow to cool, chill for 24 hours before serving.

EELS CARPIONATA

750 gr (1½ lb) eel, ready for
   cooking
2 tablespoons olive oil
2 small bay leaves
salt and pepper
½ dozen peppercorns

800 ml (28 oz or 3½ cups) wine
   vinegar
1 crushed clove garlic
½ teaspoon rosemary
2 cloves

Cut the eel into chunks, wash and dry. Arrange in one row in an oiled roasting pan. Add 1 small bay leaf. Sprinkle lightly with salt and pepper. Bake in a slow oven 150°C (300°F or Gas Mark 2) for 1 hour, then decant into a deep dish.

Bring vinegar to the boil with a pinch of salt, peppercorns, bay leaf, garlic, rosemary and cloves. Simmer for 3 minutes, pour over eels, cover and leave to marinate for 3 days, turning eel pieces from time to time.

COLD TROUT WITH PINK MAYONNAISE

Allow one trout per portion. Poach in white wine court-bouillon for 5–6 minutes. Drain, arrange on a dish and chill. Remove a strip of skin from the top middle of the trout, leaving heads and tails intact. Garnish trout with unpeeled wedges of cucumber, sprays of tarragon, and slices of lemon and hard-boiled egg.

Serve with pink mayonnaise, horseradish cream or horseradish jelly.

ASTURIAN HAKE

6 Servings

1 kg (2 lb) hake
1 sliced onion
2 sliced carrots
2 shredded leeks
½ bay leaf
1 sprig parsley
seasoning

125 ml (4 oz or ½ cup) white
  wine
2–3 boiled, sliced potatoes
2 hard-boiled eggs
200 gr (½ pint or 1 cup) cooked
  prawns
mayonnaise

Put hake in one piece, into just enough cold water, to cover, and bring to the boil. Add onion, carrots, leeks, bay leaf, parsley seasoning and wine. Simmer for 5 minutes, remove from heat and allow the fish to cool in its liquid.

Drain the fish carefully, arrange on a serving dish, garnish with slices of potato and hard-boiled egg, decorate with prawns and serve with mayonnaise.

COLD HADDOCK, RUMANIAN STYLE

4 Servings

1 kg (2 lb) haddock fillet
3 tablespoons olive oil
salt and pepper
2 chopped onions
1 pounded clove garlic
250 gr (½ lb or 1 cup) peeled,
  sliced tomatoes

2 teaspoons chopped dill
small pinch cayenne pepper
1 tablespoon lemon juice
1 tablespoon butter
1 tablespoon chopped parsley

Cut the haddock into uniform pieces, brush with oil, put in an ovenproof dish and season with salt and pepper. Heat the rest of the oil and lightly fry the onions and garlic to soften, add tomatoes, cook for 3 to 4 minutes, sprinkle with dill and cayenne pepper, stir and pour the resulting fondue over the fish.

Sprinkle with lemon juice, dot with tiny pieces of butter and bake in a moderate oven 190°C (375°F or Gas Mark 4) for 25 to 40 minutes, basting from time to time with a little melted butter. Remove allow to cool, sprinkle with chopped parsley. Serve with a simple salad.

TURBOT WITH AVOCADO DRESSING

This is a Chilean speciality and is delicious and attractive to look at. The dressing provides a change from mayonnaise and is very simple to make.

4 Servings

750 gr (1½ lb) turbot	juice of ½ lemon
court-bouillon	salt and pepper
1–2 avocado pears, depending	pinch cayenne pepper
on size	3–4 tablespoons single cream

Poach the turbot in a court-bouillon. Drain, allow to cool, arrange on a serving dish. Just before serving, mash the flesh of an avocado pear with lemon juice, season to taste, thin down with cream to desired consistency and mask the turbot with this dressing.

SMOKED HADDOCK TARTARE

4 Servings

500–750 gr (1½ lb) smoked	2 tomatoes
haddock	2 hard-boiled eggs
few tablespoons milk	60 gr (2 oz or ½ cup) peeled
2½ dcl (½ pint or 1 cup) thick	shrimps
tartare sauce (p. 212)	pinch chopped tarragon

Put the haddock in a fireproof dish with a little water, bake until cooked. Allow to cool, remove all skin and bones. Flake the fish and blend to a creamy consistency with enough milk to bind.

Put on a dish, cover with tartare sauce, garnish with slices of tomato and hard-boiled egg, decorate with shrimps, sprinkle with tarragon and serve cold.

COLD RED MULLET À L'ORIENTALE

6 Servings

6 red mullet	1 kg (2 lb) peeled tomatoes
flour	1 crushed clove garlic
oil	thyme
120 ml (4 oz or ½ cup) white	salt and pepper
wine	1 lemon

Clean, wash and dry mullet. Dredge with flour. Heat 4 tablespoons oil and fry the fish 5 minutes on each side. Transfer to a lightly buttered baking dish and pour in the wine. Heat 5 tablespoons oil, and cook tomatoes and garlic. Sprinkle with thyme, season with salt and pepper.

Cook down the sauce to concentrate and thicken and pour over the fish. Bake in the oven 205°C (400°F or Gas Mark 5) for 3 minutes.

Carefully transfer the fish to a serving dish. Serve cold, garnished with slices of lemon.

AUSTRIAN PICKLED FISH

We think this is a good way to use plain or frozen fish steaks.

4 Servings

500 gr (1 lb) cooked fish steaks
1 teaspoon chopped shallots
1 teaspoon chopped capers
1 teaspoon grated lemon zest
salt and pepper

bay leaf
2 tablespoons olive oil
3 tablespoons white wine
  vinegar

Put fish in a shallow dish. Mix shallots, capers, lemon zest, salt and pepper and bay leaf with oil and vinegar. Pour over fish and leave overnight, in a cool place.

Fish Mousses and Aspics

FISH MOUSSE

6 Servings

1 kg (2 lb) skinned, boned fish	4 whites of egg
salt	250 ml (1 pint of 2 cups)
white pepper	double cream
pinch nutmeg	

Cut the fish into pieces, put in a mortar, season with salt, pepper and nutmeg, pound into a fine smooth paste. Little by little, add whites of egg and blend in. Rub the mixture through a sieve into a bowl, or pass through a blender. Leave in a refrigerator for 2 to 3 hours.

Gradually incorporate the cream, stirring it in with a wooden spoon. Pour the mixture into a mould, filling it to about three-quarters, stand it in a pan with water and poach in the oven 190°C (375°F or Gas Mark 4), allowing 15 minutes per 250 ml (1 pint or 2 cups) of mixture. Remove from oven, allow to stand for a few seconds, then turn out, garnish and serve.

Fish mousse can be garnished with coooked prawns, shrimps, mussels, mushrooms tossed in butter, asparagus tips, etc.

If you use a ring-shaped mould, you can heap the garnish in the middle. Serve with a suitable sauce, such as cardinal, cream, lobster, Nantua, Normande, etc., recipes for which are given in this book.

This mousse can also be served cold. We have made it using haddock and, on rare occasions (such as when visiting Russian artists have overwhelmed us with several unsealed containers of fresh caviar) have served it in a plain soufflé mould, masking the top of the mousse completely with a thin layer of caviar.

Another time without the benefit of any Russian largesse, we substituted fresh garden peas for caviar—and no one complained.

SALMON CREAM IN ASPIC

4–6 Servings

1 lb (400 grs or 3 cups) fresh (or tinned) salmon
3 oz (75 grs or 6 tablespoons) butter
salt and pepper

4 oz (100 ml or ½ cup) cream
2 tablespoons plain gelatine
4 tablespoons cold water
4 oz (100 ml or ½ cup) boiling water

Poach fresh salmon, allow to cool, flake with a fork, remove all skin and bones. (If tinned salmon is used, drain off all liquid.) Cream salmon with butter by hand, or in a blender, season to taste. Whisk the cream until stiff and fold into the salmon mixture.

Dissolve gelatine in cold water, add boiling water, stir and leave to cool and thicken slightly. Line a mould with half-set jelly. To do this, pour a layer of jelly on one side of the mould at a time and put in a refrigerator to set. Proceed in this manner until all sides and bottom have a coating of jelly.

Fill the mould with salmon cream, seal and top with jelly, chill until it sets. To serve, turn out the mould on to a dish.

TROUT IN CHABLIS

Poach trout in white wine court-bouillon made with Chablis (p. 13), allow to cool in the cooking liquor. Drain, skin without breaking the flesh and dab gently with a soft cloth to dry. Put the trout on a long serving dish, coat with half-set jelly (see Aspic Jelly for Fish p. 15) prepared with the liquor in which the fish was cooked.

Glaze it by applying several layers of this jelly to give it a uniform coating, but always leave one layer to set before applying the next. Decorate with shapes cut out of cucumber, hardboiled egg, tarragon leaves, little bouquets of parsley, securing them with a little half-set aspic jelly. Pour the remainder of the jelly, if any, into a shallow pan, allow to set hard, cut into whatever shape pleases you and arrange around the fish.

TURBOT MAYONNAISE IN TOMATO ASPIC

4 Servings

Tomato aspic (p. 16)
1 kg (2 lb) turbot
court-bouillon

360 ml (¾ pint or scant 1½ cups) mayonnaise

Rinse a ring mould with cold water, pour the tomato aspic into it and leave in refrigerator to set.

Poach the turbot in court-bouillon, allow to cool in the liquid. Drain, skin, remove bones, flake the fish and mix it with mayonnaise. Turn out the tomato aspic ring on to a large round serving dish, heap the turbot mayonnaise in the centre and serve.

TURBOT WITH AVGOLEMONO SAUCE IN TOMATO ASPIC

Cook the turbot as above, dress with Avgolemono sauce.

DANISH JELLIED EEL MOULD

4–6 Servings

2 medium-sized eels	sheet gelatine (optional)
salt	few sprigs parsley
water	1 lemon
12 peppercorns	360 ml (12 oz or 1–1½ cups)
½ bay leaf	double cream
1 sliced onion	1 teaspoon castor sugar
2 cloves	pinch dry mustard
small glass port	1 tablespoon wine vinegar
rind of 1 lemon in strips	2 tablespoons grated horseradish
juice of 1 lemon	1 bunch watercress

Clean and gut the eels and cut into 5 cm (2 in.) pieces, rub with coarse salt, put in a pan with enough water to cover, add peppercorns, bay leaf, onion, cloves, port, lemon rind and lemon juice. Bring to the boil, simmer for 20 minutes. Take the pieces of eel out with a slotted spoon, remove bones. Strain the liquid in which the eel was cooked through muslin.

Rinse a ring mould with cold water and line with a little fish stock. Leave to set. (Eel liquor ought to jell by itself. Should it fail to do so, add gelatine, allowing 4 to 5 leaves per ½ litre (1 pint or 2 cups) of stock. Decorate the mould as your artistic spirit moves you, with tiny pieces of parsley and lemon, spooning over a little of the liquid jelly to secure them. Leave to set, then fill the mould with pieces of eel and the rest of the jelly. Chill.

Whisk the cream, add sugar, mustard, vinegar and horseradish, mix carefully and chill. To serve, turn out the jellied eels, fill the middle with horseradish cream and decorate with watercress and lemon slices.

JELLIED EEL IN CHABLIS

Cut small eels into pieces. Cook the eel in a concentrated fish court-bouillon made with Chablis. Drain the eel, put into a small terrine. Clarify the liquid (see Aspic p. 15) in which the eel was cooked, pour over the chunks of eel, chill until the liquid sets.

FILLETS OF SOLE IN ASPIC

6 Servings

12 small sole fillets
2 tablespoons butter
seasoning
fish fumet
1 long cucumber or 12 small
  tomatoes

2 dcl (½ pint or 1 cup) fish
  aspic
cod's roe pâté (p. 20)

Flatten sole fillets, spread with a little butter, season to taste. Roll up each one into a little horn, secure with a cocktail stick and cook slowly in good, concentrated fish fumet. While the fish is cooking, make 'stands' for the little fillet horns—either small scooped-out tomatoes, or cucumber, peeled, cut into chunks and hollowed out to make suitable pedestals. Dip both the 'pedestals' and the cooled, drained fillets in cold fish aspic jelly and fix the rolled fillets to the pedestals. Carefully extract the cocktail sticks —when the aspic has set.

Arrange on a dish, put a spoonful of cod's roe pâté into each horn and serve.

FILLETS OF SOLE IN ASPIC WITH CAVIAR

Follow above recipe but fill the sole cornets with a spoonful of caviar instead of cod's roe pâté (taramasalata).

POACHED FISH MOUSSE

6-8 Servings

1 kg (2 lb) boned fish
salt and pepper
pinch allspice

4–5 whites of egg
1 litre (2 pints or 4 cups) cream

Put the fish, cut into pieces, in a mortar. Season with salt, pepper and allspice. Pound finely, adding whites of egg a little at a time. Rub through a fine sieve, or pass through a blender. Chill for 2 hours.

Little by little stir in cream. Check seasoning, pour mixture into a ring mould deep enough to contain the mixture and be only three-quarters full. Stand in a pan of hot water and poach in a moderate oven 190°C (375°F or Gas Mark 4). Allow ½ hour cooking time per litre (quart) of mixture.

Leave to rest for a few seconds, turn out, fill the middle with a garnish of your choice—green peas dressed with butter, asparagus tips in butter, moules marinieres (p. 116), prawns in Nantua sauce, mushrooms, etc.

If you are using a plain mould without a hole in the middle for the garnish, serve with one of the following sauces poured over: Aurora, Cardinal, Cream, Lobster, Nantua, Normandy, Victoria or White Wine Sauce (see recipes).

HALIBUT MOUSSE

6 Servings

fish aspic jelly
truffle peelings or mushroom
   caps
360 gr (¾ lb or 1½ cups) poached,
   flaked halibut
1 tablespoon gelatine
125 ml (4 oz or ½ cup) dry
   white wine

6–8 tablespoons whipped cream
salt and white pepper
cucumber and horseradish for
   garnish
watercress mayonnaise

Chill a fish mould and coat the bottom and side with a thin layer of cool but still liquid fish aspic. Outline the fins, tail, and eyes with thin strips of truffles. Sprinkle some liquid aspic over each piece to set decoration. When it is firm, pour in aspic 1¼ cm (½ in.) deep.

Mash halibut and pass through a blender. Mix with gelatine softened in 2 tablespoons cold water and dissolved over hot water. Add wine and fold in cream. Season with salt and pepper. Using a pastry bag with a large round nozzle, pipe the mousse into the centre of the mould, keeping the sides clear. Chill the mousse until set. Fill the edges of the mould with aspic and chill until the aspic is firm.

Unmould on to a chilled dish, garnish with thin slices of cucumber and curls of fresh horseradish. Serve with watercress mayonnaise.

Fish Casseroles

CARP IN BEER WITH CURRANTS, RUSSIAN STYLE

4 Servings

1–1¼ kg (2–2½ lb) carp
vinegar
3–4 cloves
1 tablespoon butter
2 dcl (½ pint or 1 cup) beer

3 tablespoons freshly-grated breadcrumbs
½ teaspoon grated lemon rind
3 tablespoons washed currants

Cut the carp into portions, put in a dish, sprinkle liberally with vinegar, add cloves and allow to stand for 30–45 minutes, turning from time to time.

Melt butter, add fish with its juices, cover with beer, sprinkle in breadcrumbs evenly, cover and simmer gently for 35 to 40 minutes. Lift the fish out carefully on to a serving dish and keep hot. Add lemon rind and currants to the sauce, boil fast for 5 minutes to reduce and concentrate, pour over the carp and serve.

MISSISSIPPI FISH STEW

4 Servings

4 fillets of any white fish
4 rashers bacon
125 gr (4 oz or ¾ cup) chopped onion
500 gr (1 lb) peeled tomatoes
250 gr (½ lb) scraped new potatoes

1 tablespoon Worcestershire sauce (optional)
salt and pepper
chopped parsley

Skin plaice and cut into uniform pieces. Fry bacon and onion, and all other ingredients, except fish. Season to taste, cover and simmer for 15 minutes, stirring from time to time and adding more liquid (tomato juice, tomato sauce) if necessary. Add fish, cook for 15 minutes, sprinkle with chopped parsley and serve.

TURBOT CASSEROLE, EL SALVADOR STYLE

5-6 Servings

1-1¼ kgs (2-2½ lb) turbot
6 tablespoons olive oil
1 clove crushed garlic
salt and pepper
4 tablespoons lime (or lemon) juice

2 sliced onions
500 gr (1 lb) peeled, sliced tomatoes
2 tablespoons chopped parsley

Wash and dry the fish with a cloth. Grease an ovenproof dish with a little oil, put the turbot into it. Rub it with garlic, season with salt and pepper, sprinkle with half the lime juice and leave to macerate for 15 minutes. Cover with onions, tomatoes and parsley, sprinkle with the rest of lime juice and oil, cover with a lid and bake in the oven 190°C 375°F or Gas Mark 4) for 30 minutes, basting the turbot with the pan juices from time to time.

Remove lid, bake uncovered for 15 minutes, basting every 5 minutes, and serve.

SWEDISH MACKEREL CASSEROLE

4 Servings

4 filleted mackerel
butter
salt
2 finely shredded leeks
250 gr (½ lb or 1½ cups) peeled, chopped tomatoes

1 tablespoon chopped dill (or parsley)
½ teaspoon paprika
juice of ½ lemon
125 ml (4 oz or ½ cup) sour cream

Put the fillets in a buttered casserole, skin side down. Season with salt, cover with leek, tomatoes and dill. Sprinkle with paprika and lemon juice and pour sour cream over the top. Cover and bake in hot oven 220°C (425°F or Gas Mark 6) for 30 minutes.

EEL CASSEROLE ZUYDER ZEE

Dutch fishermen have their own way of cooking eels, celebrated throughout Holland.

Allow 250 gr (½ lb) young eel per portion and an extra 250 gr (½ lb) 'for the pot'. Chop the eels into 5 cm (2 in.) chunks and pack them tightly, in an upright position, into a sauté pan, so that they stand a little below the rim level. Put on a low heat and simmer gently until they yield up all their juices. Season with pepper, sprinkle with chopped parsley and cover with some slices of lemon cut very thin. Simmer uncovered until the liquid in the pan evaporates, but do not allow the eels to dry out. The whole cooking process should take about 25-30 minutes.

Serve with boiled potatoes.

RED MULLET, LIGURIAN STYLE

4 Servings

4 medium-sized red mullet
1 tablespoon chopped parsley
2 tablespoons olive oil
1 finely chopped onion
125 gr (4 oz or 2 cups) sliced
  mushrooms

2 chopped anchovy fillets
2½ dcl (½ pint or 1 cup)
  tomato sauce
125 ml (4 oz or ¼ cup) dry
  white wine
½ tablespoon chopped fennel

Clean, wash and dry the fish. Sprinkle it with parsley and leave in a cool place while you are preparing the sauce. Heat the oil, fry the onion lightly, add mushrooms and anchovies, stir and simmer for 5 minutes. Add tomato sauce and wine, blend. Simmer, stirring from time to time, for 15 minutes.

Put the mullet in an oiled ovenproof dish side by side, sprinkle with fennel, cover with sauce and bake in the oven 235°C (450°F or Gas Mark 7), for 20 minutes.

GREEK PLAKI

4 Servings

750 gr (1½ lb) assorted fish
  fillets
salt and pepper
1½ tablespoons lemon juice
4 tablespoons olive oil
2 large sliced onions
juice of 1–2 cloves garlic
2 tablespoons chopped parsley

125 gr (¼ lb or 1 cup) peeled
  chopped tomatoes
120 ml (4 oz or ½ cup) water
2½ dcl (½ pint or 1 cup) dry
  white wine
1 lemon sliced
2 sliced tomatoes

Trim fillets, wash, wipe with a cloth, season with salt and pepper and sprinkle with lemon juice. Heat the oil and fry the onions until transparent, add garlic juice (or crushed clove garlic) and parsley. Cook for one minute. Add tomatoes and water, and simmer, stirring until the tomatoes begin to 'melt'.

Put in fish, making sure it is well impregnated with the pan juices, moisten with wine, garnish with slices of lemon and tomato, cover, simmer for 20 minutes and serve.

CARP RUSSIAN STYLE, STUFFED WITH KASHA (BUCKWHEAT)

6 Servings

1½ kgs (2½ lb) carp, cleaned
  and scaled
salt
3–4 tablespoons butter
1 chopped onion
2 cups cooked kasha
  (buckwheat)

2 chopped hard-boiled eggs
pinch freshly ground pepper
flour
2½ dcl (8 oz or 1 cup) sour
  cream

Wash and dry the carp thoroughly, manipulate the end of a cloth to wipe the inside, and rub with salt. Melt half the butter, fry onion lightly, add buckwheat and fry together for 2–3 minutes. Remove from heat, add eggs, mix well, stuff the carp with this mixture and sew up the opening. Sprinkle with pepper, dust lightly with flour and carefully fry the fish in butter, to brown both sides.

Transfer to a buttered, fireproof dish and put in a hot oven 220°C (425°F or Gas Mark 6) for 5 minutes. Pour in sour cream and return to oven, reduce heat and continue to bake for 45 minutes, basting frequently. Serve in same dish.

NORWEGIAN BAKED WHITING

4 Servings

750 gr (1½ lbs) filleted whiting
1 chopped onion
3 shredded leeks
2 sliced carrots
2 peeled chopped tomatoes
salt and pepper
1 tablespoon lemon juice
125 ml (4 oz or ½ cup) dry white wine
125 ml (4 oz or ½ cup) sour cream
2 tablespoons grated cheese
2 tablespoons grated breadcrumbs
2 tablespoons butter

Wash and dry the whiting fillets and put two or three in a buttered ovenproof dish. Cover with a third of onion, leeks, carrots and tomatoes, season with salt and freshly ground pepper and sprinkle with lemon juice. Continue in this way with alternating layers of whiting and vegetables, seasoning each layer.

Moisten with wine, spread sour cream on top, sprinkle with mixed cheese and breadcrumbs, dot with small pieces of butter and bake in a hot oven 235°C (450°F or Gas Mark 7) for 30 minutes.

Hot Fish Dishes

BASS WITH GINGER SAUCE, CANTONESE STYLE

4–6 Servings

750 gr–1 kg (1½–2 lb) bass
water
1 dessertspoon salt
1 teaspoon oil

1 dessertspoon soya sauce
1 teaspoon ground ginger
60 gr (2 oz or ¼ cup) chopped
  spring onions

Wash and dry the fish. Bring water to the boil—enough to cover the fish. Add salt. Put in fish. As soon as boiling is re-established, reduce heat and cook for 6 minutes. Drain fish carefully and arrange on a serving dish.

Combine soya sauce, oil and ginger together, pour over the fish, garnish with spring onions and serve with plain boiled rice. For this dish, fresh finely chopped ginger is preferable to ground ginger.

BAKED STUFFED BREAM

Bream cooked this way is particularly good, but the recipe can be applied to other kinds of fish : haddock, gurnet, carp.

6 Servings

1½ kg (3 lb) bream, clean and
  ready for cooking
salt
180 gr (6 oz or ¾ cup) butter or
  margarine
1 chopped onion
3 chopped stalks celery
1 chopped apple
180 gr (6 oz or 2 cups) soft
  breadcrumbs

pinch thyme
1 tablespoon chopped parsley
salt and pepper
1–2 eggs
1 tablespoon flour
pinch paprika
lemon cut in wedges

Slit the bream along the stomach and carefully remove the backbone. Wash, dry on soft cloth and sprinkle with salt on the inside. Heat half the butter and fry onion and celery until soft. Add apple and breadcrumbs, cook together for 2–3 minutes, stirring. Remove from heat, add thyme and parsley, season to taste with salt and pepper, bind with egg and mix the stuffing well.

Pre-heat oven to 190°C (375°F or Gas Mark 4). Stuff the bream, stitch up with thread, put in a well buttered baking dish and season. Melt remaining butter and baste the fish with it. Mix flour with paprika and dust the fish with it. Bake for 50–60 minutes.

Lift the bream out on to a heated serving dish. Remove stitches, spoon the pan juices over the fish, garnish with lemon wedges and serve.

BREAM WITH HORSERADISH AND APPLES, GEORGIAN STYLE

4–6 Servings

1–1¼ kg (2–2½ lb) bream	10 peppercorns
salt	2 grated cooking apples
vinegar, brought to the boil	3 tablespoons freshly grated
bouquet garni	horseradish
1 sliced onion	1 tablespoon sugar
1 sliced leek	
1 stalk celery	

Cut the bream into portions, rub with salt, put in a dish and pour over enough boiling vinegar to cover the pieces. Allow to stand for 10 minutes. Prepare court-bouillon (p. 13) with a bouquet garni, onion, leek, celery and peppercorns.

Take bream out of its marinade and cook in court-bouillon until done. Take out the fish with a slotted slice, drain, arrange on a serving dish and keep hot.

Mix grated apples with horseradish, 1 tablespoon vinegar and sugar, dilute with strained court-bouillon to desired consistency and serve with the bream.

FRIED BREAM WITH BLACK BEANS, 'OLD FRIENDS' RECIPE

4 Servings

500–750 gr (1–1½ lb) bream	4 tablespoons oil
salt	1 dessertspoon cornflour
plain flour	1 teaspoon soya sauce
30 gr (1 oz or 2 tablespoons)	125 ml (4 oz or ½ cup) water
black soya beans	4 or 5 spring onions
1 teaspoon brandy	15 gr (½ oz or 1 tablespoon)
1 clove crushed garlic	cooked lean pork

Make a few shallow incisions, slantwise, on both sides of fish. Sprinkle with salt and coat with flour, making it adhere properly.

Scald the soya beans and mix with brandy and garlic. Heat the oil in a large pan and fry the fish until golden. Put on a large serving dish and keep hot.

Pour off surplus oil from pan, fry the black bean mixture for 2 minutes, stirring constantly. Blend cornflour with soya sauce and water, add to the pan, cooking for 2 minutes, stirring all the time. Cut spring onions into 5 cm (2 in.) strips, then with a sharp knife into as many strips lengthwise as possible. Add to the pan. Shred the pork, place in the sauce to heat it.

Pour over fish and serve with plain boiled rice.

BREAM, BASQUE STYLE

4–6 Servings

1 kg (2 lb) bream	1 crushed clove garlic
¼ teaspoon pepper	2 tablespoons lime (or lemon)
1 teaspoon salt	juice
3 tablespoons oil	

Clean, wipe and season the fish. Heat oil, fry garlic in it to flavour it. Grill the bream on a low heat, turning once. When done arrange bream on a serving dish. Remove garlic from pan, adding lime juice, boil up once, pour over the fish and serve piping hot.

CHINESE BREAM WITH TOMATOES

4 Servings

500–750 gr (1–1½ lb) whole bream, cleaned	1 teaspoon sugar
salt	1 teaspoon sherry
flour	1 teaspoon cornflour
4 tablespoons oil	125 ml (4 oz or ½ cup) water
1 crushed clove garlic	15 gr (½ oz or 2 tablespoons)
250 gr (½ lb or 1 cup) ripe, skinned, quartered tomatoes	spring onions

Make a few light incisions, slantwise, on both sides of fish, taking care not to cut too deeply. Sprinkle with salt and dredge with flour. Heat oil in pan and cook fish gently until brown. Remove and keep hot.

Pour off excess oil from pan, add garlic and tomatoes. Blend sugar, sherry and cornflour with the water and add to the pan. Simmer for 2 minutes. Cut the spring onions into 5 cm (2 in.) strips, then with a sharp knife, slice them lengthwise. Pour the sauce over the fish, sprinkle with spring onions and serve with boiled rice.

BRILL WITH SALMON FORCEMEAT

This is a gala dish for a big occasion with a garnish worthy of it : oysters and shrimps' tails, mushrooms and slivers to truffle tossed in butter, little Nantua tartlets with prawns (p. 43), poached mussels, small tomatoes stuffed with mushroom purée, artichoke hearts, quartered and simmered in butter, or any other suitable combination that strikes your fancy.

8–10 Servings

2 kg (4 lb) whole brill
salt and pepper
salmon forcement (p. 220)

½ litre (1 pint or 2 cups) white
   wine fish fumet
Normandy sauce

Make a transversal incision under the head on the dark side to clean the brill. Scale on both sides, trim all round and shorten tail. Wash and dry the brill, lay on the table, slit lengthways in the middle on the dark side and extract the central bone through this opening, taking great care not to damage the white skin. Season on the inside and stuff with salmon cream forcemeat.

Butter an ovenproof dish, lay the brill in it very flat, season, moisten with fumet (based on stock in which all the trimmed-off pieces were cooked), cover with a lid and poach gently in the oven until tender. Lift the brill out carefully, drain and arrange on a heated serving dish. Keep hot.

Cook down the pan juices to reduce, incorporate them in Normandy sauce, pour over the fish and serve.

BRILL SAINT-GERMAIN

4 Servings

Fillets from medium-sized brill
1 beaten egg
120 gr (4 oz or 1 cup)
   breadcrumbs

butter
4 halved, grilled tomatoes
Béarnaise sauce

Skin the fillets and wipe with a damp cloth. Dip in egg and breadcrumbs. Fry in very hot butter until both sides are brown. Drain, arrange on a long serving dish, garnish with tomatoes, surround with a border of thick Béarnaise sauce and serve.

TIPSY CARP, SERBIAN STYLE

There is a pretty saying in Serbia about this dish. Because of the sprinkling of brandy inside the fish, they say that its 'heart is bathed with dew'.

4 Servings
    1–1¼ kg (–2½ lb) carp
    salt
    2 tablespoons brandy
    2 peeled cloves garlic
    125 ml (4 oz or ¼ cup) oil
    freshly ground black pepper
    125 ml (4 oz or ¼ cup) dry
        white wine

Get the carp ready for cooking, season with salt and sprinkle the inside with brandy. Put whole cloves of garlic inside it, stitch up the opening and rub the fish thoroughly with oil. Season with pepper, put in a well oiled baking dish and moisten with wine.

Bake in a moderate oven 190°C (375°F or Gas Mark 4) for 45 minutes, bathing the carp's heart frequently with the tipsy dew forming in the pan.

CARP, HUNGARIAN STYLE

4 Servings
    1 kg (2 lb) carp
    salt
    2 rashers streaky bacon
    butter
    500 gr (1 lb or 2 cups) sliced,
        boiled potatoes
    250 gr (½ lb or 1 cup) peeled,
        sliced tomatoes
    2 seeded, sliced green pimentos
    pepper
    1 dcl (4 oz or ½ cup) sour
        cream
    2 teaspoons paprika

Clean out and scale the fish, but leave whole. Rub with salt. Cut the rashers into lardoons. Make incisions in the fish and insert little strips of bacon into them. Butter a fire-proof dish, line with potatoes and put the larded carp on top. Cover with tomatoes and pimentos, season to taste.

Soften 3 tablespoons butter over a low heat, add sour cream, paprika, blend well, pour over the fish and bake in a hot oven 220°C (425°F or Gas Mark 6), basting from time to time, for 45 to 50 minutes.

CARP, CZECHOSLOVAK STYLE
This is a traditional Christmas dish.

6 Servings
    1½ kg (3 lb) carp
    3–4 tablespoons butter
    1 sliced carrot
    ½ sliced parsnip
    1 sliced onion
    salt and pepper
    1 tablespoon lemon juice
    rind of ½ lemon
    small bay leaf
    ½ dozen peppercorns
    pinch thyme
    125 gr (4 oz or 1 cup)
        crumbled gingerbread
    5 dcl (1 pint or 2 cups) ale
        (dark for preference)
    1 tablespoon red currant jelly
    1 tablespoon chopped, blanched
        almonds
    1 tablespoon sultanas
    2 teaspoons sugar
    ½ teaspoon nutmeg

Clean and scale the carp, cut into uniform portions, fry in half the butter and remove. Add more butter to the same pan and fry carrot, parsnip and onion until soft. Season, add lemon juice and rind, bay leaf, peppercorns and thyme, sprinkle in gingerbread crumbs, moisten with ale, stirring from time to time, until the sauce thickens. Strain the sauce, rub through a sieve, or pass through a blender. Add jelly, almonds, sultanas, sugar and nutmeg.

Just before serving bring the sauce to the boil, check seasoning, put in carp, heat through and serve piping hot.

CHAR WITH GRUYÈRE, SWISS STYLE

4 Servings

750 gr (1½ lb) char
60 gr (2 oz or 4 tablespoons) butter
salt and pepper

pinch paprika
freshly grated breadcrumbs
120 gr (4 oz or 2/3 cup) processed Gruyère cheese

Wash and dry the fish, cut into slices. Put a layer of fish slices into a buttered ovenproof dish, season, dust with breadcrumbs and scatter a few small dots of butter on top. Cover with slices of cheese and repeat in this order until all the ingredients are used up, ending with a layer of Gruyère. Dot with tiny pieces of butter, cover with buttered greaseproof paper or a piece of foil and bake in the oven 190°C (375°F or Gas Mark 4) for 20 minutes. Remove paper and continue to cook until the top browns lightly.

BRANDADE DE MORUE

This is a great speciality of Languedoc and Provence and is one of the most delicious ways of preparing salt cod.

6 Servings

1 kg (2 lb) salt cod
360 ml (¾ pint or 1½ cups) olive oil
1 clove crushed garlic

2½ dcl (½ pint or 1 cup) cream
white pepper
chopped parsley
croutons fried in oil

Wash and soak salt cod in cold water overnight. Cut into square pieces, put into a pan with cold water, heat slowly, bring to the boil, simmer for 5 minutes and drain. Skin and bone the cod and flake the flesh.

Heat 120 ml (4 oz or ½ cup) oil in a heavy flat-bottomed pan, put in the cod and garlic, keep on a very low heat, using a very hard wooden spoon, crush the fish to a creamy paste. Keep the rest of the oil in a small pan over low heat, so that it is warm.

Do the same with the cream—it is essential to keep cod, oil and cream at the same temperature, just tepid.

Stirring all the time, alternately add a little oil and a litle cream to the cod paste until all has been used up and the brandade acquires the texture of good creamy mashed potatoes.

Season with white pepper and serve in small round bowls, moulding the brandade into a dome and smoothing the surface. Sprinkle with parsley. Garnish with croûtons—slices of white bread, cut into small triangles and fried in oil.

BRANDADE À LA NANTUA

Prepare the brandade as above, but garnish with crayfish tails and slivers of truffle tossed in butter and croûtons of white bread fried in oil.

COD WITH LOBSTER BUTTER

This dish is called 'Cardinal' in French, because the fish is 'robed' in pink.

4 Servings

4 cod steaks	2 tablespoons tomato purée
salt and pepper	prawn of lobster butter
1 tablespoon butter	
2 dcl (½ pint or 1 cup) Béchamel sauce	

Season the cod steaks, brush with butter and bake in a moderate oven 190°C (375°F or Gas Mark 4) for 20 minutes. Heat the sauce, and tomato purée, adjust seasoning and finish off with a little prawn or lobster butter to add flavour and colouring.

CURRIED COD, INDIAN STYLE

4 Servings

1 kg (2 lb) fillet of Cod	½ teaspoon ground turmeric
60 gr (2 oz or 4 tablespoons) butter	½ teaspoon ground mustard seed
1 finely chopped onion	1 teaspoon rice flour
2 cloves chopped garlic	2 dcl (½ pint or 1 cup) coconut milk
1 dried seeded, chopped chilli	juice of ½ lemon
1 teaspoon ground coriander	salt
½ teaspoon ground chilli	

Slice the fish. Heat butter, fry the onion until it softens and becomes transparent, add garlic, chilli and all the ground spices, stir and reduce heat. Dilute rice flour with coconut milk, pour the mixture into the pan and blend well. Add lemon juice, season with salt to taste, simmer gently, stirring until the sauce thickens, add fish, make sure it is completely immersed in the sauce, simmer until tender and serve with rice.

GRILLED COD OR HADDOCK STEAKS WITH ROSEMARY

4 Servings

8 fresh or frozen fish steaks
2 tablespoons melted butter
1 tablespoon chopped fresh
   rosemary

salt and pepper
1 sliced lemon, as garnish

Pat the fish dry and brush with melted butter. If frozen fish is used, follow instruction on packet for thawing before cooking. (See also p. 10). Put on a pre-heated grill and sprinkle with half the rosemary. Season with salt and pepper to taste. Grill for 4 minutes. Turn over, sprinkle with the rest of the rosemary, season and grill for another 4 minutes. Serve garnished with slices of lemon.

CODLIFLOWER CHEESE

4–6 Servings

1 nice cauliflower
500 gr (1 lb) fresh or frozen cod
   (or any other white fish)
125 ml (¼ pint or ½ cup) milk
2 tablespoons grated Parmesan
250 ml (½ pint or 1 cup) hot
   Mornay sauce

salt and pepper
2 tablespoons butter
125 gr (4 oz or 1 cup) dry
   breadcrumbs

Divide the cauliflower into neat flowerets and put in a saucepan with just enough water to cover. Add salt, cover and bring to the boil. Remove from heat without uncovering. Poach cod in milk for 15 minutes, drain and flake. Add the Parmesan to the hot sauce and season to taste. Mix with fish.

Melt butter in a frying pan and stir in the breadcrumbs until they are crisp and golden brown. Drain the cauliflower and arrange in a ring (stalks inwards) on a warmed serving dish. Heap the cod mixture into the centre and sprinkle with fried breadcrumbs.

COD STEAKS WITH TOMATOES

4 Servings

8 frozen cod steaks
juice of 2 lemons
½ cup oil

3 chopped onions
4 peeled and chopped tomatoes
salt and pepper

Thaw cod steaks and pat dry. Sprinkle with lemon juice. Heat oil in a large frying pan and fry onions until transparent. Add fish, chopped tomatoes and salt and pepper to taste. Simmer for 15 minutes.

CZECH SPICED COD IN HERBS

6 Servings

1½ kg (3 lb) cod (or 12 thawed cod steaks or any other white fish)
250 ml (½ pint or 1 cup) milk
1 tablespoon vinegar
1 tablespoon lemon juice
salt
1 tablespoon flour
4 tablespoons butter

1 tablespoon chopped shallots
½ teaspoon basil
½ teaspoon chopped rosemary
½ teaspoon chopped parsley
1 tablespoon cornflour
180 ml (6 oz or ¾ cup) dry white wine
125 ml (¼ pint or ½ cup) sour cream

Skin and bone fish and marinate for an hour in milk and vinegar. Pat dry and cut into slices 2 cm (¾ in.) thick. Sprinkle with lemon juice and salt to taste. Dip in flour and fry on both sides in 2 tablespoons butter. In another pan, fry shallots in remaining butter until golden. Add herbs. Stir cornflour into wine and add gradually to shallots. Bring up to boil and remove from heat. Add sour cream.

Put the fried fish slices into the herb sauce and simmer for 10 minutes, but do not allow to boil.

COD FILLETS IN SAVOURY CUSTARD

4 Servings

1 tablespoon butter
4 portions cod fillet
3 beaten eggs
360 ml (¾ pint or 1½ cups) milk
120 ml (4 oz or ½ cup) single cream

salt and pepper
1 tablespoon chopped spring onions

Butter an ovenproof dish and arrange the fillets in it. Beat the eggs with milk and cream, season, pour over the fish and bake in a slow oven 150°C (300°F or Gas Mark 2) until the fish is done and custard set. Sprinkle with spring onions and serve.

COD, SINGAPORE STYLE

4 Servings

2 fresh coconuts
500 gr (1 lb) cod fillet
salt and pepper
2–3 dried chillis
pinch coriander
¼ teaspoons cumin

1 clove garlic
crushed tamarind
1 chopped onion
¼ teaspoon powdered turmeric
2 tablespoons oil

Use the coconuts to extract half a pint of fairly thick coconut milk. Cut the cod into uniform small pieces and season with salt and pepper. Pound chillis, coriander, cumin, garlic, tamarind and onion in a mortar, or pass through a blender, to make curry paste.

Add turmeric, blend well. Fry the mixture in oil for a few minutes, stirring briskly to hasten amalgamation. Add cod and coconut milk, simmer gently for 7 to 8 minutes and serve.

COD, NORWEGIAN STYLE

This recipe was first brought to my attention by a Norwegian professor at a terribly learned international conference. We have since tried it, and it certainly does things for dear old cod.

4 Servings

500–750 gr (1–1½ lb) cod fillets
2 carrots
90 gr (3 oz or ¾ cup) celery
6 slices white bread
120 gr (4 oz or ½ cup) butter

1 medium-sized chopped onion
3 tablespoons chopped parsley
salt and pepper
3 tablespoons breadcrumbs

Wash and dry cod fillets. Grate the carrot and dice the celery. Cut the crusts off and dice the bread. Melt the butter (reserving a quarter of it for later use) in a bowl, add carrots, celery, diced bread, onion and parsley, season to taste and mix well. Put the fish in a well buttered ovenproof dish, season, cover with the mixed vegetables, sprinkle with bread-crumbs, dot with remainder of the butter in tiny pieces, bake in a pre-heated oven 233°C (450°F or Gas Mark 7) for 30 minutes.

DANISH BAKED COD WITH APPLE AND CELERY

4 Servings

750 gr (1½ lb) cod fillet
120 gr (4 oz or 1 cup) shredded celery
1 finely chopped onion
3 diced cooking apples
salt and pepper

4 tablespoons tomato purée
1 dcl (14 oz or ½ cup) milk
2 tablespoons butter

Wash and dry the cod fillets. Lightly butter an ovenproof dish, put in celery, onion and apples, mix and spread out evenly and put the fish on this foundation. Season with salt and pepper. Dilute tomato purée with milk, pour over the fillets. Dot the top with small pieces of butter. Bake in the oven, 233°C (450°F or Gas Mark 7) for 30 minutes. Serve with mashed potatoes or rice.

BAKED COD, SPANISH STYLE

4 Servings

4 cod steaks	1 small onion
a little butter	1 clove garlic
salt and pepper	1 tablespoon chopped parsley
25 gr (½ lb) skinned tomatoes	1 tablespoon olive oil

Heat oven to 175°C (350°F or Gas Mark 3). Put the fish steaks into a lightly buttered ovenproof dish, season to taste. Purée the tomatoes in a blender. Add onion, garlic, parsley and oil. Switch on and blend until smooth and well amalgamated. Cover the fish with this dressing and bake for 25 minutes.

DRIED COD CANARY ISLANDS

Marina Pereyra de Aznar, who has a genius for Spanish dishes, has a way of preparing salt dried cod which is delicious.

4 Servings

1 kg (2 lb) salt cod	1–2 cloves chopped garlic
3 tablespoons flour	2 sliced red pimentos
4 tablespoons oil	1 teaspoon salt
3 medium-sized sliced onions	½ teaspoon pepper
750 gr (1½ lb) peeled, ripe tomatoes	cinnamon
60 gr (2 oz or 1½ cups) chopped parsley	

Soak the cod in water overnight, change the water once or twice. Just before cooking, scale the fish but without removing the skin, because this gives the sauce the right glazed consistency. Cut into pieces, squeeze surplus water out of them, roll in flour and fry in oil until golden. Remove and keep hot.

Pour a little of the oil left from frying into a deep sauté pan, put in a layer of onions, then a layer of tomatoes and follow with a layer of cod. Continue in this way, seasoning each layer lightly. Sprinkle with parsley and garlic, cover with pimentos and sprinkle in the rest of the oil.

Check seasoning, add a tiny pinch of cinnamon, cover and simmer gently for 1½ hours, without stirring but shaking the pan from time to time. If too much juice forms in the pan, take the lid off for the last 10 minutes to evaporate. Serve with rice.

DRIED COD, ITALIAN STYLE

4 Servings

1 kg (2 lb) dried cod
flour
125 ml (4 oz or ½ cup) olive oil
1 clove crushed garlic
freshly grated black pepper
125 ml (4 oz or ½ cup) wine
   vinegar

180 ml (6 oz or ¾ cup) water
2 tablespoons seedless raisins
1½ tablespoons fresh chopped
   mint
1½ tablespoons shelled
   pistachio nuts

Soak the cod overnight. Scale, rinse, wipe with a cloth, cut into portions and dredge with flour. Heat oil in sauté pan, fry the garlic in it just to flavour and remove. In the same oil fry cod portions 4 to 5 minutes each side. The fish should become quite soft and acquire a pale brown colour. Season with pepper.

In a saucepan combine vinegar, water, raisins, mint and pistachio nuts, bring to the boil, simmer for 6 to 7 minutes to reduce and concentrate, pour over the cod, simmer gently for 5 minutes and serve with a lettuce salad.

CONGER EEL, CANARY ISLANDS

6 Servings

1–1½ kg (2–3 lb) eel, cleaned
   and skinned
2 chopped carrots
1 chopped onion
6 tablespoons olive oil
1 tablespoon flour
500 gr (1 lb or 2 cups) shelled
   peas

salt and pepper
2 tablespoons sherry
250 ml (½ pint or 1 cup) fish
   stock, made from the pieces
   trimmed off the eel

Trim the eel, cut into portions and use trimmings to make a little concentrated stock. Fry carrot and onion in oil until onion becomes transparent, blend in flour, add peas and simmer together until the onion begins to colour.

Season eel, sprinkle with sherry, add to pan, pour in stock, cover, bring to the boil, simmer on low heat for 20 minutes and serve.

CONGER EEL IN GREEN SAUCE

6 Servings

1–1½ kg (2–3 lb) cleaned and
   skinned conger eel
1 chopped onion
3 tablespoons oil
salt and pepper
120 gr (4 oz or 3 cups) chopped
   parsley

1 glass dry white wine
120 ml (4 oz or ½ cup) fish
   stock made from pieces
   trimmed off the eel

Wash, dry and cut eel into portions. Brown onion lightly in oil, add eel, cook together for 5 minutes, season, add parsley and wine. Simmer for 15 minutes, add stock, cover the pan and simmer for another 15 minutes.

GREY MULLET BLACK SEA STYLE

4 Servings

4 grey mullets
2 tablespoons flour
salt and pepper
3 tablespoons butter

pinch saffron
125 ml (4 oz or ½ cup) sour cream

Clean and scale the fish, roll in flour seasoned with salt and pepper and fry in butter, turning once carefully to brown both sides. Transfer to a buttered fireproof dish, sprinkle with saffron, cover with sour cream, put in the oven or under the grill for 5 minutes to set the top and serve in the same dish.

INDONESIAN SPICED FISH FILLETS

4 Servings

500 gr (1 lb) fish fillets (mullet for preference)
walnut-size piece of tamarind
3–4 tablespoons peanut oil
2 finely chopped onions
2 finely chopped cloves garlic

½ teaspoon fresh chillis (optional)
1 tablespoon soya sauce
2 tablespoons water
1 teaspoon soft brown sugar
juice of 1 lime (or lemon)

Rub the fish fillets with tamarind, then fry them in hot oil to brown both sides. Reduce heat, add onions and garlic and cook for 3–4 minutes. Add chilli and fry lightly. Mix soya sauce, water, sugar and lime juice and pour over the fish. Bring to the boil, simmer for 3–4 seconds and serve.

FRIED GUDGEON

Clean the fish, remove entrails and gills, but do not scale. Rinse dry on a cloth, dip in egg and breadcrumbs, leaving the heads and tails uncoated, and fry in butter for about 5 minutes, by which time they should be nicely browned.

STUFFED GURNET

4 Servings

2 medium-sized gurnet
120 gr (4 oz or 1 cup) grated
  breadcrumbs
90 gr (3 oz or 6 tablespoons)
  butter
1 tablespoon chopped parsley
pinch mixed herbs
¼ teaspoon nutmeg

½ teaspoon grated lemon rind
salt and pepper
1 beaten egg
4 rashers bacon
2½ dcl (½ pint or 1 cup) white
  sauce
1½ teaspoon anchovy essence

Clean the gurnet, remove fins and gills, but leave the head on. Rinse and dry. Mix breadcrumbs, 60 grs (2 oz or 4 tablespoons) butter, parsley, herbs, nutmeg and lemon rind. Season with salt and pepper, bind with egg and blend into a smooth forcemeat. Stuff the fish with the forecemeat, stitch up the opening, coax the gurnet into holding its tail in its mouth, put in a baking dish. Melt the rest of the butter, pour over the fish.

Cover the fish with bacon rashers and bake in the oven 190°C (375°F or Gas Mark 4) for 40 minutes.

Blend anchovy essence into white sauce and serve with stuffed gurnet.

This recipe can also be recommended for Shad.

FINNAN HADDIE

Among the great debts we owe to Scotland, the excellence of her ways of dealing with fish must be universally recognised. Smoking fish slowly and lovingly over smouldering oak chips in Scotland has always been an art. No wonder finnan haddie is immortalised in Scottish literature!

4 Servings

1 Finnan haddock
3 tablespoons butter
small chopped onion
1 tablespoon flour

1 teaspoon paprika
½ litre (1 pint or 2 cups) milk
breadcrumbs

Butter an ovenproof dish, put in haddock. Heat 2 tablespoons butter, soften the onion in it, blend in flour and paprika, gradually dilute with milk, simmer until the sauce thickens slightly and pour over the haddock. Sprinkle with breadcrumbs, dot with small pieces of butter and bake in the oven 190°C (375°F or Gas Mark 4) for 25 minutes.

Or, as a delectable variation, you could put the haddock in a cocotte, garnish it on one side with potatoes, on the other with onions, both cut in 3/5 cm (¼ in.) slices, cooked in unsalted water for 10 minutes. Cover with the sauce, made as above but omitting the cheese and using 2½ dcl (½ pint or 1 cup) of milk and equal amount of cream, and bake in the oven. The potatoes will be tender and the sauce full of playful bubbles and a beautiful golden colour.

HADDOCK WITH MINT AND CAPERS, ITALIAN STYLE

4 Servings

1 kg (2 lb) boned haddock
flour seasoned with salt and pepper
2–3 tablespoons olive oil
1 clove crushed garlic

3 tablespoons tomato purée
120 ml (4 oz or ½ cup) warm water
2 sprigs fresh mint
1 teaspoon capers

Wash and dry the fish, cut into portions. Season a little flour with salt and pepper and dredge the haddock with it. Heat oil, fry the garlic for a couple of minutes, then remove and in the same oil fry haddock about 4 minutes each side, or until golden. Dilute tomato purée with warm water, pour over haddock, add mint and capers, taste for seasoning, simmer for 7 to 8 minutes under a lid and serve.

SMOKED HADDOCK COTTAGE PIE

6–8 Servings

500–750 gr (1–1½ lb) smoked haddock
125 ml (¼ pint or ½ cup) milk
250 gr (8 oz or 1 cup) cottage cheese
125 ml (1¼ pint or ½ cup) béchamel sauce
1 egg lightly beaten

1 tablespoon Dijon mustard
1 tablespoon chopped chives
salt and pepper
500 gr (1 lb or 2 cups) potatoes, cooked and mashed
2 tablespoons grated Parmesan
2 tablespoons butter

Poach smoked haddock in milk for 5–10 minutes until tender. Drain and flake, removing skin and bones. Sieve the cottage cheese into the béchamel, or put both through a blender, and add egg, mustard, chives and seasoning to taste. Fold into flaked fish and turn mixture into a buttered ovenproof dish. Cover with layer of mashed potato. Mark the top of the potato with a fork. Sprinkle with Parmesan, dot with small pieces of butter and cook in the oven pre-heated to 200°C (400°F or Gas Mark 5), until nicely brown on top.

90

SCANDINAVIAN HADDOCK PUDDING

4 Servings

1 kg (2 lb) haddock fillets	salt and pepper
1 tablespoon potato flour	1 litre (1 quart) milk
1 tablespoon plain flour	mushroom sauce
90 gr (3 oz or 6 tablespoons) butter	

Skin the fillets, discard all bones and put the flesh through a mincer. Add potato flour, plain flour and butter, season with salt and pepper to taste and stir until the mixture is blended into a smooth paste.

Add milk little by little. It is important to carry out this operation very, very gradually. Begin by blending in a tablespoon of milk at a time, increasing the amount as more and more milk is absorbed. Stir well. Pour the pudding mixture into a well buttered ovenproof dish. Pre-heat the oven and bake the pudding in a moderately hot oven, 204°C (400°F or Gas Mark 5) for 1 hour. Serve with mushroom sauce.

SCRAMBLED HADDOCK

Flake left-over piece of haddock, remove all skin and bones. Allow 60 gr (2 oz or ¼ cup) of fish for each egg. Beat the eggs and haddock, season, thin down with a little milk if necessary. Heat butter in a saucepan and scramble the mixture in the ordinary way.

Serve on rice, mashed potatoes, or buttered toast, garnished with watercress, tomatoes or whatever you happen to have in the larder that would harmonise with the mixture.

HAKE CARDINAL, WITH LOBSTER SAUCE

4 Servings

4 portions of hake	30 gr (1 oz or 2 tablespoons) butter
court-bouillon (p. 13)	
3 tablespoons grated cheese	lobster sauce (p. 209)
3 tablespoons fresh breadcrumbs	

Simmer the hake in court-bouillon for 10 minutes, drain and put in a buttered ovenproof dish. Mix cheese with breadcrumbs and sprinkle the mixture liberally over each portion of fish. Spoon the sauce carefully all around the pieces of hake, without masking the cheese-and-breadcrumb coating. Dot this un-sauced surface with tiny pieces of butter. Put in the oven or under the grill to brown the top and serve.

HALIBUT WITH PISTACHIO NUTS, PERSIAN STYLE

4 Servings

750 gr–1 kg (1¾–2 lb) halibut
4 tablespoons olive oil
salt and pepper
small pinch saffron
2½ dcl (½ pint or 1 cup) tomato
   sauce

60 gr (2 oz or 6 tablespoons)
   blanched pistachio nuts
60 gr (2 oz or 6 tablespoons)
   washed, seedless raisins
1 teaspoon chopped parsley

Wash and dry the fish, score with a knife, brush with olive oil, season with salt and pepper, put in a well greased baking dish, sprinkle with saffron and 2 tablespoons oil and bake in the oven 175°C (350°F or Gas Mark 3) for 30 minutes, basting from time to time. Add tomato sauce and continue to bake for another ¼ hour.

Toss the pistachio nuts and raisins in 1 tablespoons oil, sprinkle over fish, put back in the oven for 5 minutes. Sprinkle with parsley and serve.

HALIBUT, SCANDINAVIAN STYLE

6 Servings

750 gr (1½ lb) halibut
8 bacon rashers
250 gr (½ lb) sliced carrots
1 chopped onion
125 gr (4 oz or 1½ cups)
   chopped mushrooms
2 teaspoons chopped dill

1 tablespoon chopped parsley
salt and pepper
4 slices lemon
125 ml (4 oz or ½ cup) dry
   white wine
2 tablespoons butter

Cut the fish into uniform slices. Line a buttered ovenproof dish with bacon rashers, cover with carrots, then onions and mushrooms. Sprinkle with dill and parsley and season. Having made this bed, lay the halibut on it. Season to taste, put lemon slices on top, moisten with wine, dot with small pieces of butter, cover and bake in a hot oven 220°C (425°F or Gas Mark 6) for 25 minutes.

HALIBUT À LA SOUBISE

4 Servings

1 kg (2 lb) halibut steak
white wine fumet

Soubise sauce (p. 211)
chopped parsley

Have the fishmonger skin the halibut for you and ask for all the trimmings, head, tail, bones of the halibut, and other fish, to use as a basis for your fumet. Clarify and strain the fumet as described (p. 15).

Wrap the halibut in butter muslin, put carefully into a fish kettle, cover with fumet, and simmer over such gentle heat that the water in the kettle no more than 'smiles'. Cook for about 30 minutes, or until the fish begins to come away easily from the bone.

Remove halibut, drain, unwrap, arrange on a dish, cover with Soubise sauce—prepared while the fish is cooking—sprinkle with parsley and serve.

BAKED HALIBUT, GREEK STYLE

4 Servings

1 kg (2 lb) halibut
salt and pepper
1 teaspoon lemon juice
olive oil
2 sliced onions
2 chopped cloves garlic
4 tablespoons chopped parsley

500 gr (1 lb) peeled tomatoes
3 tablespoons water
125 ml (4 oz or ½ cup) white wine
1 sliced lemon
60 gr (2 oz or 1/3 cup) black olives

Wash and dry the halibut, season with salt and pepper and sprinkle with lemon juice. Oil an ovenproof dish lightly, put in the fish.

Heat 3 tablespoons oil, fry onions and garlic until they soften, add parsley and tomatoes, simmer for 5 minutes, pressing down with a wooden spoon to make the tomatoes render up their juices. Add water, stir, cook for 2 minutes. Add wine, bring to the boil. Garnish with slices of lemon and bake in the oven 190°C (375°F or Gas Mark 4) for 40 minutes. Garnish with olives, return to oven for 5 minutes and serve.

SCOTTISH HERRING IN OATMEAL

4 Servings

4 plump filleted fresh herrings
salt and pepper
milk

fine oatmeal
fat for deep frying
lemon

Season the herrings, dip in milk, coat with oatmeal and deep fry in hot fat until golden brown. Drain, garnish with lemon wedges and serve.

HERRINGS STUFFED WITH PRAWNS OR SHRIMPS

4 Servings

4 fresh herrings
1–2 slices white bread
milk
60 gr (2 oz or ½ cup) peeled prawns or shrimps

seasoning
anchovy essence
1 beaten egg
toasted breadcrumbs
butter

Wash and dry the herrings, cut off heads. Split the fish open and remove backbone. Soak the bread in a little milk, squeeze out and flake. Chop the prawns or shrimps, mix with bread, chop together for a couple of minutes, season with salt and pepper, add a few drops of anchovy essence and blend well, adding a little butter, to make a homogeneous stuffing. Spread a quarter of the stuffing on each herring, on the inside.

Starting at the head end, roll up the herrings to enclose all filling and secure with a cocktail stick. Dip in beaten egg and breadcrumbs, put in a buttered fireproof dish, dot with pieces of butter and bake in very moderate oven 175°C (350°F or Gas Mark 3) for 30 minutes.

HERRINGS, BRITTANY STYLE

4 Servings

4 soft-roed herrings	$\frac{1}{2}$ teaspoon French mustard
salt and pepper	fried parsley
beaten egg	lemon
breadcrumbs	
60 gr (2 oz or 4 tablespoons) butter	

Fillet the herrings and remove roes. Season fish and half the roes to taste, dip in egg and breadcrumbs, fry in half the butter, drain and keep hot. Toss unbreadcrumbed roes in the same butter, pass through a blender, or rub through a fine sieve. Flavour with mustard and blend with the rest of the butter.

Arrange the fried herrings and roes on a dish, garnish with fried parsley and wedges of lemon and serve with roe dressing.

HERRINGS, BURGUNDY STYLE

4 Servings

4 filleted herrings	red Burgundy wine
1 chopped onion	fish stock
1 chopped carrot	125 gr (4 oz or 2 cups) button
2 stalks shredded celery	mushrooms
butter	bread for croûtons
salt and pepper	

Wash and dry the herring fillets with a cloth. Toss the onion, carrot and celery in one tablespoon butter. Put in a casserole, season and moisten with as much wine as you can spare. Cover and simmer until the vegetables are tender.

Add fish and mushrooms and, if you have been mean with the wine, enough fish stock or water, just to cover the herrings.

Simmer until the fish is done, put herring fillets on a serving dish, surround with mushrooms and keep hot.

Cook down the sauce to reduce and concentrate it, pour over the fish and serve with croûtons fried in butter.

SWEDISH BAKED HERRINGS

4 Servings

4 filleted herrings	2 tablespoons chopped dill
2 tablespoons butter	(or parsley)
salt and pepper	2 tablespoons breadcrumbs
12 poached mussels (p. 116)	120 ml (4 oz or ½ cup) cream

Put half the herring fillets in a buttered ovenproof dish, skin side down. Season with salt and freshly ground black pepper. Cover with mussels, sprinkle with dill and lay the rest of the fillets on top. Season, sprinkle with breadcrumbs, dot with small pieces of butter and bake in a hot oven 235°C (450°F or Gas Mark 7) for 15 minutes. Coat with cream, return to oven for 10 minutes.

Serve with new boiled potatoes and a green salad.

JOHN DORY GRILLED OVER DRY FENNEL

Allow one medium-sized John Dory and 45 gr (1½ oz or 1 cup) dried fennel per portion.

Clean, wash and dry the fish, make several shallow incisions on each side, brush with butter or oil and grill 4–5 minutes each side. Pile fennel on a metal dish, spread evenly, erect a grill rack above it, place the fish on the rack and set the fennel alight. Cook the John Dory in these aromatic fumes, for as long as the fennel lasts, turn once or twice to make sure the delicate fish is thoroughly impregnated with the delicious aroma and serve.

GRILLED JOHN DORY, GALILEE

This is an old dish dating back to Biblical times. The fish used in Galilee, then as now, is the John Dory. It is also called 'St Peter's Fish' since it has, it is said, the marks of St Peter's thumbs on its back—a distinction it shares with haddock.

If John Dory is not available, red mullet, small bass and, of course, trout, are all good cooked this way. Traditionally the fish should be cooked over glowing charcoal.

4 Servings

4 John Dory, whole, ready for	salt and pepper
cooking	4 sprigs parsley
2 onions	4 halved lemon slices
oil	lemon juice

Wash and dry the fish. Cut onions into fairly thick slices. Brush the fish with oil on the inside, season, stuff each with a portion of sliced onion, a sprig of parsley and 2 semi-circles of lemon. Oil grill rack and heat grill. Brush fish with oil on the outside and grill for 6–7 minutes each side, turning once and basting with lemon juice and oil during cooking.

MACKEREL WITH MUSHROOMS AND SHRIMPS

4 Servings

4 filleted mackerel
white wine court-bouillon
125 gr (4 oz or 2 cups) button
  mushrooms
8–12 poached mussels (p. 116)
60 gr (2 oz or 1 cup) peeled
  shrimps

2 dcl (½ pint or 1 cup) white
  sauce
2–3 tablespoons cream
1 tablespoon butter

Poach the mackerel in court-bouillon with mushrooms. Drain, skin, arrange on a dish and garnish with mushrooms, mussels and shrimps.

Make white sauce incorporating in it the liquor in which the fish was poached, add cream, blend in butter, adding it in tiny pieces. Pour over the mackerel, put under the grill or in the oven to brown the top and serve.

ISRAELI MACKEREL WITH CARROTS AND LEEKS

4 Servings

4 filleted mackerel
salt
1 chopped onion
2 chopped leeks
120 gr (4 oz or 1¼ cups) sliced
  carrots

1 tablespoon butter
2 tablespoons vinegar
1 dcl (4 oz or ½ cup) olive oil
2 tablespoons chopped dill
  (or parsley)

Wash and dry fillets, season with salt and put in a buttered ovenproof dish, skin side down. Cover with onion, leeks and carrots, moisten with vinegar and oil. Top with small pieces of butter, cover and bake in a hot oven 233°C (450°F or Gas Mark 7) for 30 minutes.

Before serving, sprinkle with chopped dill. Serve with baked potatoes.

MACKEREL CÔTES DU NORD

4 Servings

4 mackerel
court-bouillon
2 raw yolks
1 teaspoon mustard
salt and pepper
dash vinegar

1 tablespoon chopped parsley
1 tablespoon chopped chives
60 gr (2 oz or 4 tablespoons)
  butter
1 lemon

Poach the fish in court-bouillon, allow to cool, skin, fillet and arrange on a dish. Put the yolks in a bowl, add mustard, salt, pepper, vinegar, parsley and chives and mix thoroughly, warm the butter enough to melt it, add it in a trickle to the ingredients in the bowl, stirring to blend it in, until the sauce acquires the consistency of mayonnaise. Pour over the mackerel, garnish with wedges of lemon and serve at once. If the dish has to be kept waiting, serve the sauce separately.

MACKEREL À LA FLAMANDE

4 Servings

1 litre (2 pints or 5 cups) water
2½ dcl (½ pint or 1 cup) vinegar
3 chopped carrots
1 chopped onion
2–3 chopped shallots
½ bay leaf
sprig thyme

few sprigs parsley
1 teaspoon salt
10 peppercorns
2 filleted mackerel
2 dcl (½ pint or 1 cup) white
  sauce
1 tablespoon French mustard

Cook water with vinegar, carrots, onion, shallots, bay leaf, thyme, parsley and salt, to make court-bouillon. Bring to the boil, then simmer gently for 45 minutes without covering the pan. Add peppercorns, simmer for a further 10 minutes, strain and leave the court-bouillon until it is just tepid. Put the fish into court-bouillon, bring to the boil, simmer for 10 minutes. Drain the mackerel carefully and keep warm.

Incorporate the liquid left from cooking the fish into the white sauce, blend in mustard, cook down to reduce. Serve this sauce with the mackerel.

BAKED MACKEREL WITH FENNEL

2–4 Servings

2 mackerel
salt and pepper

1 tablespoon fennel seeds
1 tablespoon butter

Clean, wash and dry the mackerel. Cut four shallow diagonal slits in both sides of the fish. Rub inside the fish and the slits with salt and pepper to taste and fennel seeds. Place mackerel on

D

a sheet of kitchen foil, dot with butter and wrap up, leaving some air space between fish and foil. Lay on a baking sheet and cook for 30 minutes at 190°C (375°F or Gas Mark 4).

BAKED MACKEREL WITH CURRY

As above, substituting 2 teaspoons curry powder for the fennel seeds.

BAKED MACKEREL WITH ROSEMARY

As above, substituting 2 teaspoons fresh rosemary needles for fennel seeds. It is best to place a whole sprig of fresh rosemary inside the fish.

NOTE: There are many variations for Baked Mackerel with paprika, ginger, garlic, etc. Those on a diet can leave out the butter, as mackerel is an oily fish.

All these dishes are equally good served hot or cold.

GRILLED MACKEREL WITH GOOSEBERRY SAUCE

4 Servings

4 mackerel about 250–375 gr (½–¾ lb) each	250 gr (½ lb or 1½ cups) gooseberries
2 tablespoons seasoned flour	½ teaspoon sugar (optional)
30 gr (1 oz or 2 tablespoons) butter	¼ teaspoon grated nutmeg grilled tomatoes

Fillet the mackerel, wash, dry and dip in flour seasoned with a pinch of salt and a grating of pepper. Brush with melted butter and grill, basting with butter from time to time and allowing 4 minutes for each side. Top and tail the gooseberries, add sugar and stew with a little water. Put through a blender or rub through a sieve. Add nutmeg, stir, boil down if the sauce needs thickening and serve with mackerel.

Garnish with grilled tomatoes.

MACKEREL, MOUNT ATHOS MONASTERY STYLE

This is an authentic monastery recipe.

6 Servings

4 tablespoons olive oil	pinch wild marjoram
2 medium-sized chopped onions	juice of 1 lemon
3 large filleted mackerel	125 gr (4 oz or 2/3 cup) black olives
salt and pepper	
1 crushed bayleaf	

Heat half the oil and lightly fry the onions. Oil an ovenproof dish, line with half the onions, lay the mackerel fillets on top, season with salt and pepper, sprinkle with bay leaf, marjoram and lemon juice, cover with the remaining onions. Sprinkle with whatever oil is left, surround with olives, cover with a lid and bake in the oven 205°C (400°F or Gas Mark 5) for 20 minutes.

Serve in the same dish and hand boiled potatoes separately.

PERCH, SWISS STYLE

4 Servings

4 medium-sized perch	butter or oil for frying
beer	maitre d'hôtel butter
flour	lemon
salt and pepper	

Prepare the perch for cooking, rinse, dry, put in a deep dish, cover with beer and leave to stand for an hour. Drain, dredge lightly with flour, seasoned with salt and pepper, and fry. When golden on both sides, remove from pan, drain on absorbent paper, arrange on a heated serving dish, put a piece of maitre d'hôtel butter on each fish, garnish with lemon wedges and serve.

PERCH, BOHEMIAN STYLE

4 Servings

4 medium-sized filleted perch	60 gr (2 oz or ¼ cup) sliced carrot
salt and pepper	
60 gr (2 oz or 4 tablespoons) butter	60 gr (2 oz or ¼ cup) shredded celery
1 chopped onion	2½ dcl (½ pint or 1 cup) sour cream
60 gr (2 oz or ¼ cup) chopped ham	1 tablespoon chopped parsley

Trim, wash and dry the fillets carefully, season with pepper and salt. Melt the butter, pour half of it into an ovenproof dish. Line the dish with half the onion, ham, carrot and celery. Put the fish on this foundation, cover with the rest of the ham and vegetables, sprinkle with remaining butter, mask with sour cream and bake in a hot oven 220°C (425°F or Gas Mark 6) for 30 minutes.

Before serving, sprinkle with parsley.

PERCH IN BEER BATTER, GERMAN STYLE

4 Servings

750 gr (1½ lb) perch fillets
salt and pepper
3 tablespoons chopped onion
1 tablespoon chopped parsley
1 tablespoon lemon juice
2 tablespoons flour

fat for deep frying
for batter:
180 gr (6 oz or 1½ cups) flour
small pinch salt
2 eggs
2½ dcl (½ pint or 1 cup) beer

Season perch fillets with salt and pepper, put in a dish, cover with onion and parsley, sprinkle with lemon juice and leave to macerate for half an hour, turning from time to time.

Sift flour into a mixing bowl, add salt. Separate yolks from whites and add yolks to flour. Beat in beer little by little, whisk vigorously to make sure there are no lumps and leave to stand for 20 minutes. Beat the whites into a stiff foam, fold into the batter.

Drain the fillets, dip in flour, shake off surplus, coat with batter, deep fry until golden, drain and serve.

PERCH, YUGOSLAV STYLE

4 Servings

1 kg (2 lb) perch
salt
3 tablespoons olive oil
2 tablespoons butter

180 gr (6 oz or 3 cups) sliced
mushrooms
2½ dcl (½ pint or 1 cup) sour
cream

Gut and fillet the fish, cut into portions, season with salt and fry until pale golden in oil—about 2½ minutes each side. Transfer to a buttered baking dish.

Toss the mushrooms in butter for 1 minute and heap on fish. Pour sour cream over the top and bake in a very moderate oven 175°C (350°F or Gas Mark 3) for 15 minutes.

Serve with new potatoes and a mixed tomato and green pepper salad.

SINAI PERCH

This is an ancient recipe and is suitable for any fresh water fish. Its distinctive feature is the top dressing of tahina used for the gratin surface.

4 Servings

4 medium-sized perch
salt and pepper
juice of ½ lemon
oil
1 tablespoon breadcrumbs

2 tablespoons chopped parsley
1 clove chopped garlic
2 sliced onions
180 gr (6 oz or ¼ cup) tahina

Score both sides of the fish, season, sprinkle with lemon juice. Pre-heat oven to 205°C (400°F or Gas Mark 5). Oil an ovenproof dish. Mix breadcrumbs with 1 tablespoon chopped parsley and sprinkle the mixture over the inside of the dish. Heat 2–3 tablespoons oil, gently fry the fish until pale golden on both sides. Carefully remove, without breaking, and put in the prepared dish.

Heat the oil left from cooking the fish. Fry the garlic for 1 minute. Add onions and fry together. Season. As soon as onions become soft and transparent, spoon them over the fish. Sprinkle in any remaining lemon juice. Spread tahina over the surface and cook in oven for about 15 minutes. Sprinkle with parsley and serve.

MONASTERY PIKE-PERCH

An 1890 edition of a Russian cookery book says : 'When this dish is served in Orthodox monasteries as lenten fare, the ham and rum are left out and vegetable oil is used instead of butter.'

4–5 Servings

1–1½ kg (2–2½ lb) pike-perch
250 gr (½ lb) lean ham, shredded
30 gr (1 oz or ¾ cup) chopped parsley
salt and pepper
4 tablespoons butter
1 litre (2 pints or 4 cups) strained fish stock (p. 14)

2 tablespoons vinegar
12 peppercorns
125 gr (4 oz or 2 cups) sliced mushrooms
4 tablespoons rum
4 tablespoons olive oil
2–3 slices lemon

Clean the fish, stuff with mixed ham and parsley and season with salt and pepper to taste. Wrap the pike-perch in a clean napkin, folded in four and generously spread with butter, tie with string. Bring stock to the boil, add vinegar and peppercorns, put in wrapped fish and simmer for 15 minutes.

Lightly fry the mushrooms. Unwrap the pike-perch, put on a serving dish and keep hot. Pour rum into a small saucepan, set it alight for a moment, then add olive oil, half a pint of the strained liquid in which the fish was cooked, mushrooms, lemon and whatever seasoning is required. Stir briskly, bring to the boil, pour over the fish and serve.

GILA MICHAELI'S HUNGARIAN PIKE GOULASH

4 Servings

750 gr–1 kg (1½–2 lb) pike
2 tablespoons butter or oil
1 finely chopped onion
2 peeled chopped tomatoes
salt

freshly ground pepper
1 litre (2 pints or 4 cups) strained fish stock
500 gr (1 lb) new potatoes
1 teaspoon paprika

Clean, skin and bone the fish. Use the heads and trimmings for making fish stock.

Fry onion in butter until transparent, add fish and tomatoes, season to taste and fry together for 5 minutes over moderate heat. Pour in stock. Scrape potatoes and add to the pan. As soon as boiling is re-established, add paprika, cover and simmer for 15 to 18 minutes. As soon as potatoes are done, serve. Goulash, like Bouillabaisse, should be served in deep soup plates.

BROCHET À LA CRÈME (BAKED PIKE IN SOUR CREAM, ALSACE STYLE)

8 Servings

1½ kg (3 lb) pike
salt
3 tablespoons butter

180 ml (6 oz or ¾ cup) sour cream

Wash the pike inside and out and pat dry with a clean cloth. Rub the fish all over with salt. Heat butter in a long narrow baking dish, lay the fish in this and pour over 125 ml (4 oz or ½ cup) sour cream. Bake for 30 minutes in the oven pre-heated to 180°C (350°F or Gas Mark 3), basting frequently with remaining sour cream.

PIKE, POLISH STYLE

4 Servings

1 kg (2 lb) pike fillets
salt and pepper
3 tablespoons butter
1 chopped onion
250 gr (8 oz or 3½ cups) sliced mushrooms

2 tablespoons chopped parsley
1 teaspoon grated lemon rind
3 tablespoons white wine
2½ dcl (½ pint or 1 cup) single cream
2 fresh egg yolks

Cut the fillets into uniform pieces and season to taste. Heat butter, soften the onion in it, add mushrooms and simmer until done. Sprinkle with parsley and lemon rind, stir, put in pike fillets, moisten with wine, cover and simmer for 10 minutes.

Add cream (all but 2 tabelespoons), blend it in carefully, without breaking up the fish. Simmer for another 10 minutes. Dilute yolks with the reserve 2 tablespoons cream, pour into the pan, stir, remove from heat and serve.

PIKE, SWISS STYLE

Fish-minded Swiss friends never tire of telling us how good their pike dishes are. We have been fortunate enough to sample some of the specialities of several lake districts : Zug, Leman, Lucerne and Lugano.

4 Servings

1–1½ kg (2–2½ lb) cleaned pike
salt and pepper
1 peeled carrot
4 bacon rashers
1 sliced onion
2–3 fresh sage leaves
2 cloves
120 ml (4 oz or ½ cup) fish
  fumet

120 ml (4 oz or ½ cup) dry
  white wine
60 gr (2 oz or 4 tablespoons)
  butter
4 tablespoons cream
1 teaspoon anchovy essence
few drops lemon juice

Wash and dry the pike, season on the inside with salt and pepper. Wrap the carrot in a bacon rasher and put it inside the pike—this allows the bacon to flavour the fish from the inside and helps it to preserve its shape.

Line an ovenproof dish with the rest of the bacon strips, cover with onion and place the pike on top of this foundation. Add sage, cloves, fumet and wine. Dot the surface generously with small pieces of butter and bake in the oven 190°C (375°F or Gas Mark 4) for 40 to 45 minutes, basting at intervals.

Carefully drain off the cooking liquor, without damaging the fish, into a small saucepan. Bring to the boil, cook down to reduce by one-third and to concentrate the sauce, check seasoning, blend in cream and anchovy essence, sharpen with a little lemon juice, pour the sauce over the pike and serve.

LITHUANIAN PIKE WITH MUSHROOMS

This recipe can be used with equal success for any other kind of fish fillets, cod, haddock, hake, halibut, etc.

6 Servings

1 kg (2 lb) pike fillets
salt and pepper
4 tablespoons butter or
  margarine
1 large chopped onion
240 gr (8 oz or 2½ cups) sliced
  fresh mushrooms
1 tablespoon chopped dill or
  parsley

1 teaspoon grated lemon rind
180 ml (6 oz or ¾ cup) fish
  stock or water
180 ml (6 oz or ¾ cup) cream
1 teaspoon cornflour
1 tablespoon cold water
2 raw yolks

Cut the fish into pieces, season with salt and pepper. Heat butter, fry onion until transparent, add mushrooms and simmer until they soften. Add dill or parsley and lemon rind, stir and put in fish. Little by little add stock, blend in cream, cover and simmer on very low heat for 20 minutes.

Transfer fish and mushrooms with a perforated spoon to a fairly deep, heated serving dish and keep warm while you finish off the sauce.

Blend cornflour with cold water, add to the pan juices and simmer gently, stirring until the sauce thickens. Remove from heat. Dilute yolks with a couple of tablespoons of hot but not boiling sauce, mix, then stir the diluted yolks into the sauce. Reheat if necessary, without allowing the sauce to come to the boil, pour over fish and serve.

FILLETS OF PLAICE WITH CHINESE SWEET AND SOUR SAUCE

2 Servings

250 gr ($\frac{1}{2}$ lb) plaice fillets
1 egg
$\frac{1}{2}$ cup cornflour

1 tablespoon oil
sweet and sour sauce
1 cup rice

Slice the fillets thinly and dip in beaten egg and dry cornflour. Heat oil in pan and fry fish, stirring carefully, for 3 minutes. When fish turns white, add sauce, stir, simmer for 2 minutes and serve with boiled rice.

FILLETS OF PLAICE CRÉCY

4 Servings

fish fumet
seasoning
3 tablespoons Béchamel sauce

3 tablespoons cooked carrot
purée
glazed new carrots

Roll the fillets and poach in enough fumet to cover, drain and arrange on a serving dish. Boil down the cooking liquid to reduce by half, add Béchamel sauce and carrot purée. Check the seasoning and pour the sauce over the fillets. Garnish with small glazed carrots and serve.

AMERICAN FILLETS OF PLAICE

In the original American recipe, flounder was recommended.

4 Servings

4 large or 8 small plaice fillets
2–2$\frac{1}{2}$ tablespoons flour
salt and pepper
120 ml (4 oz or $\frac{1}{2}$ cup) milk

250 gr (8 oz or 2 cups) crushed
cornflakes
60 gr (2 oz or 4 tablespoons)
butter

Wash, dry and trim the fillets. Season flour with salt and pepper and dredge the fish with it. Dip the fillets in milk, coat with cornflakes and fry in butter until golden. Serve with a green salad.

SANDWICHED PLAICE FILLETS

4 Servings

8 small plaice fillets
salt and pepper
500 gr (1 lb or 2 cups) mashed
  potatoes
4 tablespoons cream
1 raw egg
2 hard-boiled egg yolks
60 gr (2 oz or 1 cup) chopped
  mushrooms

30 gr (1 oz or ½ cup) chopped
  onion
butter
1 beaten egg
1 tablespoon olive oil
1 tablespoon water
grated breadcrumbs
1 teaspoon capers
lemon

Trim the fillets, skin and season with salt and pepper. Season mashed potatoes, mix with cream and raw egg. Rub hard-boiled yolks through fine sieve. Cook the mushrooms and onions together in a little butter. Mix yolks, mushrooms and onions with mashed potato. Put a little of this mixture on half the fillets, cover each with another fillet and press gently to sandwich.

Blend beaten egg with oil and water, dip the sandwiched fillets in this mixture, coat with breadcrumbs and fry in butter, browning lightly on both sides. Heat the remaining mashed potatoes, spread on a dish, arrange the fillets on this foundation.

Heat 2–3 tablespoons butter, add capers, heat through and pour over the dish. Serve garnished with lemon butterflies.

FRIED PLAICE, HONG KONG STYLE

2 Servings

oil
60 gr (2 oz or 6 tablespoons)
  chopped onion
30 gr (1 oz or 3 tablespoons)
  diced celery
60 gr (2 oz or 6 tablespoons)
  sliced water chestnuts
100 gr (3 oz or 8 tablespoons)
  sliced bamboo shoots
60 gr (2 oz or 6 tablespoons)
  sliced cucumber

30 gr (1 oz or 3 tablespoons)
  sliced mushrooms
250 gr (½ lb) filleted plaice
stock
½ teaspoon pepper
1 tablespoon Chinese wine or
  sherry
1 teaspoon cornflour
1 teaspoon soya sauce
few drops sesame oil

Heat a little oil in a pan and quick-fry the vegetables, allowing no more than 1 minute. Add enough stock to cover and simmer under a lid for one minute. Meanwhile cut the fish into thin slices. Remove vegetables from pan and arrange on a dish.

Put fish in another hot, oiled pan, add a little pepper and sherry. Cook for one minute, turning carefully. Add vegetables to the fish and cook for 2 minutes. Pour in cornflour diluted with enough water to make a thin paste, season with soya sauce, sprinkle with sesame oil, cook for one minute and serve.

PAPRIKA PLAICE

6 Servings

6 large plaice fillets
120 gr (4 oz or ½ cup) peeled
  prawns
8 tablespoons fresh breadcrumbs
1 tablespoon lemon juice
1 lightly beaten egg

3 teaspoons paprika
salt
4 teaspoons butter
3 tablespoons tomato purée
3 tablespoons white wine

Skin the plaice fillets (p. 11) and pat dry. Chop prawns and add to breadcrumbs. Stir lemon juice into beaten egg, add to prawns and breadcrumbs, season with 1 teaspoon paprika and salt to taste and blend well. Divide mixture into 6 portions and spread on fillets, leaving 0.25 cm (⅛ in.) at the narrow end uncovered. Roll up plaice fillets around stuffing finishing up with the tail end. Put in a lightly buttered dish, cover and bake for 30 minutes in the oven pre-heated to 200°C (400°F or Gas Mark 5).

Heat butter, remaining paprika, tomato purée and wine in a small saucepan. Arrange the plaice on a warmed serving dish, pour the sauce over and serve with plain boiled rice.

MADRAS PLAICE CURRY

This is known as a dry fish curry.

6 Servings

6 plaice fillets
1 egg
1 teaspoon ground turmeric
¼ teaspoon ground chillis
1 finely chopped onion

1 pounded clove of garlic
2 tablespoons lemon juice
pinch salt
oil for deep frying

Trim and skin the fillets. Beat the egg in a bowl, add turmeric, chillis, onion, garlic, lemon juice and salt, mix and put the plaice to marinate in the mixture for 45–50 minutes, turning from time to time to flavour it evenly. Heat oil until it sizzles, fry the plaice flllets until golden, drain on kitchen paper to remove grease and serve.

TRINIDAD PLAICE WITH BANANAS

6 Servings

6 plaice fillets
  salt and pepper
½ lemon
1 beaten egg
breadcrumbs

100 gr (3 oz or 6 tablespoons)
  butter
3 bananas
1 tablespoon chopped parlsey

Wash and dry the fillets, season, squeeze a few drops of lemon juice on each, dip in egg and breadcrumbs, fry in butter until golden on both sides, drain and keep hot.

Peel bananas, cut in half lengthwise, sprinkle with lemon juice and fry in butter, just to soften the fruit. Do not overcook or it will become difficult to handle and misshapen to look at. Put half a banana on each plaice fillet garnish with parsley and serve immediately.

PLAICE IN CHRYSANTHEMUM WREATHS, JAPANESE STYLE

6 Servings

6 plaice fillets	pinch sugar
6 tablespoons soya sauce	salt
cucumber	5 tablespoons mirin (or any
1 tablespoon sake (or sherry)	sweet white wine)
1 tablespoon vinegar	sweet red pepper

Put plaice in a dish, moisten with soya sauce and leave to marinate for 3 hours.

Peel cucumber, cut lengthwise into slices 0.5 cm (¼ in.) thick and the wider the better. Cut 'chrysanthemum petals' along one side without cutting right through, sprinkle with a pinch of salt and leave to soften, then moisten with sake and vinegar and sprinkle with sugar. Allow to stand for one hour.

Drain fish, but keep the soya sauce. Sprinkle it with salt on both sides, impale on skewers. Mix the soya sauce in which the plaice was steeped with mirin, dip the skewered fish in the sauce and grill until golden on both sides. Baste with the sauce two or three times during grilling.

Arrange the plaice fillets on a serving dish. Twist cucumber strips to look like chrysanthemums and crown the fish with these wreaths. Cut small disks out of red pimento, put one in the centre of each chrysanthemum. Serve.

RED MULLET, ADRIATIC STYLE

4 Servings

4 medium-sized red mullets	1 clove chopped garlic
3 tablespoons olive oil	1 tablespoon capers
3 salted anchovies	1 lemon
1½ tablespoons chopped parsley	

Clean, wash and dry the mullets. Heat the oil, chop the anchovies, add to oil, stir for a minute, put in mullets and brown, about 3–4 minutes each side. Sprinkle with parsley and garlic, reduce heat and simmer for 10 minutes. Lift the fish out carefully, put on heated serving dish and keep hot.

Add capers to the pan juices, heat through, pour the sauce over the fish and serve garnished with lemon wedges.

RED MULLET, COSTA BRAVA STYLE

Catalan fisherman, Joachim, used to reserve for us the best of his catch, with magnificent disregard for the profit he could make by taking his choice mullets to the local fish market.

4 Servings

4 red mullets	1 teaspoon salt
1 clove chopped garlic	½ teaspoon pepper
60 gr (2 oz or ½ cup) breadcrumbs	1 tablespoon chopped parsley
3 tablespoons olive oil	120 ml (4 oz or ½ cup) sherry
250 gr (½ lb or 1½ cups) peeled shallots	

Scrape the fish and cut off the fins but leave head and tail on. Mix garlic with breadcrumbs and coat the fish with this mixture. Grease a baking dish with a little oil, put in mullets, surround with shallots, season to taste, sprinkle with parsley and sherry and bake in the oven for 20 minutes.

RED MULLET, ORIENTAL STYLE

Choose very small fish, allowing 1–2 per portion. Season with salt and pepper, roll in flour and deep fry in hot oil.

Arrange the fish on an oiled baking dish. Cover with tomato fondue, spiced with a little bit of saffron, fennel, thyme, powdered bay leaf, some grains of coriander, garlic and chopped parsley. Bring to the boil. Cover the dish and finish cooking in the oven for 8–10 minutes. Sprinkle with chopped parsley.

RED MULLET WITH TOMATOES, ANCHOVIES AND OLIVES (cold)

4 Servings

4 small mullets	500 gr (1 lb or 3 cups) peeled, chopped tomatoes
salt and pepper	
2 tablespoons olive oil	12 anchovy fillets
3 chopped shallots	60 gr (2 oz or 1/3 cup) stoned olives
1 crushed clove garlic	

Scale the fish, cut off fins, clean out, but leave the livers. Wash and gently dab with a cloth to dry. Season on the inside with salt and pepper. Rub with a little olive oil and grill until done and both sides are uniformly browned.

While the fish is grilling, prepare the sauce. Heat the rest of the oil and gently fry the shallots with garlic for 2 to 3 minutes. Add tomatoes and increase heat to cook down the sauce to a thick consistency. Season to taste.

Arrange the fish in a serving dish, pour the sauce over it and leave until cold. Decorate the top with anchovies in a crisscross patterns, stud with olives and serve.

SALMON ALICANTE

4 Servings

4 salmon steaks
salt and pepper
120 ml (4 oz or ½ cup) olive oil
juice of 1 lime (or lemon)
small sliced onion

1 sliced pimento
2 sprigs chopped parsley
1 tablespoon butter
mayonnaise

Put the salmon steaks into a shallow dish, season with salt and pepper, sprinkle with olive oil and lime juice and cover with onion, pimento, and parsley. Leave in this marinade for one hour. Brush salmon steaks with butter, grill and serve with mayonnaise.

SALMON STEAKS FLAMBÉS IN WHISKY

4 Servings

4 salmon steaks
butter
salt and pepper
pinch grated nutmeg

2 small chopped shallots
ccoked sliced lobster tail
4 tablespoons whisky

Wipe the salmon steaks with a damp cloth, brush with melted butter, season with salt, pepper and nutmeg, put on a well-greased grill rack. Grill 4 to 5 minutes each side, basting with butter. Fry shallot in butter, add lobster slices, brown lightly. Put salmon steaks on a dish, garnish each with slices of lobster, keep hot.

Add more butter to the pan, including whatever is left of the basting butter, and as soon as it gets frothy pour over the salmon. Add a splash of whisky, set alight and serve at once, before the flame dies down.

SALMON CUTLETS, MOSCOW STYLE

6 Servings

6 slices of salmon 2 cm (¾ inch)
   thick
salt water court-bouillon
aspic jelly for fish
sliced cucumber
3 hard-boiled eggs
red caviar

For lining paste:
125 gr (4 oz or 1 cup) flour
60 gr (2 oz or 4 tablespoons)
   butter
60 gr (2 oz or 4 tablespoons)
   whipped cooking fat
iced water

Poach the salmon in court-bouillon, allow to cool in the liquid, drain, remove skin, dab gently with a cloth to dry, arrange on a dish and coat with half-set aspic jelly. (For details of coating and glazing fish with jelly see recipe for Trout in Chablis p. 68.) Decorate with sliced cucumber and quarters of hard-boiled egg.

Make ordinary lining paste (see Buckling Flan, p. 41), bake small oval shaped tartlet cases 'blind'. Garnish them with red caviar and place these barquettes around the salmon cutlets.

CANADIAN WHOLE BAKED SALMON

This is one of the finest ways of cooking whole salmon and salmon trout. After all, however good the liquid in which you poach the fish, some of its flavour goes towards enriching the stock. Baked slowly this way, the fish preserves all its juices and flavour.

It is impossible to indicate the number of servings—all depends on the size of the salmon and the appetites of your guests.

Cut a piece of kitchen metal foil big enough to enclose the whole fish and allow for overlap. Spread the foil with butter, put the salmon on it, season to taste, wrap up and put in a baking pan.

Pre-heat oven to 120°C (250°F or Gas Mark ½) and bake, allowing 2 hours cooking time for a 4-pound salmon and adding 15 minutes for each additional pound.

Serve hot with its own juices, garnished with cucumber salad, black olives, lemon wedges and pats of tarragon butter.

SARDINE MERINGUE, PORTUGUESE STYLE

4 Servings

1 large tin sardines	butter
2½ dcl (½ pint or 1 cup) white sauce	3 whites of egg
	onions cut in rings
seasoning	stuffed olives
3 yolks	

Drain the sardines, remove tails and bones, mash and mix with white sauce. Season to taste, allow to cool. Add yolks, stir well and pour into a lightly buttered soufflé dish. Beat the whites with a small pinch of salt until stiff, pile over the sardine mixture.

Smooth the top lightly and decorate by carefully arranging a layer of thin onion rings in whatever pattern pleases you. Put an olive, stuffing upwards, in the centre of each onion ring, put in the oven pre-heated to 190°C (375°F or Gas Mark 4), bake for 25–30 minutes and serve.

SKATE IN BROWNED BUTTER

If you buy skate unskinned, you will have an infallible way of testing its freshness, for the viscous coating which covers it goes on re-forming for ten hours after death. By wiping the skate with a cloth and watching whether the coating will re-form, it is possible to establish its degree of freshness.

4 Servings

750 gr (1½ lb) skate
court-bouillon
salt and pepper

180 gr (6 oz or ¾ cup) butter
1½ tablespoons chopped parsley
1½ tablespoons vinegar

Poach the skate in court-bouillon for 15–20 minutes, drain, put on a heated serving dish, season to taste and sprinkle with parsley. Melt the butter and cook unil it acquires a dark brown colour, but do not allow it to burn black. Pour butter over the skate. In the same pan heat the vinegar, cook briskly until it is reduced by half, sprinkle over the fish and serve.

Delicious with new potatoes.

SKATE HOLLANDAISE

Poach skate as above. Serve with boiled potatoes and Hollandaise sauce.

SOLE VERONIQUE

4 Servings

4 fillets of sole
½ litre (1 pint or 2 cups) milk
125 gr (4 oz or 1½ cups) sliced
  mushrooms
4 tablespoons butter
seasoning

2 tablespoons flour
3 tablespoons grated cheese
125 ml (¼ pint or ½ cup) cup
  cream
175 gr (6 oz or 2¼ cups) peeled
  white grapes

Put the fish in an ovenproof dish, cover with milk and poach in the oven 175°C (350°F or Gas Mark 3). Toss the mushrooms in 1½ tablespoons butter, season. Drain fillets (keeping the liquid) and put them in a buttered ovenproof dish. Cook flour in the rest of the butter, dilute with the milk left from poaching the fillets to make white sauce, stir until it thickens, add cheese and cream and blend well.

Put the mushrooms and grapes around the fillets, cover with sauce, bake in a hot oven 235°C (450°F or Gas Mark 7) for 10 minutes and serve.

SOLE BERCY

2 Servings

2 medium-sized soles
4 chopped shallots
2 tablespoons butter
1 tablespoon chopped parsley
salt and pepper

lemon juice
125 gr (4 oz or 2 cups)
mushrooms
4 tablespoons wine, either dry
white wine or red Burgundy

Trim the soles to the edges of fillets. Fry shallots lightly in 1 tablespoon butter, add parsley, cook together for 30 seconds. Transfer to a buttered baking dish and lay the soles on this foundation. Season with salt and pepper, squeeze a little lemon juice over the fish, surround with mushrooms, moisten with wine, dot with pieces of butter and bake in the oven 205°C (400°F or Gas Mark 5) for 20 minutes, basting frequently to glaze the fish nicely.

FILLETS OF SOLE BORDELAISE

4 Servings

4 large sole fillets
red wine court-bouillon
250 grs (½ lb) cooked button
mushrooms

250 grs (½ lb) small glazed
onions
1 tablespoon kneaded butter

Poach the fillets in red wine court-bouillon for 8 minutes, drain, arrange on a serving dish garnish with button mushrooms and glazed onions. Boil down 1 cup of the liquid in which the fillets were cooked, thicken with kneaded butter, pour over the fish and serve.

SOLE BONNE FEMME

4 Servings

4 medium-sized soles
salt and pepper
butter
125 gr (4 oz or 1½ cups)
chopped mushrooms
2 chopped shallots

2 teaspoons chopped parsley
a few drops lemon juice
125 ml (4 oz or ½ cup) dry
white wine
1 tablespoon kneaded butter

Trim the soles to the edge of the fillets, slit longways on skinned side and with the tip of the knife raise the fillets a little to loosen the backbone. Season with salt and pepper. Butter a shallow pan, line with mushrooms, shallots and parsley, put the soles on top. Sprinkle with lemon juice, moisten with wine, dot with pieces of butter, bring to the boil, then put in a hot oven 220°C (425°F or Gas Mark 6) and bake for 10 to 15 minutes, depending on size of fish.

Drain off liquor, boil it down and thicken with a tablespoon kneaded butter. Pour the sauce over the soles, put back in the oven for a few moments to glaze and serve.

SOLE BROCHETTE
2 Servings

2–3 sole fillets	salt and pepper
2 chopped hard-boiled yolks	½ chopped onion
½ tablespoon breadcrumbs	1 chopped shallot
½ tablespoon chopped parsley	small pinch nutmeg
butter	125 ml (4 oz or ½ cup) velouté
125 grs (4 oz or 2 cups)	sauce
mushrooms	

Cut the fillets into square pieces of equal size. Mix yolks with freshly grated breadcrumbs and parsley, add a little melted butter to bind the mixture and use if for sandwiching pieces of sole, two by two.

Dip the best mushroom heads in melted butter and thread sole 'sandwiches' and mushrooms, alternately, on greased skewers. Season with salt and pepper, brush lightly with melted butter and grill.

Chop up left over mushrooms and all stalks and peelings to make duxelles as follows : squeeze out chopped mushrooms, stalks, and trimmed off or broken pieces of mushroom in a cloth, to extract all liquid. Heat a tablespoon butter and lightly fry the onion. As soon as it becomes transparent, add shallot, seasoning, nutmeg and chopped mushroom mixture. Cook, stirring constantly, over a brisk flame to evaporate all moisture. Add duxelles to velouté sauce, mix well. Line a serving dish with this thick sauce, arrange sole on top and serve.

FILLETS OF SOLE COLBERT
4 Servings

4 skinned fillets of sole	2 tablespoons sieved
milk	breadcrumbs
2 tablespoons flour	fat for deep frying
pinch salt	maître d'hôtel butter
1 beaten egg	lemon

Split the fillets in half, roll up, skewer, dip in milk and dredge with salted flour. Shake off surplus flour, dip in beaten egg, then in breadcrumbs, deep fry for 5 minutes. Drain, arrange on a dish, fill the middle of the rolled fillets with maître d'hôtel butter, garnish with sliecs of lemon and serve.

FRIED DOVER SOLE WITH PARSLEY BUTTER

Allow one sole per portion. Either fillet fish or leave on the bone, dredge with flour seasoned with salt and freshly ground pepper, then dip in beaten egg and breadcrumbs and fry in butter until both sides are golden, starting with the side to be served uppermost. Drain on kitchen paper.

Garnish with wedges of lemon on top with maître d'hôtel butter.

SOLE FLORENTINE

4 Servings

4 medium-sized sole fillets
125 gr (4 oz or ½ cup) butter
juice of one lemon
salt and pepper
1 kg (2 lb or 5 cups) cooked spinach

2½ dcl (½ pint or 1 cup) Mornay sauce
2 tablespoons grated Parmesan cheese

Cook the fillets in butter and lemon juice in a sauté pan for about 5 minutes, season. Toss the cooked spinach in butter, and spread it in an ovenproof dish. Put the fillets on the spinach, cover with sauce, sprinkle with cheese and put in a hot oven or under a grill to brown the top.

BAKED SOLE STUFFED WITH MUSHROOMS AND PRAWNS

4 Servings

4 soles
60 gr (2 oz or ¾ cup) chopped mushrooms
60 gr (2 oz or ¾ cup) chopped prawns (or shrimps)
2 tablespoons chopped onion
2 tablespoons peeled, chopped lemon

1 tablespoon chopped parsley
salt and pepper
oil
butter
1½–2 dcl (6 oz or ¾ cup) dry white Chianti

Trim and skin the soles. Make an incision down the centre as for filleting, and raise the flesh from the bone as far as possible. Insert into each a quarter of the mixed mushrooms, prawns, onion, lemon and parsley. Season, put into an ovenproof dish greased with a mixture of butter and oil.

Moisten with wine, sprinkle the top generously with melted butter and oil, cover and bake for about 20 minutes in a moderate oven 190°C (375°F or Gas Mark 4) basting frequently with the pan juices. The sole must not be allowed to brown. Cooked this way it conserves all its juices and has a delectable, clean flavour.

FILLETS OF SOLE MEUNIÈRE

4 Servings

4 large sole fillets
flour
salt, pepper
125 gr (4 oz or ½ cup) butter

1 tablespoon lemon juice
1 tablespoon chopped parsley
lemon slices

Trim and wipe the fillets. Season a little flour with salt and pepper, mix, and dredge the fillets with it. Fry in butter, 3 minutes each side. By this time both sides should be golden brown. Arrange the fillets on a heated serving dish, sprinkle with parsley and lemon juice.

Reheat the butter left in the frying pan, cook until it browns, pour over the fish. Garnish with twisted lemon slices and serve.

SOLE NORMANDY WITH CREAM SAUCE AND POACHED MUSSELS

There are innumerable variations of this pleasant dish. Half a pint of dry white wine may be used instead of cider, and fleurons—little crescents of puff pastry—instead of croûtes.

4 Servings

4 fillets of sole
4 tablespoons butter
2 chopped shallots
salt and pepper
2½ dcl (½ pint or 1 cup) cider
1 tablespoon flour
1 teaspoon chopped parsley

4 tablespoons cream
8–12 poached mussels
60 gr (2 oz or ¾ cup) peeled shrimps
125 gr (4 oz or 1½ cups) fried button mushrooms
8 thin croûtes

Wipe the fillets with a damp cloth, fold and put in a buttered ovenproof dish. Sprinkle with shallots, season with salt and pepper, cover with cider and cook in a moderate oven 190°C (375°F or Gas Mark 4) for 20 minutes.

Strain off liquor, carefully place the fillets on a hot serving dish and keep warm.

Melt butter, stir in flour, little by little add the liquid in which the fish was cooked, cook gently, stirring constantly until the sauce thickens and becomes smooth. Add parsley and cream, stir and pour the sauce over the fillets. Garnish with mussels, shrimps, mushrooms and croûtes and serve.

To make the croûtes, cut a French loaf into thin slices and brown in the oven.

SOLE OR PLAICE CHORON

4 Servings

8 fillets of sole or plaice of 60 gr (2 oz) each
salt and pepper
butter

4 tablespoons fish stock
small bunch asparagus
2½ dcl (½ pint or 1 cup) choron sauce

Wipe fillets with a cloth, season with salt and pepper, fold in three, put in a lightly buttered ovenproof dish, add stock, cover and cook in a fairly hot oven 190°C (375°F or Gas Mark 5) for 20 minutes. Drain the fillets, arrange on a serving dish, garnish with asparagus tips cooked in butter and serve with Choron sauce.

SOLE OR PLAICE, CRIMEAN STYLE

4 Servings

4 small sole, plaice or dabs
1 large chopped onion
2 cloves chopped garlic
2 tablespoons oil
1 tablespoon butter
2–3 large tomatoes, peeled, seeded and chopped
250 gr (½ lb) leaf spinach
250 gr (½ lb) sorrel

bunch spring onions
1 teaspoon salt
½ teaspoon pepper
1 tablespoon chopped parsley
½ tablespoon chopped dill
2½ dcl (½ pint or 1 cup) dry white wine
1 sliced lemon

Wash and wipe the fish. Fry onion and garlic in oil and butter, using a fairly deep pan. When the onion becomes transparent, add tomatoes and simmer gently. Chop spinach, sorrel and spring onions and add to pan. Add fish, season with salt and pepper, sprinkle with parsley and dill, moisten with wine, cover and simmer until fish is cooked.

Remove the fish, arrange on a serving dish and keep hot. Add lemon to the pan, boil to reduce the liquid by one-third, pour over the fish and serve.

SOLE, VENETIAN STYLE

This is a delicious way of serving sole. It is traditionally served in Venice on the Feast of the Redemption, 19th July.

4 Servings

2 large skinned soles
1 tablespoon flour
salt and pepper
3 tablespoons oil
3 chopped onions
45 gr (1½ oz or 4 tablespoons) sultanas

45 gr (1½ oz or 4 tablespoons) pine kernels
2½ dcl (½ pint or 1 cup) wine vinegar

Trim the soles, cut off heads and fins, but do not remove backbone. Dip in flour, season to taste. Heat oil, fry the onions, remove. In the same fat start frying the soles, brown on one side, turn, add sultanas and pine kernels, continue to cook until the other side is brown. Put the soles on serving dish.

Reheat the onions in the pan in which the soles were cooked. Add vinegar, bring to the boil, simmer to reduce by one-third, remove from heat and allow to cool completely. Pour over the soles and serve.

FILLETS OF SOLE WITH COD ROE QUENELLES

4 Servings

8 sole fillets	3 eggs
60 gr (2 oz or 5/8 cup) fresh sliced mushrooms	3 tablespoons oil
	breadcrumbs
½ litre (1 pint or 2 cups) good fish stock	2 medium-sized sliced onions
	120 ml (4 oz or ½ cup) dry white wine
240 gr (8 oz or 1 cup) smoked cod's roe	½ teaspoon grated lemon rind
1 slice stale bread	1 teaspoon cornflour
salt and pepper	strained juice of 2 lemons
1 tablespoon chopped parsley	pinch cayenne pepper

Wash and dry the fillets of sole. Put a few slices of mushroom on each fillet, roll it up and secure with a cocktail stick. Make a good strong fish stock and strain.

Dip the roe in water, leave for a few minutes to remove excess salt, then squeeze out. Soak bread in water, squeeze and add to roe. Season with salt and pepper, add parsley and pound in a mortar or put through a blender. Work in 1 tablespoon oil and add 1 lightly beaten egg. If the mixture is too liquid, sprinkle in a tablespoon breadcrumbs. Mix well.

Heat remaining oil in a casserole and lightly fry onions. Put in rolled fillets, season, add wine and enough stock just to cover the fish. Bring to the boil, cover, reduce heat and simmer for 7–8 minutes. Taking a little of the cod's roe mixture at a time shape into little quenelles, add to sole fillets, continue to simmer for 15 minutes.

Take the fillets out of the casserole, arrange on a heated serving dish, surround with quenelles and keep hot. Strain the liquor in which the fish was cooked, add to it remaining stock and bring to the boil. Add lemon rind. Dilute cornflour with 2 tablespoons lemon juice, blend into stock, simmer stirring for 2–3 minutes, until the sauce thickens, keep hot without allowing to boil.

Heat remaining eggs with the rest of the lemon juice until

frothy. Dilute with 2 ladlefuls of hot, but not boiling, stock, adding it a little at a time, Remove stock from heat. Pour the egg liaison into the stock, stir, ladle some of the sauce over the fish, sprinkle with cayenne and serve. Serve the rest of the sauce separately.

Don't let the sauce boil after adding the egg liaison, or it will curdle.

SPRATS IN PINK CREAM

4 Servings

750 gr (1½ lb) sprats	2 teaspoons French mustard
2 tablespoons butter	salt and pepper
1 tablespoon breadcrumbs	2 tablespoons tomato purée
2 dcl (8 oz or 1 cup) cream	1 tablespoon chopped chives

Open sprats, clean out and remove bone carefully, without breaking up the little fish. Wash and pat dry. Butter a pie dish, sprinkle with breadcrumbs. Blend cream with mustard and whip until stiff. Season sprats with salt and pepper, spread with cream on the inside and roll up like rollmops. Arrange the sprats in the pie dish in neat rows.

Blend tomato purée into the cream, pour over the sprats, sprinkle with chives, dot with small pieces of butter and bake in a hot oven, 204°C (400°F or Gas Mark 6) for 30 minutes.

STURGEON

Sturgeon figures prominently on Russian menus. Smoked, as an hors-d'oeuvre, we have had it offered to us in expensive restaurants in Moscow and Leningrad and in railway station and snack-bars, in private houses and even in a self-service shop on a collective farm. All rather a long way from its source. Cooks of the Caspian region say that the best way of preparing sturgeon is poaching and baking. It is excellent in pies and coulibiacs and makes superb 'ukha', which is the Volga boatmen's answer tp bouillabaisse.

Ever since the mists of legend began to crystallise into recorded culinary essays, sturgeon has been part of that lore. Perhaps because even the ones that do not get away need no exaggeration —they weigh several hundred pounds! One particular anecdote crops up again and again.

Alexandre Dumas, the novelist, in his *Le Grand Dictionnaire de la Cuisine* (1873) tells the story of a banquet given by the High Chancellor of the Empire, Cambacérès, later Duke of Parma, when as a *pièce de résistance* a 300-pound sturgeon was carried in a solemn procession by several footmen, accompanied by musicians and torchbearers. The host, who appears to have cared more about the effect he was making than for good food, with satisfaction observed the shudder which shook his guests as one of the footmen slipped and dropped the gorgeous fish on the floor . . . whereupon, at a signal from Cambacérès, a second sturgeon, double the size, with twice the number of servants and attendants was ushered in among even louder fanfares.

We have heard many versions of this story, including several Russian ones, in which all sorts of likely and unlikely men are named as the hosts perpetrating the atrocity described above, from Ivan the Terrible to Balakirev.

VOLGA STURGEON

6–8 Servings

1–1¼ kg (2–2½ lb) sturgeon
salt
fish stock
125 ml (4 oz or ½ cup) dry
  white wine
1 tablespoon butter

250 grs (½ lb or 2 cups) sliced
  mushrooms
250 ml (2 pints or 1½ cups)
  cooked prawns (or shrimps)
sour cream sauce

Scald the sturgeon with boiling water several times to loosen the skin. Remove skin and trim the fish. (Skin, trimmings and fish bones should be used for making the stock.) Sprinkle with salt and leave for 1 hour.

Put the sturgeon into cold strained stock, add wine and simmer until done. Drain, arrange on a dish and keep hot. Toss the mushrooms in butter.

Garnish the fish with mushrooms and prawns and serve with sour cream sauce.

STURGEON À LA BALAKIREV

This is studded with truffles and simmered in champagne, and Balakirev insisted that the fish stock had to be strengthened with champagne. The dish should on no account be dropped!

8 Servings

1 skinned medium-sized
  sturgeon 1½–1¾ kg (3–3½ lb)
truffles
salt
pepper
1 glass brandy
fish fumet
125 gr (4 oz or ½ cup) shredded
  carrot

125 gr (4 oz or ½ cup)
  shredded celery
2 tablespoons finely chopped
  onion
100 gr (3 oz or 5–6 tablespoons)
  butter
2½ dcl (½ pint or 1 cup) dry
  champagne

Stud the sturgeon with slivers of truffle, sprinkle with salt, pepper and brandy and marinate for 1 hour. Put the sturgeon on a buttered grid in a fish kettle, moisten with fumet. Simmer the carrot, celery and onion in 2 tablespoons butter until tender and add to fish. Add champagne, bring to the boil, cover with a well-fitting lid and braise slowly in the oven, basting frequently.

When done carefully take out and drain the sturgeon. Put it in the oven to glaze the surface and arrange on a serving dish. Garnish as desired. (The garnish recommended for this dish consists of button mushrooms cooked in butter, braised cucumbers and boiled prawns.)

Cook down the pan juices to reduce to desired consistency, incorporating the rest of the butter, adding it in small pieces and blending it in, strain and serve.

CAUCASIAN MOUNTAIN LAKE TROUT

6 Servings

½ litre (1 pint or 2 cups) mayonnaise (p. 209)	1½ kgs (3 lb) trout fillets salt
1 tablespoon chopped parsley	pepper
2 teaspoons chopped chives	flour
2 chopped dill cucumbers	3 lbs butter
1 tablespoon chopped capers	lemon

Mix mayonnaise with parsley, chives, cucumbers and capers and keep cold until required.

Wash the trout fillets, season with salt and pepper, dip in flour lightly and shake off surplus. Heat the butter until it sizzles, fry the fillets, turning once, until golden.

Garnish with wedges of lemon and serve at once. Serve the sauce separately.

PAN-FRIED RENKEN OR TROUT, STARNBERG STYLE

Marianne de Barde's recipe. Renken are similar to trout and found in lakes near Munich. This recipe is a speciality of the area around Lake Starnberg.

4 Servings

4 renken or trout	juice of 1 lemon
2 teaspoons Worcestershire sauce	1½ tablespoons chopped parsley
2 teaspoons salt	3–4 chopped shallots
5 tablespoons vegetable cooking fat	2 teaspoons fresh chopped tarragon
4 tablespoons flour	2 teaspoons finely chopped capers
3 tablespoons butter	

Clean and wash the fish. Dry thoroughly inside and out. Sprinkle inside with Worcestershire sauce and rub with salt. Heat vegetable fat in a pan large enough to take all the fish. Roll fish in flour and fry 2 minutes on each side, till golden. Pour off fat and add butter, lemon juice, parsley, shallots, tarragon and capers. Sauté for 2 more minutes.

Serve with buttered new potatoes and a green salad dressed with vinaigrette sauce.

YUGOSLAV TROUT WITH PRUNES

6 Servings

250 gr (8 oz or 2 cups) prunes	4 tablespoons wine vinegar
1½ kg (3 lb) trout	4 tablespoons water
salt	4 beaten eggs
250 ml (½ pint or 1 cup) oil	1 tablespoon lemon juice
6 tablespoons chopped parsley	lemon quarters for garnish
2 cloves pounded garlic	

Soak the prunes in water to soften and make them plump. Scald trout, clean out inside, wipe with a cloth, sprinkle with salt. Drain the prunes thoroughly and dry. Cut a few slanting incisions in the fleshy part of the trout and put a prune in each slit. Grease an ovenproof dish with oil, sprinkle with parsley and garlic, lay the fish on top, add oil, vinegar and water and bake in a hot oven 235°C (450°F or Gas Mark 7) for 35 to 40 minutes.

Carefully transfer the trout to a heated serving dish. Heat the pan juices left from cooking the fish, pour the eggs into the pan, sprinkle with lemon juice, scramble briskly and use as garnish for the trout.

Decorate with lemon wedges and serve.

TRUITES AUX AMANDES

4 Servings

4 brook trout	125 gr (4 oz or ¾ cup) blanched
1 dcl (4 oz or ½ cup) milk	almonds
flour	squeeze lemon juice
salt and pepper	
100 gr (3 oz or 6 tablespoons) butter	

Clean the trout, wash, dry on a cloth, dip in milk and roll in flour seasoned with salt and pepper. Fry in 2 tablespoons butter until golden on both sides, remove, put on a heated serving dish and keep hot.

Slice the almonds longwise into slivers. Add the rest of the butter to the frying pan in which the fish was cooked, heat, put in almonds and brown them and the butter. Spoon a portion of the almonds over each trout. Add a dash of lemon to the browned butter and serve with the fish.

Delicious with new boiled potatoes tossed in butter and sprinkled with chopped chervil.

TURBOT DUGLÉRÉ

4–5 Servings

1 kg (2 lb) turbot
4 tablespoons butter
1 tablespoon chopped onion
250 gr (½ lb or 2 cups) peeled,
   chopped tomatoes
1 tablespoon chopped parsley
½ clove grated garlic

1 sprig thyme
¼ bay leaf
125 ml (4 oz or ½ cup) dry white
   wine
2 tablespoons flour
salt and pepper

Cut the fish into portions of uniform size. Melt half the butter and sauté the onion with tomatoes, parsley, garlic, thyme and bay leaf. Put the fish on this foundation, moisten with wine, bring to the boil, cover and cook in the oven 205°C (400°F or Gas Mark 5) for 20 minutes. Remove the fish carefully, arrange on a long dish and keep hot. (In France the cooks often re-form the pieces in the shape of the fish.)

Discard thyme and bay leaf. Melt the remainder of the butter, add flour and cook for a couple of minutes. Add contents of the pan in which the turbot was cooked, stirring constantly. Simmer for 5 to 6 minutes, thinning down the sauce with a little water, if necessary. Taste, season, pour the sauce over the turbot and serve.

INDIAN TURBOT IN ALMOND AND YOGHOURT SAUCE

4–5 Servings

1 kg (2 lb) turbot fillet
1 teaspoon turmeric
salt and pepper
60 gr (2 oz or 4 tablespoons)
   butter
4 chopped onions

5 cm (2 inch) cinnamon stick
400 ml (¾ pint or 1¾ cups) milk
250 grs (8 oz or 2 z 2/3 cups)
   ground almonds
250 ml (½ pint or 1 cup)
   yoghourt

Wash and dry the fillets, cut into portions, dust with turmeric and season with salt and pepper. Heat butter, put in onions and cinnamon stick, cook gently until the onions soften and become transparent. Add turbot, brown quickly, turn, then pour in milk, let it reach boiling point, lower the heat and simmer gently for 15 minutes.

Pound the almonds in a mortar, or pass through a blender, moisten with yoghourt, adding it a little at a time, until you have a creamy paste, pour over the fish, cover, simmer gently for 10 minutes and serve.

CHINESE STEAMED TURBOT

4 Servings

30 gr (1 oz or 4 tablespoons) sliced onion	500 gr (1 lb) turbot
125 gr (4 oz or 1½ cups) sliced mushrooms	1 teaspoon vinegar
	2 tablespoons oil or other cooking fat
1 tablespoon soya sauce	salt and pepper

Combine the mushrooms and onions and season with soya sauce. Wash fish, put in a deep dish, cover with mushrooms and onions, put in a steamer and steam for 15 minutes with a lid on. Season with vinegar, salt and pepper and serve with boiled rice.

This recipe is equally successful with halibut, sole and plaice.

TURBOT, ENGLISH STYLE

4 Servings

4 portions turbot	2½ dcl (½ pint or 1 cup) béchamel sauce
125 ml (4 oz or ½ cup) milk	
butter	2 tablespoons cream
salt and pepper	60 gr (2 oz or ½ cup) grated cheese
1 dozen oysters	

Simmer the turbot gently in a shallow pan in milk with a little butter for 15 minutes, season to taste. When done, drain, put on an ovenproof serving dish, garnish with oysters.

Add cream to sauce and pour it over the fish. Sprinkle with cheese, dot with small pieces of butter and brown the top lightly in the oven or under a grill.

TURBOT AU GRATIN

4 Servings

4 portions of turbot fillet	sifted breadcrumbs
salt and pepper	60 gr (2 oz or ½ cup) grated Parmesan cheese
4 tablespoons melted butter	
4 tablespoons dry Vermouth	

Season the fish with salt and pepper, brush with butter, sprinkle with Vermouth. Grill, allowing 3 minutes for each side and basting two or three times with butter and Vermouth.

Mix breadcrumbs with cheese, sprinkle turbot portions with the mixture, return to grill, cook for one more minute each side and serve.

TURBOT, HONG KONG STYLE

4–6 Servings

750 gr (1½ lb) filleted turbot
salt and pepper
flour
oil
16 gr (½ oz or 4 teaspoons) fresh
  ginger
30 gr (1 oz or 6 tablespoons)
  mushrooms
60 gr (2 oz or 4 tablespoons)
  pork (lean)

15 gr (½ oz or 2 tablespoons)
  onions
soya sauce
1 teaspoon sugar
stock
1 teaspoon cornflour
few drops sesame oil

Skin the fish, put in a dish, sprinkle with salt and pepper and dredge with flour. Deep fry in boiling oil, for about 3 minutes. Slice finely the ginger, mushrooms, pork and onions and put all these ingredients into a pot or pan with a little salt and the soya sauce. Quick fry for 1 minute.

Add fish, sugar and enough stock to cover. Simmer for 10 minutes, add cornflour diluted with enough water to make a thin paste, and sesame oil, cook for 1 minute. Serve with boiled rice.

WHITING ORLY

4 Servings

8 fillets of whiting
juice of ½ lemon
2 tablespoons olive oil
small sliced onion
1 tablespoon chopped parsley

salt and pepper
flour
oil for deep frying
sprigs of parsley
tomato sauce

Wipe the fillets, put in a shallow dish, sprinkle with lemon juice, oil, onion, parsley, salt and freshly ground black pepper, and leave to stand for 45 to 50 minutes, turning from time to time.

Drain the fillets, roll in flour, deep fry for 5 minutes, drain, arrange on a napkin covered dish, garnish with sprigs of fresh or fried parsley and serve. Serve tomato sauce separately.

WHITING WITH PEAS, ITALIAN STYLE

4 Servings

4 cleaned whiting
500 gr (1 lb or 2 cups) shelled
  peas (or large packet frozen
  peas)
salt
1 tablespoon olive oil

1 medium-sized chopped onion
1 tablespoon chopped parsley
freshley ground black pepper
1 tablespoon tomatoe purée
4 tablespoons boiling water

Wash and dry the whiting. Cook the peas for 5 minutes in

salted water and drain (or 1 minute if frozen peas are used). Heat oil, fry the onion lightly, add whiting, brown gently on both sides, sprinkle with parsley and pepper.

Dilute tomato purée with water, pour into the pan, add peas, bring to the boil, cover, simmer on low heat for 12 to 15 minutes and serve.

WHITING COLBERT

Allow one fish per portion.

Slit whiting along the back, remove backbone, season with salt and pepper, sprinkle with flour, dip in egg and breadcrumbs and deep fry. Drain, arrange on a dish, fill the slit with maître d'hôtel butter.

WHITING MEUNIÈRE

Proceed as described in the recipe for Fillets of Sole Meunière (p. 115) using whiting.

CHINESE FISH BALLS IN SWEET AND SOUR SAUCE

4 Servings

500–750 gr (1–1½ lb) boned chopped (white) fish	oil for deep frying
salt and pepper	sweet and sour sauce (p. 212)
1 egg	4 or 5 spring onions, chopped
120 gr (¼ lb or ¾ cup) cornflour	boiled rice

Season the chopped fish with salt and pepper, add egg and cornflour. Stir until the mixture is smooth, shape into small balls, deep fry them in oil until golden, drain and cover with sweet and sour sauce.

Garnish with chopped spring onions and serve plain boiled rice separately.

BAKED FISH RAMEKINS

4 Servings

375 gr (12 oz or 1½ cups) cooked (or tinned) white or pink fish	2 tablespoons lemon juice
1 large packet frozen spinach	2 teaspoons finely chopped onion
salt and pepper	125 ml (4 oz or ½ cup) sour cream (or yoghourt)
butter	1 tablespoon sherry
125 gr (4 oz or 1 cup) grated cheese	pinch nutmeg
	4 small peeled tomatoes

Flake the fish with a fork, remove all skin and bones. Cook

spinach in lightly salted water and drain. Butter 4 ramekin dishes and dust with a little cheese. Fill each dish with quarter of the spinach and fish and sprinke with a dash of lemon juice. Mix onion, sour cream, and sherry. Season to taste with salt, pepper and nutmeg and spoon over the fish. Put a whole tomato on top, sprinkle with cheese, dot with a small piece of butter and bake for ½ hour at 190°C (375°F or Gas Mark 4).

This recipe can be used equally successfully with prawns, shrimps, crab, etc.

SWEDISH FISH BALLS

4 Servings

500 gr (1 lb) cod or haddock
  fillets
150 gr (5 oz or 10 tablespoons)
  butter
salt and pepper
2 fresh egg yolks
120 ml (4 oz or ½ cup) single
  cream

120 ml (4 oz or ½ cup) double
  cream
2 stiffly beaten egg whites
½ litre (1 pint or 2 cups)
  strained fish stock
30 grs (1 oz or ¼ cup) flour
1 tablespoon prawn butter

Wash the fillets, dry and mince finely. Pound with 120 grs (4 oz or 8 tablespoons) butter, season to taste and rub through a sieve, or pass through a blender. Blend yolks with single cream and gradually incorporate in the fish forcemeat, stirring all the time.

Add double cream, trickling it in a little at a time and blending well before adding any more. Fold in egg whites carefully. Poach the fish balls for 10 minutes in boiling stock, taking up a spoonful at a time and shaping them as you scoop them up. Dip the spoon into boiling liquid each time, to prevent the mixture sticking to it. When done, drain and keep hot.

Using the remaining 30 grs (1 oz or 2 tablespoons) of butter and the flour, make a white roux, dilute with strained liquor in which the fish balls were poached and make a white sauce.

Finsh off with a little prawn butter, stir it in, pour over the fish balls and serve.

FRIED FILLETS OF FISH

4 Servings

750 gr (1½ lb) fish fillets (plaice,
  sole, halibut, cod, haddock,
  hake, etc.)
1 egg
1 tablespoon milk

salt and pepper
pinch mace
breadcrumbs
oil

Wash and dry the fillets carefully. Mix egg with milk, season with salt, pepper and mace. Dip fillets in egg, then in breadcrumbs. Pat down to coat all over, then shake lightly to shed surplus crumbs.

Use enough oil to submerge the fillets. Heat oil until a blueish haze begins to rise. Put the fillets in a few at a time, to prevent sudden cooling of the oil temperature, as this would make the fillets soggy. Fry until brown all over, drain on paper, garnish with fried parsley and serve piping hot.

BOURRIDE

This is a great favourite in Provence and there are innumerable variations. Various small fish or fillets or larger fish can be used. The one indispensable ingredient is aioli (p. 203).

4 Servings

4 portions of brill (halibut or turbot) fillet	2 tablespoons cream
court-bouillon à la mineport	2 dcl (½ pint or 1 cup) aioli
2 tablespoons olive oil	chopped parsley
small piece bitter orange peel	boiled potatoes
pinch saffron	croutons fried in oil

Using head, bones and trimmings of the fish, prepare court-bouillon, add oil, orrange peel and saffron and poach the fish in it for 15 to 20 minutes. Drain the fish and put on a heated serving dish, cover and keep hot.

Reduce the court-bouillon by rapid boiling by two-thirds, strain, pressing the vegetables through the sieve, return to heat and blend in cream. Mix the aioli with the hot sauce. The best way is to have the aioli ready and waiting and to pour the reduced hot court-bouillon on it in a steady stream, stirring constantly to ensure smooth amalgamation. The texture should be that of a thick cream and the colour a lovely, shiny yellow.

Pour the sauce over the fish, sprinkle with parsley and serve with potatoes and croûtons.

CORNISH FISH AND POTATO CAKES

4 Servings

360 gr (¾ lb) raw potatoes	1 teaspoon chopped onion
500 gr (1 lb) flaked or minced cooked (white) fish	salt and pepper
60 gr (2 oz or ½ cup) flour	125 gr (4 oz or ½ cup) butter for frying

Peel potatoes and grate, raw, into a bowl of cold water. Drain and pat dry on a cloth. Mix fish with potato. Add flour, onion and salt and pepper to taste.

Shape into 7½ cm (3 in.) fish cakes and fry in hot butter until crisp and golden. Serve at once.

BREADED FISH CAKES

6 Servings

750 gr (1½ lb) (white) fish
125 gr (4 oz) streaky bacon
500 gr (1 lb) potatoes, boiled
1 small chopped onion
2 tablespoons butter
1 tablespoon chopped parsley
salt and pepper
pinch marjoram, thyme or basil
  or to taste

125 gr (3 oz or 1 cup) fresh breadcrumbs
180 ml (6 oz or ¾ cup) warm milk
60 gr (2 oz or ½ cup) toasted breadcrumbs for coating
125 grs (4 oz or ½ cup) butter or oil for frying

Chop up fish and bacon together; mince, if you like a finer texture. Mash the potatoes and blend in fish and bacon. Fry onion in butter and add to fish mixture. Add parsley, salt and pepper to taste and herbs. Add fresh breadcrumbs and milk and blend well.

Shape into 18 flat fish cakes, coat with breadcrumbs and fry in butter on both sides until nice and brown. Serve at once.

Fish Fritters and Croquettes

TEMPURA (JAPAN)

The three syllables of the word *tempura* have their roots in three characters symbolising heaven, woman and veil. In less romantic terms, tempura is food, mainly fish and shell-fish, dipped in tempura batter, deep fried and served with tempura sauce.

It is delicious and the success lies in everything being freshly done : the batter prepared just before frying and kept cold, the oil kept absolutely clear, and the cooked tempura served as soon as it is done. The oil should be at least 2 in. deep and kept at a temperature between 150°–175°C (300°F–350°F). Japanese housewives who do not use a thermometer test the temperature by dropping a small lump of batter into the oil. At 150°C (350°F) the batter cooks through completely in precisely 1 minute.

Skim the oil carefully during frying without allowing little bits of batter to burn in it.

Tempura batter

125 gr (4 oz 1 cup) unsifted flour	2½ dcl (½ pint or 1 cup) cold water
1 egg	

Mix flour, egg and water together, whisking lightly, without trying to make the mixture too smooth. A few lumps won't matter, as tempura batter is intended for immediate use. Never let it stand, and do not allow it to get warm.

SIMPLE PRAWN TEMPURA

4 Servings

8 large Pacific or Dublin Bay prawns	3–4 teaspoons finely grated radish
tempura batter	3–4 teaspoons finely grated ginger
oil for deep frying	tempura sauce (p. 213)

Allow two large prawns per portion. Leaving the tails on, remove the head, shell, slash down the back with a sharp knife and remove the dark vein inside. Cut lengthwise in several places, but not right through, to prevent shrinking during frying. Pat the prawns with a dry cloth to remove all moisture and make sure the oil doesn't spatter.

Dip in batter, deep fry in hot oil until pale golden. Take out and drain on kitchen paper to remove excess fat. Arrange on a dish, garnish with tiny mounds of grated radish and ginger.

Serve with plain boiled rice and hand tempura sauce separately.

CHRYSANTHEMUM PRAWN TEMPURA

This is a delicious and most decorative dish—excellent for cocktail parties.

4 Servings

125 gr (4 oz or 1 cup) peeled prawns	1 packet harusame noodles
2 egg whites	oil for deep frying
pinch salt	6–8 chrysanthemum leaves
1 tablespoon cornflour	tempura sauce
pinch Aji-no-Moto	grated radish
	grated ginger

Put the prawns through a mincer, then pound in a mortar to a smooth paste. Add egg whites, salt, cornflour and Aji-no-Moto. Blend well and shape into 2½ cm (1 in.) round patties. Cut harusame noodles into strips 4–5 cm (1½–2 in.) long.

To make chrysanthemum petals : press the prawn patties on one side only gently but firmly into the harusame strips.

The idea is to preserve the round shape of the patties and at the same time to make them pick up as many 'petals' as will stick. Deep fry, drain on absorbent paper and arrange the newly cooked 'chrysanthemums' in the form of a bouquet in a large dish—a flat straw one is ideal. Decorate with washed and dried chrysanthemum leaves to complete the illusion and serve.

Hand tempura sauce, grated radish and grated ginger in separate dishes.

FRITTO MISTO MARE

It is impossible to give a list of ingredients for this most popular of seaside specialities. Signora Dell'Omo prepares it the Venetian way and says various small fish may be included, but the 'musts' are red mullet (2 per portion), scampi (cooked unshelled), squids cut in rings, and tiny octopus. Prepare all these for cooking as described in appropriate recipes, dredge lightly with flour, season, fry in sizzling hot oil, drain, garnish with lemon wedges and serve piping hot.

FINNISH HERRING CROQUETTES

4 Servings

2 plump salt herrings	1 tablespoon finely chopped
2½ dcl (½ pint or 1 cup) milk	onion
250 gr (½ lb or 1 cup) boiled	1 teaspoon cornflour
potatoes	pepper
125 gr (4 oz or ½ cup) cold	breadcrumbs
cooked beef	fat for frying

Leave the herrings in a dish covered with milk for several hours, better still, overnight. Drain, remove skin, fins, bones, etc. Put the herrings, potatoes and beef (roast or boiled left-overs will do very well) through a mincer. Add onion and cornflour. Sprinkle with freshly grated pepper and blend the mixture until smooth.

Shape into small croquettes, roll in breadcrumbs, fry both sides until golden, drain on greaseproof paper and serve. Excellent with Hollandaise sauce.

FISH CROQUETTES

4–5 Servings

500 grs (1 lb) white fish	2 eggs
2–3 slices of crustless bread	1–2 tablespoons flour
2–3 tablespoons milk	breadcrumbs
1 small onion	oil for deep frying
salt and pepper	anchovy sauce

Skin the fish and remove bones, if any. Soak the bread in a little milk. Put the fish, onion and bread through a mincer. Season to taste, add one egg and mix well.

Shape into croquettes, dip in flour, then in beaten egg and breadcrumbs. Deep fry in hot fat until crisp and brown. Avoid too high a heat, otherwise you find the croquettes will be too dark on the outside without being cooked properly on the inside. Drain on kitchen paper.

Serve with anchovy sauce.

VIENNESE PIKE FRITTERS

6 Servings

1 kg (2 lb) pike	1 teaspoon chopped parsley
1 teaspoon salt	beer batter
2 tablespoons chopped onion	fat for deep frying

Clean out, wash and dry pike. Cut into slices removing bones as you do so. Lay on a plate and cover with salt, onion and parsley. Allow to stand for an hour. Brush off the onion and parsley, dip pike slices into beer batter.

Deep fry, drain on paper towels and serve at once with a sauce of your choice.

SPANISH HERRING FRITTERS

4 Servings

4 filleted fresh herrings
pepper
milk
2 tablespoons flour
2 tablespoons warm milk
1 egg yolk

pinch salt
2 teaspoons olive oil
1 stiffly beaten white of egg
oil for deep frying
lemon

Rinse the fillets, sprinkle with freshly ground pepper, put in a bowl, cover with milk and leave to steep for an hour.

To make batter, mix flour with warm milk, add egg yolk, salt and olive oil, stir until smooth and leave for an hour. Fold in white of egg just before the batter is needed.

Heat oil, coat the herring fillets with batter, deep fry until golden, drain well on kitchen paper to remove surplus fat. Serve with lemon quarters and fried parsley (p. 224).

SPANISH DRIED COD FRITTERS

8–10 Servings

1 kg (2 lb) dry cod
3 tablespoons flour
1 tablespoon water
2 tablespoons olive oil

1 raw egg yolk
2 tablespoons rum
oil for deep frying

This is a Canary Islands' speciality and well worth the trouble.

Soak the cod overnight in water to de-salt it. Drain, boil until tender enough to be easily flaked with a fork. Drain, flake, combine with flour, water, olive oil, yolk and rum. Blend well and leave for 2 hours.

Heat oil for deep frying, and taking a small quantity of the mixture (about the size of a hazel nut) on the tip of a fork, drop each pellet into fat, about a dozen at a time. Fry until golden, remove, drain and serve at once.

SHRIMP AND CHEESE FRITTERS

4 Servings

120 grs (4 oz or 1 cup) plain
    flour
salt and pepper
120 ml (4 oz or ½ cup) milk
1 egg

120 gr (4 oz or ½ cup) peeled
    shrimps
120 gr (4 oz or ½ cup) grated
    cheese
fat for frying

Sift flour into a mixing bowl, season, gradually whisk in milk. Beat egg lightly and whisk into batter mixture. Add shrimps and cheese and mix well. Taking a teaspoon at a time fry in hot fat until crisp all over. Drain on kitchen paper and serve at once.

MUSSEL FRITTERS À LA DUXELLES

Choose large mussels, poach in white wine, take them out of their shells, de-beard, dry well, cover with a teaspoon of thick Duxelles sauce. Dip in frying batter and fry.

HERRING FRITTERS

Use marinated herrings. Drain and dry on a cloth, spread with a thin layer of fish forcemeat. Roll up, dip rolls in frying batter and fry. Drain well and serve hot.

ANCHOVY FRITTERS

Roll anchovy fillets into rings and put them on thin round slices of bread, about 3–3½ cm (1½ inches) in diameter. Sandwich these rounds together two by two, dip them in frying batter and fry just before serving.

Fish Pancakes and Pies

GRANDFATHER'S KIPPERS WITH BLINI

This delectable variation on a Russian theme was invented by George John Froud. Being an engineer by profession, an artist at heart and often impecunious, he was determined to serve blini with fish during Lent but could not afford smoked salmon. The result of his famous experiment was so wonderfully good that we have adopted it into our regular repertoire.

6 Servings

1 cake of yeast	½ teaspoon salt
2½ dcl (½ pint or 1 cup) lukewarm water	2 teaspoons sugar
	2 tablespoons melted butter
½ litre (1 pint or 2 cups) lukewarm milk	4 egg whites
	2 plump smoked kippers
250 gr (½ lb or 2 cups) buckwheat flour	butter
	sour cream
4 egg yolks	2 hard boiled eggs

Dissolve yeast in water and 125 ml (4 oz or ½ cup) milk. Add half the flour and mix well. Cover the mixing bowl with a tea towel and leave in a warm place for 3 hours.

Beat egg yolks with salt and sugar, add the rest of the lukewarm milk, mix, add melted butter, mix again and add to the yeast mixture, stirring thoroughly. Incorporate the rest of the flour. Beat the whites until stiff, fold into the batter, cover and allow to stand for 45 to 50 minutes without disturbing the batter, which should have the consistency of thick cream.

We use special cast iron pancake frying pans about 7–8 cm (3 in.) in diameter, but blini can be baked in any good lightly greased frying pan or on a griddle. Take care to measure out the correct amount of batter to keep the blini of uniform size. Brown on both sides, stack on a dish and keep warm until all batter is used up.

Do not cook the kipper in any way at all, just carefully remove the bone, slice thinly as you would smoked salmon and arrange on a dish. Serve the kippers and the blini together with melted butter and sour cream handed in separate sauceboats. Let your guests spread their blini with melted butter with chopped hard boiled egg added to it, put a slice of kipper over it, and top with a spoonful of sour cream.

BLINI WITH CAVIAR

This is one of the best of Russian inventions and a traditional way of serving caviar. Make blini as described in recipe Grandfather's Kippers with Blini, and serve with caviar. Red or black caviar can be used.

If you are serving red caviar, sprinkle it with chopped spring onions and hand melted butter and sour cream separately.

BLINI WITH SMOKED SALMON

Follow above recipe substituting sliced smoked salmon for kippers.

CHINESE SPRING ROLLS WITH PRAWNS AND PORK

6 Servings

Batter:

2 eggs	salt
1 dcl (4 oz or ½ cup) milk	60 gr (2 oz or ½ cup) flour

Mix all ingredients till smooth, adding flour little by little. Grease a pan and heat over moderate flame (ideally the diameter of the pan should be about 12½ cm (5 in.)) : Gently pour in a thin layer of batter. Cook for one minute on one side only. Turn out to cool on paper towel. Repeat until all batter is used up.

Filling:

2 tablespoons butter	1 tablespoon diced celery
60 gr (2 oz or ½ cup) sliced bamboo shoots	salt and pepper
	1 tablespoon nut oil
60 gr (2 oz or 4 tablespoons) cooked shredded pork	½ tablespoon Ve-Tsin
	125 gr (4 oz) peeled prawns
2 tablespoons diced onions	oil for deep frying

Heat butter in a pan, put in all ingredients except prawns, cook for 5 minutes, add prawns, mix well, simmer for 5 minutes. Leave to cool. Put a spoonful of filling on cooked side of each pancake, roll up, tucking in and sealing the edges with beaten egg or left-over batter. Chill 20 minutes. Deep fry in hot oil, drain and serve.

If necessary, spring rolls can be kept in a low oven, though care must be taken not to allow them to dry up.

RUSSIAN RICE AND SALMON COULIBIAC

6–8 Servings

brioche dough or puff pastry
velouté sauce
125 gr (4 oz or ½ cup)
buckwheat or rice
½ kg (1 lb or 2¾ cups) cooked,
peeled, boned salmon
1 finely chopped onion
1 tablespoon butter
3–4 sliced hard-boiled eggs

salt and pepper
2–3 tablespoons chopped
parsley, chervil and
tarragon
125 gr (4 oz or 8 tablespoons)
melted butter
1 egg yolk mixed with 1
teaspoon water

Prepare dough or pastry and the sauce. Cook rice and cool. Flake or cut salmon into very thin slices. Lightly fry the onion in a tablespoon butter. Add to it the mushrooms which were cooked in the sauce. (Or lightly fry some sliced mushrooms in butter.)

Roll out the pastry into a thin rectangle and cut in two. Place one of the sheets of rolled out pastry on a lightly buttered baking sheet, moisten the edges. Leaving the edges uncovered, spread a layer of rice on the pastry evenly. Follow with a layer of egg slices, then salmon. Season with salt and pepper. Sprinkle with chopped herbs, onions and mushrooms. Spoon some melted butter over each layer. Finish off with the remaining rice. Season, sprinkle liberally with butter. Cover with the second sheet of pastry, press down to seal the edges.

If using brioche dough, brush with yolk, prick with a fork to provide outlet for steam and bake in a hot oven 220°C (425°F or Gas Mark 6) for 30–35 minutes.

If using puff pastry, put in a refrigerator for half an hour. Then paint the whole surface with egg and bake in a hot oven for 20 minutes.

AVOCADO CRÊPES WITH CRABMEAT

8 Servings

1 large ripe avocado pear
6 eggs
90 gr (3 oz or ¾ cup) flour
salt and pepper
180 ml (6 oz or ¾ cup) milk
180 ml (6 oz or ¾ cup) water
butter
¾ litre (1½ pints or 3 cups)
bechamel or velouté sauce

120 gr (4 oz or 2/3 cup) diced
Gruyère cheese
1 tablespoon Worcestershire
sauce
¾ kg (1½ lb) flaked crab meat
60 grs (2 oz or ½ cup) grated
cheese

Mash avocado, add eggs, flour and pinch of salt, beat until smooth and gradually stir in milk and water. Heat a 15 cm (6 in.) pan, melt in it 1/3 teaspoon butter, pour in 4 tablespoons of the avocado batter, tilt the pan to cover the bottom and cook the pancake until underside is brown, turn and cook the other side. Continue in this manner until all the batter is used up.

Heat the sauce, add Gruyère cheese and cook until the sauce thickens. Remove from heat, add Worcestershire sauce, season with salt and pepper to taste, and stir in crab meat.

Put a little filling on each pancake and roll up. Arrange pancakes in a single layer in a large buttered shallow baking dish, sprinkle with grated cheese and dot with tiny pieces of butter. Bake in a hot oven 220°C (425°F or Gas Mark 6) until the cheese melts.

ITALIAN WHITEBAIT PANCAKES

4 Servings

500 gr (1 lb) whitebait
2 beaten eggs
salt and pepper
3 tablespoons grated Parmesan
    cheese
½ teaspoon chopped basil
1 tablespoon chopped parsley
4 tablespoons breadcrumbs
1 clove chopped garlic
5–6 tablespoons flour
125 ml (4 oz or ¼ cup) oil

Keep the whitebait with a piece of ice in a basin until required. Drain, spread on a cloth to dry and pat gently. Put in a mixing bowl with eggs, seasoning, cheese, basil, parsley, breadcrumbs, garlic and enough flour to form a manageable mixture. Shape into 7–8 cm (3 in.) pancakes, dust with flour.

Fry briskly in very hot oil and serve piping hot.

Fish with Rice and Pasta

PAELLA A LA VALENCIANA

For all Spanish rice dishes or paella, a large, deep frying-pan is essential. It is paella, the pan, which gave the dish its name.

Paella is the most typical of Spanish dishes and is not difficult to make. It relies on the blending of flavours for its effect and combines meat with fish and shellfish.

8–10 Servings

3 tablespoons oil
1 jointed chicken
½ kg (1 lb or 2 cups) pork, cut in large dice
1 finely chopped onion
3 ripe tomatoes, peeled and chopped
750 gr (1½ lb or 3 cups) rice
250 gr (½ lb or 1 cup) runner beans and/or peas
1 dozen artichoke hearts (optional)
3 red peppers, seeded and sliced

360 gr (¾ lb or 1½ cups) fish (hake, eel, etc.) cut in pieces
1 crayfish cut in pieces
250 gr (½ pint or 1½ cups) peeled prawns (or shrimps)
a few slices octopus
½ litre (1 pint) mussels
1 teaspoon salt
½ teaspoon pepper
a pinch of saffron
1¼ litres (2½ pints or 5 cups) stock

Heat the oil, add chicken and pork. Brown lightly, add onion. When the onion is golden, add tomatoes. Cook for a few minutes then put in the rice and simmer for 10 minutes. Add runner beans and/or peas, artichoke hearts and cook for five minutes. Add peppers and fish, crab or lobster, shrimps or prawns, octopus and any other interesting sea food. Scrub mussels, rinse well, discard all open ones. Test carefully: they should shut tightly if given a sharp tap. Add to rice.

Season to taste and boil fast for 8 minutes. Reduce heat and simmer for 8 minutes. Add the saffron and stock or water with a bouillon cube.

When the rice is cooked and all the water has been absorbed, put the paella in the oven for five minutes to give it a nice golden colour. Take it out of the oven and let it stand for a couple of minutes to settle before serving.

FISH AND RICE CROQUETTES

4 Servings

500 gr (1 lb) cooked (white) fish
180 gr (6 oz or 7/8 cup) rice
salt and pepper
1 tablespoon chopped parsley or chives
125 ml (¼ pint of ½ cup) béchamel sauce

seasoned flour
1 egg, lightly beaten
60 gr (2 oz or ½ cup) dry breadcrumbs
oil for frying

Flake cooked fish into rice, season to taste and add parsley. Bind mixture with béchamel and shape into 8 croquettes. Roll in seasoned flour. Dip in egg, then in breadcrumbs. Fry in oil until crisp and brown. Drain well.

To make seasoned flour, put a few tablespoons flour into a paper bag, add salt and pepper and shake well.

BASQUE RICE

6 Servings

1 onion
oil for frying
½ kg (1 lb or 2 cups) sliced hake
1 clove chopped garlic
big bunch parsley

½ kg (1 lb or 2 cups) rice
1½ litres (3 pints or 6 cups) boiling water
salt and pepper
bay leaf

Chop and fry the onion lightly in oil for 3–4 minutes. Add garlic, parsley and rice. Add boiling water, season, put in bay leaf, simmer 15 minutes, add fish, continue to simmer for 15 minutes. Serve.

CHINESE FRIED RICE WITH PRAWNS, HONG KONG STYLE

4 Servings

1 tablespoon lard or oil
½ kg (1 lb or 2 cups and 4 tablespoons) cooked rice
125 gr (4 oz or ¾ cup) cooked peeled prawns

2 beaten eggs
3–4 chopped spring onions
1 tablespoon soya sauce

Heat lard in pan. Fry the rice quickly stirring all the time. Stir in prawns. Pour eggs over rice, fry slowly together for 4–5 minutes. Sprinkle with spring onions, season with soya and serve.

For Chinese fried rice, it is best to use boiled rice. It has exactly the right consistency.

SPANISH FISHERMAN'S RICE

6–8 Servings

250 ml (½ pint or 1 cup) olive oil
2 chopped onions
½ kg (1 lb or 3 cups) peeled chopped tomatoes
bouquet garni
2 litres (4 pints or 8 cups) water
1 tablespoon salt
pinch freshly ground pepper

180 gr (6 oz) monkfish
180 gr (6 oz) conger eel
180 gr (6 oz) sea bass or halibut
180 gr (6 oz) prawns
6 small crayfish
1 dozen small mussels or clams
pinch saffron
2–3 cloves garlic
½ kg (1 lb or 2 cups) rice

Heat the oil and cook onions until they brown lightly. Add tomatoes, bouquet garni, water, salt and pepper. Bring to the boil, add all fish heads and trimmings and simmer to make a good fish stock. Cook for 18–20 minutes and strain.

Wash the fish, cut into portions. Wash the shell-fish and scrub the mussels. Toss the mussels in a little water in a frying-pan over a high flame until they open and discard half the shells. Put all fish, shell-fish and mussels into a pan, add the prepared stock and simmer gently for 6–7 minutes.

Pound the saffron with garlic in a mortar, dilute with a tablespoon stock and add to pan. Simmer for a further 6–7 minutes. Remove from heat.

Draw off 1 litre (2 pints or 4 cups) of the liquid in which the fish was cooked. Bring to the boil in another pan, sprinkle rice into it and cook on low heat for 20 minutes. Arrange the rice on a dish. Reheat the fish and serve with the rice on a separate dish.

MOST PRECIOUS RICE

Most Precious Rice is so called because it contains an interesting variety of ingredients, including a mixture of crab meat and pork.

6 Servings

125 gr (4 oz or ¾ cup) crab meat
250 gr (8 oz or 1 cup) lean pork
250 gr (8 oz or 1 cup) shelled peas (or beans, topped and tailed and sliced)
125 gr (4 oz or 1¼ cups) sliced mushrooms

1–2 tablespoons chopped spring onions
2–3 eggs
1 dessertspoon soya sauce
oil
salt and pepper
750 gr–1 kg (1½–2 lb or 3–4 cups) cold cooked rice

See that all ingredients are cut to a uniform size, determining the size and shape by the smallest natural ingredient; thus, if peas are used, the rest of the ingredients must be cut into dice no bigger than a pea.

Beat eggs with soya sauce and keep by. Cook all other ingredients in a deep oiled pan, season to taste, add rice, stirring until it becomes separate and quite hot. Stir to mix well.

Pour the eggs over the whole mixture. Increase heat to cook quickly and keep stirring until the eggs have been integrated into the mixture and are quite dry.

PRAWNS WITH WILD RICE

4 Servings

1 cup wild rice
1 litre (1 quart or 4 cups) clear chicken stock (or water with a bouillon cube)
salt
4 tablespoons butter
1 clove chopped garlic
1 large chopped onion
250 gr (8 oz or 3 cups) sliced mushrooms

1 chopped green pepper
120 ml (4 oz or ½ cup) dry white wine
pepper
1 tablespoon cornflour
2 tablespoons cold water
375 gr (12 oz or 1½ cups) cooked, peeled prawns

Wash the wild rice in several waters and leave in water to soak for an hour. Drain, put in a saucepan with 3 cups of chicken stock. Add a pinch of salt, cover and bring to the boil. Reduce heat, remove lid and cook for 30 minutes, without stirring. The rice should not need any draining, all the liquid ought to be absorbed. When done, add a tablespoon of butter to the rice. Keep warm.

Heat 2 tablespoons of butter and lightly fry the garlic, onion, mushrooms and pepper. Add wine and the rest of the stock, simmer for 5 minutes, season to taste. Blend corn-flour with 2 tablespoons cold water, stir into the sauce, cook until the sauce thickens, add prawns and remove from heat.

Arrange the rice as a border in a buttered ovenproof dish, fill the centre with the prawns and their sauce, dot with small pieces of butter, put in a moderate oven, 190°C (375°F or Gas Mark 4) for 15 to 20 minutes and serve.

INDIAN PULAU WITH FISH

6 Servings

500–750 gr (1–1½ lbs) fish
    fillets (hake, cod, haddock)
1½ cups rice
3 tablespoons butter
1 teaspoon turmeric
2 chopped sprigs coriander
small pinch chilli powder
1 teaspoon garam-masala

1 teaspoon salt
1 tablespoon lemon juice
1 chopped onion
750 ml (3 pints or 2¼ cups) hot
    water
250 grs (1½ pint or cup)
    cooked, shelled prawns

Wash the fish, wipe with a cloth and cut into portions. Wash the rice and leave in water while preparing the other ingredients. Heat half the butter, add turmeric, coriander, chilli powder, garam-masala and a good pinch of salt. Cook the herb mixture for 2 minutes. Moisten with lemon juice, continue to cook over a lively flame, stirring all the time, until all surplus moisture evaporates.

Add fish and fry on both sides, allowing it to pick up as much of the herb mixture as will adhere, patting lightly with a fish slice. Be careful not to break the fish portions. Cook for 5 to 6 minutes and remove from pan.

In a saucepan big enough eventually to take all the ingredients, heat the rest of the butter and fry the onion. Drain the rice, add to saucepan, season with salt, mix well, cook for 2 minutes, add the herbs and juices left from frying the fish, stir to mix well, add hot water, bring to the boil, reduce heat, cover and simmer for 30 minutes.

Stir the rice mixture gently with the clean handle of a wooden spoon, put the portions of fish on top, cover and simmer for 7 to 8 minutes, garnish with prawns and serve.

CREOLE RICE WITH SHRIMPS

4 Servings

180 gr (6 oz or ¾ cup) rice
1 finely chopped onion
30 gr (1 oz or 2 tablespoons)
    butter
15 gr (½ oz or 2 tablespoons)
    flour
1 teaspoon thyme
250 ml (½ pint or 1 cup) sour
    cream

2 eggs yolks
salt
cayenne pepper
½ litre (1 pint or 2 cups) cooked
    and shelled shrimps or
    prawns
2 tablespoons paprika
4 tablespoons grated parmesan

Boil rice and while it is cooking prepare sauce.

Fry onion in butter until golden brown. Stir in flour and thyme. Add sour cream, stirring all the time and when the sauce begins to get hot beat in egg yolks. Season to taste with salt and cayenne pepper.

Stir in shrimps. Spoon hot rice on a heated serving dish and cover with the shrimps. Serve at once with a little bowl of paprika and parmesan mixed together for everyone to help himself to at table.

RICE WITH LOBSTER TENDON, TOKYO STYLE

This is a delicious way of serving deep-fried lobster in the tempura style.

4 Servings

oil for deep frying	125 grs (4 oz or 1/3 cup)
½ kg (1 lb or 2½ cups) lobster,	grated daikon radish
cut in chunks	tempura sauce
tempura batter	pinch grated ginger
4 cups freshly cooked rice	

Heat oil for deep frying. Dip pieces of lobster in batter, deep fry until crisp and golden, remove, drain quickly, arrange on a mound of steaming rice. Add radish to hot tempura sauce, pour over the lobster, sprinkle with ginger and serve at once.

FISH SAMBAL TO SERVE WITH RICE

4 Servings

3 cloves garlic	2½ cm (1 inch) piece finely
2 seeded fresh red chillis (or 1	chopped ginger
teaspoon chilli powder)	500 gr (1 lb) fish (any firm
½ teaspoon cumin seed	white fish) boiled, skinned
¼ teaspoon turmeric	and boned
2–3 tablespoons peanut oil	salt
1 seeded, sliced green pepper	2½ dcl (½ pint or 1 cup)
1 large finely sliced onion	coconut milk

Pound together in a mortar or blend in a liquidiser the garlic, chillis, cumin and turmeric until they form a smooth paste. Heat oil and fry green pepper, onion and ginger for 2 minutes. Add spice paste and stir quickly.

Add fish (which should not be overcooked), cut into portions. Cook gently to heat the fish and permeate it by the spices, for 2–3 minutes. Season with salt to taste.

Add coconut milk, simmer for 5–6 minutes.

PRAWN SAMBAL TO SERVE WITH RICE

As Fish Sambal, substituting equivalent amount of peeled prawns for fish.

SPAGHETTI ALLE VONGOLE

4–6 Servings

500 gr (1 lb) spaghetti   clam sauce (p. 206)

Boil the spaghetti in salted water. Do not overcook. Drain, arrange in a heated serving dish. Pour very hot clam sauce over it and serve.

SPAGHETTI WITH TUNNY SAUCE

4–6 Servings

60 gr (2 oz or 4 tablespoons) butter
60 ml (2 oz or 4 tablespoons) oil
1 clove garlic
small tin tomato paste
¼ litre (½ pint or 1 cup) water

180 gr (6 oz or ¾ cup) tin tunny in oil
3 finely chopped anchovy fillets
2 tablespoons chopped parsley
salt and pepper
½ kg (1 lb) spaghetti

Heat butter and oil together, fry the garlic until golden. Then discard garlic. Dilute tomato paste with water, add to butter and oil. Simmer for half an hour.

Flake the tunny and add with its oil and anchovies. Stir, add parsley, season to taste and simmer for 10 minutes. Boil spaghetti for 10–11 minutes, stirring from time to time. Do not overcook. Drain, mix with the sauce and serve.

SPAGHETTINI WITH ANCHOVY SAUCE

3–4 Servings

120 ml (4 oz or ½ cup) olive oil
2 cloves garlic
2–3 ripe tomatoes, peeled and chopped

4–5 finely chopped anchovy fillets
salt and pepper
375 gr (12 oz) thin spaghetti

Heat the oil, fry garlic in it until it browns. Remove and throw away the garlic. Add tomatoes, cook on low heat, stirring for 15 minutes.

Add anchovies, simmer for a couple of minutes. Season to taste and bear in mind the salt content of the anchovies. Leave on lowest possible heat.

Boil spaghetti without overcooking. Drain, mix with the sauce and serve at once.

UMBRIAN SPAGHETTI (WITH ANCHOVY, TOMATO PASTE AND TRUFFLES)

4 Servings

60 ml (2 oz or 4 tablespoons)
   olive oil
1 clove garlic
4–5 anchovy fillets
1 small tin tomato paste

360 ml ($\frac{3}{4}$ pint of $1\frac{1}{2}$ cups)
   warm water
salt and pepper
2 fresh or tinned black or
   white truffles (optional)
375 grs (12 oz) spaghetti

Heat the oil and brown the garlic to flavour the oil. Discard the garlic. Pound anchovies or liquidise in a blender. Add to pan. Dilute tomato paste with water and stir into the pan. Simmer on low heat for half an hour, and season.

Cook the spaghetti. While it is boiling, chop the truffle. As soon as the spaghetti is cooked, drain well, mix with sauce, sprinkle with truffles and serve.

CHINESE STEAMED PRAWN DUMPLINGS

6–8 Servings

1 tablespoon lard
125 gr (4 oz or $\frac{1}{2}$ cup) raw
   pork, minced
2 tablespoons mushrooms,
   finely chopped
2 spring onions, finely chopped
4 peeled and chopped Pacific
   prawns
2 tablespoons bamboo shoots,
   diced
1 thin slice ginger, finely
   chopped
$\frac{1}{2}$ teaspoon sesame oil

pinch salt
pinch Ve-Tsin
2 teaspoons light soya sauce
$\frac{1}{4}$ teaspoon sugar
1 tablespoon wine (or sherry)
$\frac{1}{2}$ teaspoon cornflour
2 tablespoons cold water
180 gr (6 oz or $1\frac{1}{2}$ cups)
   Chinese wheat starch (or
   flour)
180 ml (6 oz or $\frac{3}{4}$ cup) boiling
   water

Heat lard in frying pan and toss the pork for 30 seconds. Add mushrooms, spring onions, prawns, bamboo shoots, ginger and sesame oil. 'Scramble' for 30 seconds, season with salt, Ve-Tsin, soya sauce and sugar. Sprinkle in wine. Dilute cornflour in cold water, pour over the contents of the frying-pan, stir well and turn out the dumpling filling into a bowl.

Mix wheat starch with hot water into a stiff dough, adding the water very gradually. Knead well, sprinkle with dry flour and roll into a long sausage. Pinch off small pieces of dough of uniform size, roll out into circles $7\frac{1}{2}$ cm (3 in.) in diameter, taking care to fray the edges by scraping them with the lip of a bowl or sauce. Put a good teaspoon of the filling in the middle of each circlet of dough, pinch the edges together to form a semi-circle, steam for 12 minutes and serve piping hot.

Prawns, Lobster
and other Shellfish

BUTTERFLY PRAWNS
HONG KONG RECIPE

6 Servings

750 gr (1½ lb) fresh large
    prawns
2 egg whites
¼ teaspoon salt
4 tablespoons flour
4 rashers lean bacon
2 tablespoons oil

1 finely chopped onion
1 teaspoon tomato purée
2½ dcl (½ pint or 1 cup)
    chicken stock
1 tablespoon cornflour
3 tablespoons cold water

Wash and shell the prawns, rinse and drain. Slash down the back of each with a sharp knife, remove the dark vein, then make a few slanting cuts on each prawn. Mix egg whites, salt and flour. Put a thin layer of this mixture into the long cut of each prawn.

Cut bacon rashers into pieces about 4 cm (1½ in.) across, put a piece on the prawns on top of the egg white mixture and press lightly with your palm. Heat oil in a pan, lay prawns in it, bacon side down, and cook until the bacon is crisp. Turn carefully to cook the other side. As soon as the prawns turn red skewer them on cocktail sticks and serve with the following sauce :

Fry onion until pale golden in the fat left over from the prawns. Add tomato purée and chicken stock (bouillon cube diluted in boiling water will do, in an emergency). Cook for 2 minutes, stirring all the time. Mix cornflour with cold water, pour into the pan, blend in, simmer until the sauce thickens and pour over the prawns.

PRAWNS IN ASPIC

8 Servings

½ litre (1 pint or 2 cups) aspic jelly
8 stuffed olives
½ litre (1 pint or 1¾ cups) shelled prawns

croûtons
butter
maître d'hôtel butter

Line 8 small individual moulds with a thin layer of jelly. When nearly set, arrange thinly sliced olives in a decorative pattern. Put a portion of prawns in each mould, cover with jelly and allow to set. Cut croûtons to slightly larger diameter than jelly moulds, fry them in butter, and just before serving, spread with maître d'hôtel butter. Turn out the jellied prawns on to the croûtons and serve.

BAVARIAN BRANDIED PRAWNS

6 Servings

1 kg (2 lb) fresh prawns or shrimps (cooked ones just do not give the same effect—so down to the sea and out with the shrimping nets)
2 chopped shallots
60 ml (2 oz or ¼ cup) olive oil
60 ml (2 oz or ¼ cup) brandy

125 ml (4 oz or ½ cup) dry white wine
1 tablespoon tomato purée
sugar, salt and cayenne pepper to taste
1 tablespoon butter
1 tablespoon flour

Shell the prawns and de-vein. Fry shallots in oil until transparent, add prawns. Pour brandy over the pan and set alight. When the flame dies down add wine, tomato purée, sugar, salt and cayenne pepper to taste. Simmer, stirring occasionally, for 15 minutes. Remove prawns to a heated serving dish.

In a small saucepan, melt butter, stir in flour and a couple of spoonfuls of the prawn gravy. Pour this mixture into the rest of the gravy and stir and gently bring to the boil. Strain over the prawns and serve at once.

SPICED PRAWNS WITH POPPY SEEDS OR SESAME SEEDS

6 Servings

12 large prawns
2 tablespoons vinegar
1½ teaspoons sugar
1½ teaspoons salt
pinch Aji-no-Moto

30 grs (1 oz) fresh ginger
2 tablespoons shoyu
2 teaspoons poppy seeds or sesame seeds

Wash prawns, pull out intestinal tract (lying just under the tail) and, to keep them straight, insert a toothpick between shell and flesh at the head until it emerges just above the tail tip. This prevents the prawns from curling up during cooking.

Ideally, prawns should be boiled in sea water strained through muslin, when they will not need any further seasoning. When this is not possible, boil them in lightly salted water for 8 minutes, allowing about 15 gr ($\frac{1}{2}$ oz or one tablespoon) salt to $\frac{1}{2}$ litre (1 pint or 2 cups) water. Drain prawns, leave until completely cold, or, better still, chill in refrigerator, then shell and remove toothpick. Put in a deep dish.

Mix vinegar with the sugar and half the salt, add a good pinch of Aji-no-Moto, blend well, sprinkle the mixture over the prawns and leave to marinate for 40–45 minutes. Peel and chop ginger finely, or put it through a mincer. Add shoyu and Aji-no-Moto and cook over gentle heat, stirring constantly, until the liquid is completely reduced.

Take prawns out of marinade, cut into 2$\frac{1}{2}$ cm ($\frac{1}{2}$ inch) pieces, arrange on a dish. Put ginger on top, sprinkle with poppy or sesame seeds and serve.

TOKYO PRAWNS WITH ASPARAGUS

Long hard bamboo skewers which do not burn are used in Japan.

4 Servings

8 large prawns	12 asparagus tips
1 tablespoon salt	3 tablespoons vinegar
4 tablespoons soya sauce	small pinch sugar
1 tablespoon sake (or brandy)	$\frac{1}{2}$ teaspoon cayenne pepper
pinch powdered ginger	

Boil prawns in salted water for 5 minutes. Peel, wash and dry on a cloth. Slit half way through and marinate for half an hour in a sauce made of soya sauce, sake and salt. Put on skewers and grill, basting with the marinade from time to time. Before serving, sprinkle with ginger.

Slice asparagus tips and boil in salted water for a few minutes, rinse with cold water, drain. Mix vinegar, sugar and cayenne pepper, pour this dressing over asparagus and serve with the prawns.

PRAWN SAMPANS

8 Servings

240 gr (8 oz or 1$\frac{1}{2}$ cups) peeled prawns	2 teaspoons Ve-Tsin
3 egg whites	pepper and salt
2 chopped spring onions	8 slices French bread
1 teaspoon ground ginger	oil for frying

Chop the prawns coarsely. Mix egg whites, onions, ginger, Ve-Tsin, add prawns, season to taste and whisk vigorously. Cut crusts off bread slices and trim into boat shapes to make 16 'sampans'. Spread generously with prawn mixture, piling it up and patting down well.

Heat the oil. Put 'sampans' into frying basket and lower into oil for 10 seconds, which is ample time to deep fry them pale golden. Drain well and serve at once.

PRAWN 'MEDALS'

4–6 Servings

240 gr (8 oz or 1½ cups) peeled prawns
3 egg whites
1 tablespoon butter
1 tablespoon soya sauce

1 tablespoon cornflour
bread
oil for deep frying
lettuce

Chop prawns finely, mix with egg whites, butter, soya sauce and cornflour and shape mixture into small balls. Cut bread into round slices with 3¼ cm (1½ in.) pastry cutter. Put a ball of filling on each slice, press down to form 'medals', deep fry in hot oil until golden, drain and serve on lettuce shells.

The above amount should make about 18–20 'medals'.

PRAWN JAMBALAYA, NEW ORLEANS STYLE

4–6 Servings

½–¾ litre (1–1½ pints) peeled prawns
butter
1 large chopped onion
1 chopped clove garlic
120 gr (4 oz or ½ cup) chopped bacon
250 gr (½ lb or 1 cup) peeled, sliced tomatoes

1–2 seeded, sliced sweet peppers
salt and pepper
pinch cayenne pepper
250 gr (½ lb or 1 cup) cooked rice

Toss the prawns in butter for half a minute and remove. In a saucepan large enough to take all the ingredients, melt 60 gr (2 oz or 4 tablespoons) butter. Brown the onion and garlic lightly. Add bacon and tomatoes, stir and cook until the tomatoes yield their juices. Add peppers and prawns, season with salt and pepper, heighten with a little cayenne pepper.

Add rice, mix well, dot with little pieces of butter, cover and simmer until the peppers are done. Serve piping hot.

PRAWNS WITH BRANDY OR RUM

4 Servings

olive oil
1 finely chopped onion
125 gr (4 oz or ½ cup) peeled,
  chopped tomatoes
500 gr (1 lb or 2 cups) large
  peeled prawns

salt and pepper
2 tablespoons brandy or rum
water
2 sliced onions
flour

Heat 3 tablespoons oil and lightly fry chopped onion. Add tomatoes, cook for 2 minutes. Put in prawns, cook for 5 minutes, season, mix well. Sprinkle with brandy or rum and set it alight. When it has burnt out, add 1 to 2 tablespoons water, cover and simmer on low heat for 10 minutes.

Shake sliced onions into rings, dredge with flour, deep fry in smoking hot olive oil until golden, drain and serve as garnish for prawns.

PRAWNS WITH CELERY, CANTONESE STYLE

4 Servings

1 dessertspoon olive oil
250 gr (8 oz or 1 cup) cooked,
  peeled prawns
1 small sliced onion
60 gr (2 oz or 8 tablespoons)
  chopped mushrooms
90 gr (3 oz or 6 tablespoons)
  sliced celery

pinch pepper
1 teaspoon soya sauce
1 teaspoon brandy
1 teaspoon cornflour
120 ml (4 oz or ½ cup) water
4–5 spring onions, cut in 5 cm
  (2 inch) strips

Heat oil in pan and fry prawns and onion together for 3 minutes, stirring constantly. Add mushrooms, celery and pepper. Cook for 4 minutes. Mix soya sauce, brandy, cornflour and water, pour into the pan, stir, cook for 1 minute, remove from heat, sprinkle with spring onions and serve.

SINGAPORE PRAWNS IN YOGHOURT

4 Servings

30 gr (1 oz or 2 tablespoons)
  butter
2 medium-sized chopped onions
1 chopped sweet green pepper
1 pounded red chilli
1 dessertspoon curry powder

500 gr (1 lb or 2 cups) shelled
  prawns
salt
½ litre (1 pint or 2 cups)
  yoghourt

Heat butter and fry the onions until they become transparent. Add green pepper and chilli, cook together for 3 to 4 minutes. Add curry powder, blend well, cover and simmer for 15 minutes. Put in prawns, season with salt. Add yoghourt, bring to the boil, stirring all the time. Simmer for 2 to 3 minutes and serve with plain boiled rice.

MACAO PRAWNS WITH PEPPERS AND CUCUMBER

4–6 Servings

500 gr (1 lb or 2 cups) shelled uncooked prawns
500 gr (1 lb or 3 cups) sweet peppers
2 tablespoons oil
salt
water
1 knob shredded green ginger
1 teaspoon sugar
2 teaspoons soya sauce
4 tablespoons sliced cucumber
1 teaspoon sherry
1 teaspoon cornflour

Split prawns lengthwise and remove intestinal cord. Cut peppers, discard core and seeds, and slice into half rings. Heat 1 tablespoon oil in a pan, add ½ teaspoon salt and toss peppers for 7–8 seconds. Add 1 tablespoon water, simmer for 3 minutes, remove from pan and keep hot.

Heat the rest of the oil, add ½ teaspoon salt and the ginger and sauté the prawns on a lively heat for half a minute. Add sugar, soya sauce, cucumber, sherry and 2 tablespoons water. Simmer for 3 minutes. Add peppers and their juice, mix, cook together for 1 minute.

Dilute cornflour with just enough water to make a thin paste, blend in. Serve with plain boiled rice or noodles.

PRAWNS OR SHRIMPS BORDEAUX STYLE

4 Servings

125 gr (4 oz or ½ cup) butter
1 chopped onion
1 chopped carrot
1 tablespoon chopped chives
375 gr (12 oz or 1½ cups) raw, peeled, de-veined prawns or shrimps
1 tablespoon brandy
2 tablespoons tomato purée
120 ml (4 oz or ½ cup) red wine
salt and pepper
1 tablespoon chopped parsley

Melt 90 gr (3 oz or 6 tablespoons) butter and fry onion and carrot. Add chives and prawns and sauté for 7 to 8 minutes, shaking the pan at intervals. Sprinkle with brandy, set alight for a moment.

Stir in tomato purée, gradually dilute with wine. Season to taste, cover and cook gently for 10 to 12 minutes. Remove the prawns with a perforated spoon, arrange on a heated serving dish and keep warm.

Boil down the sauce to reduce by half, amalgamate the remainder of the butter, adding it in tiny pieces and stirring constantly. Pour sauce over the prawns, sprinkle with parsley and serve.

JAPANESE PEPPERED PRAWNS

2–3 Servings

6 large shelled prawns
6 tablespoons mirin (or sweet white wine)

6 tablespoons soya sauce
freshly ground black pepper

Thread prawns on skewers. Boil mirin and soya sauce until the mixture becomes syrupy in texture. Grill the prawns, basting them with the mirin-soya liquid, season with pepper to taste and serve.

PACIFIC PRAWNS WITH LETTUCE

4 Servings

500 gr (1 lb or 2 cups) large raw prawns
salt
2–3 slices pounded ginger
2 teaspoons cornflour

1 crisp washed lettuce
1 tablespoon oil
1 crushed clove garlic
freshly ground pepper
124 ml (4 oz or ½ cup) water

Peel prawns (Dublin Bay or the large Pacific kind are best for this dish), leaving tail tips on. Split lengthwise and remove intestinal cord. Put prawns on a plate, sprinkle with a pinch of salt, ginger and cornflour. Shred lettuce coarsely.

Heat oil in a pan with garlic, add prawns and sauté briskly. As soon as the prawns change colour, add lettuce. Cook for 1 minute, season with pepper, add more salt if necessary, pour in water, bring to the boil, stir and serve.

PRAWNS RIVABELLA

6–8 Servings

1 kg (2 lb or 4 cups) fresh prawns
flour
125 ml (4 oz or ½ cup) olive oil

salt and pepper
2 sliced seeded green peppers
125 ml (4 oz or ½ cup) dry vermouth

Wash and shell prawns, dip in flour and fry briskly in sizzling hot oil for 5 minutes. Season and remove from pan. In the same oil, fry the peppers until soft. Add prawns, stir, pour in vermouth, bring up flame, cook for 2 minutes.

Serve with rice and brocoli or baby marrows.

CHINESE PRAWNS STUFFED WITH ALMONDS

4 Servings

500 gr (1 lb or 2 cups) uncooked
   large prawns
2 rashers lean bacon
60 gr (2 oz or 1/3 cup)
   blanched roasted almonds

salt
1 beaten egg
flour
oil for deep frying

Peel the prawns, leaving the tail tips on. Make 2 slits in each prawn without opening them out. Shred bacon and almonds. Put ½ to ¾ teaspoon of this mixture into each slit in the prawn. Press edge of slits gently together to seal. Season with salt to taste.

Dip in egg, dredge lightly with flour. Deep fry in smoking hot oil until golden. Drain on paper and serve at once.

SCAMPI, MODENA STYLE

4 Servings

24–36 scampi
30 gr (1 oz or 2 tablespoons)
   butter
1 chopped onion
1 shredded carrot
1 tablespoon chopped parsley

pinch chopped thyme
125 ml (4 oz or ½ cup) white
   wine
3 tablespoons white wine
   vinegar

Shell the scampi. Heat butter, add onion and carrot, cook gently to soften. Add parsley, thyme, wine and vinegar and simmer on very low heat for 15 minutes. Add scampi, stir to coat all with the sauce, cover, simmer gently for 15 minutes and serve scampi piping hot with the pan juices poured over.

SCAMPI, LOMBARDY STYLE

4 Servings

24–36 large scampi (or Dublin
   Bay prawns)
3 tablespoons white wine
   vinegar
½ bay leaf
1 clove crushed garlic

2–3 cloves
1 chopped shallot
1 tablespoon chopped parsley
1 teaspoon chopped fennel
salt and pepper

Wash and shell the scampi. Combine the rest of the ingredients in a large enough saucepan to take everything, bring to the boil, simmer for 3–4 minutes, put in scampi, stir, cover, simmer for 15 minutes shaking the pan at intervals. Serve at once.

BUTTERFLY SCAMPI

6–12 Servings

250 gr (1 lb) scampi (fresh or
    frozen)
1 egg
2 tablespoons flour

salt and pepper
1 teaspoon ground ginger
oil for deep frying
Chinese seafood sauce

If frozen scampi are used, thaw carefully, drain and dry on kitchen paper.

Mix egg and flour gradually, to make batter, season with salt and pepper to taste, add ginger. Impale 2 scampi on a cocktail stick to form a 'butterfly'. Dip in batter, deep fry in hot nut oil for 30 seconds. Drain and serve with Chinese seafood sauce.

MEXICAN SHRIMP TAMALES

In Mexico the ingredients would be packed into corn husks and steamed or baked in hot ashes. If you happen to come by some corn husks, that will be your chance of presenting tamales in the traditional way. Fill them with the ingredients in layers and cook as described. When done, just peel and eat. When no such natural containers are at hand, use an ovenproof dish.

6 Servings

½ litre (1 pint or 2 cups) water
salt
125 gr (4 oz or 2/3 cup) corn
    meal (maize) (or a tin of
    creamed sweet corn)
pepper
2–3 tablespoons butter
4 chopped bacon rashers

2 chopped onions
125 gr (4 oz or 1½ cups) sliced
    mushrooms
2 tablespoons tomato purée
250 gr (8 oz or 1 cup) diced ham
2 tablespoons tequila (or brandy)
1 litre (1 quart) peeled shrimps
butter

Bring water to the boil, add salt, pour in the corn meal little by little, stirring all the time to prevent the formation of lumps. Simmer for 20 to 25 minutes, stirring and adding salt and pepper to taste, until the corn meal acquires the consistency of good mashed potatoes.

Fry the bacon in 2 tablespoons butter, add onion, fry until it becomes transparent. Add mushrooms, stir, cook for 1 minute. Add tomato purée and ham, moisten with tequila and simmer gently for 10 minutes.

Butter an ovenproof dish and fill it with alternate layers of corn meal, the fried mixture and shrimps. Dot with tiny pieces of butter, cover and bake in the oven 205°C (400°F or Gas Mark 5) for 30 minutes.

SHRIMP LOLLIES

A shrimp 'lolly' is one of the treats traditionally served in Japan at Girls' Festival (3rd March). The amount given below is calculated for 4 servings, allowing 2 'lollies' per portion.

32 small peeled shrimps	3 tablespoons sugar
6 tablespoons mirin (or sweet sherry)	8 cocktail sticks (long bamboo ones, whenever possible)
8 tablespoons soya sauce	

Thread 4 shrimps on each cocktail stick. Mix the rest of the ingredients, dip the skewered shrimps in the mixture and grill on gentle heat. Dip twice more in the basting mixture during grilling.

Put two shrimp lollies on each small pastel-coloured or natural (straw) mat, and serve.

LOBSTERS

Lobsters, more often than not, are bought ready boiled, but there are occasions when one may have to do it at home. There are two schools of thought as to the best method. One is to put the lobster into a big pot and slowly pour warm water over it, then gradually bring to the boil. It is said that this method has an anaesthetising effect on the lobster and that it becomes unconscious without realising it is being cooked.

The other method, more popular on the Continent, is to plunge the lobster, head first into a pan of boiling salted water, which is supposed to kill it instantly.

We consulted the R.S.P.C.A. and they kindly sent us their instructions for the humane killing of lobsters. They advocate the second method as the best found so far, and offer the following advice :

1. Make sure that there is at least 4–5 litres ($3\frac{2}{3}$–4 quarts) of boiling water per lobster;
2. Keep the flame very hot under the pot;
3. See that the water into which the lobster is to be plunged is boiling very fast;
4. Ensure that the lobster is completely immersed. Hold it under the boiling water with tongs or wooden spoons for 2 minutes.

With these precautions the lobster should die with seconds. If these rules are not observed, unnecessary suffering will be caused, because the water will go off the boil if the temperature is allowed to fall by the immersion of the cold lobster in it.

BOILED LOBSTER

Allow 20 minutes' boiling time per 500 gr (1 lb) of lobster. It is important to judge the cooking time correctly, as over-boiling ruins the texture and insufficient boiling prevents the coral turning red.

4 Servings

12 litres (9 quarts) water
2 sliced carrots
1 sliced onion
salt and pepper
2½ dcl (½ pint or 1 cup) wine
  vinegar

2 sprigs thyme
½ bay leaf
3 sprigs parsley
1 kg (2 lb) lobster
olive oil
mayonnaise

Put carrots, onion, seasoning, vinegar, thyme, bay leaf and parsley into water, bring to the boil, skim, simmer for 1 hour and strain. Return liquid to deep pot, make sure the amount is not less than 11 litres (8 quarts), put in lobster, do *not* allow the liquid to go off the boil. Cook for 35–40 minutes, drain and allow to cool.

If the lobster is to be served cold in the shell, rub it with a little olive oil to enhance the colour and make it more vivid. Serve with mayonnaise.

LOBSTER THERMIDOR

4 Servings

2 small boiled lobsters
1 chopped shallot
125 ml (4 oz or ½ cup) white
  wine
pinch chopped chervil
pinch chopped tarragon
2½ dcl (½ pint or 1 cup) thick
  bechamel sauce

120 gr (4 oz or 1½ cups) sliced
  mushrooms
60 gr (2 oz or ¼ cup) butter
salt and pepper
1 teaspoon mixed mustard
pinch cayenne pepper
grated Parmesan cheese

Cut the lobsters in half lengthwise, pick out stomach and intestinal cord. Remove meat from shell and claws and slice. Keep the shells.

Simmer the shallot in wine with chervil and tarragon until soft and the wine reduced by half, mix with béchamel sauce and put the lobster meat into it to heat through.

Toss mushrooms in 1 tablespoon butter and add to sauce. Check seasoning, stir in mustard and heighten with cayenne pepper, mix and spoon the lobster mixture and the sauce into the shells. Sprinkle with a little grated cheese, brown under a hot grill and serve at once.

GINGER LOBSTER

2 Servings

1 tablespoon cornflour
water
125 gr (¼ lb or 1½ cups) sliced
  mushrooms
125 gr (¼ lb or 2/3 cup)
  shredded lettuce hearts

30 gr (1 oz or 2 tablespoons)
  oil
250 gr (½ lb or 1 cup) diced
  lobster meat
1 teaspoon minced fresh ginger
4 or 5 chopped spring onions

Mix cornflour with enough water to make a thin paste. Fry mushrooms and lettuce in half the oil for 3 minutes. Remove. Add rest of oil. Dip lobster into cornflour paste and fry for 3 minutes. Then add fried vegetables and cook together for 3 minutes.

Add ginger and spring onions, stir and serve.

LOBSTER NEWBURG

4 Servings

two 500 gr (1 lb) cooked
  lobsters
125 gr (4 oz or ½ cup) butter
salt and pepper
pinch paprika

125 ml (4 oz or ½ cup) sherry
2½ dcl (½ pint or 1 cup) single
  cream
3 fresh raw egg yolks
few drops Tabasco (optional)

Slice the lobster meat, pick out the coral and keep for later use. Heat half the butter, put in lobster and cook gently to brown lightly on all sides. Season with salt and pepper to taste. Sprinkle with paprika, cover and cook for 10 minutes. Sprinkle with sherry and cook down over strong heat to reduce the liquid.

Blend 3 tablespoons cream with the egg yolks. Reduce heat and add rest of cream to sauce. Stir, taste for seasoning, heighten with a few drops Tabasco. Cream remaining butter with lobster coral until smooth. Add yolks to sauce, then little by little whisk in the coral butter and serve.

In France a few slices of truffle are often added at the last moment.

LOBSTER IN COCONUT, BALI STYLE

4 Servings

4 fresh coconuts
½ litre (1 pint or 2 cups) water
2–3 tablespoons butter
1 chopped onion
1 pounded clove garlic
375 gr (12 oz or 1½ cups)
  shelled, sliced lobster meat

2 sliced sweet green peppers
125 gr (¼ lb or 1 cup) peeled,
  sliced tomatoes
salt and pepper
1 teaspoon kneaded butter
flour and water paste
4 dessertspoons rum

Ask the greengrocer to saw off the tops of the coconuts, but keep the lids. Extract the coconut flesh and soak in water for 2 to 3 hours, to soften and make them yield up their milk. Squeeze out two or three times to get as much thick milk as you can—you need about 2½ dcl (½ pint or 1 cup). Shred the remainder of the coconuts.

Heat the butter and lightly cook the onion and the garlic until soft. Add lobster and green pepper, cook stirring constantly for 5 minutes. Add tomatoes, seasoning, pour in coconut milk, cover and simmer for 20 minutes. Check seasoning, incorporate kneaded butter, stirring it in in small pieces.

Fill the coconut shells with the cooked lobster and its sauce to just over half way. Fill to the top with shredded coconut and carefully put the 'lids' on again, sealing them with a little flour and water paste. Put into a baking tin with water, to come about a quarter way up the height of the coconuts, and put in a slow oven 150°C (300°F or Gas Mark 2) for 1 to 1¼ hours. Spoon a little water over the sealed coconuts from time to time to preserve their appearance.

Remove from pan, dry off the bottoms on a cloth, put each coconut on a serving plate, take off 'lids', pour a dessertspoon of rum over each coconut, set alight and serve.

CHINESE LOBSTER WITH BEAN SPROUTS

2–3 Servings

1 tablespoon oil	1 teaspoon sugar
250 gr (8 oz or 1 cup) sliced	1 teaspoon cornflour
lobster meat	water
salt	15 gr (½ oz or 2 tablespoons)
750 gr (1½ lbs) bean sprouts	spring onions
stock (any available)	1 teaspoon sesame oil
pepper	

Heat oil in pan, put in the lobster, cook for 1 minute and season with salt to taste. Add bean sprouts, toss together for 2 seconds. Cover with stock and simmer for 1 minute. Add pepper, sugar and cornflour diluted with enough water to make a thin paste, and cook for 1 minute.

Cut the spring onions into 5 cm (2 in.) pieces and add to the pan. Sprinkle in sesame oil. Cook for 1 minute, and serve with boiled rice.

LOBSTER IN MARSALA

2 Servings

750 gr (1½ lb) lobster	salt and pepper
2 tablespoons oil	1 tablespoon chopped parsley
2 tablespoons butter	1 dcl (4 oz or ½ cup) marsala
2 crushed cloves garlic	

Wash the lobster and chop and split into 3–4 pieces, without removing shell; crack claws. Heat the oil and butter and cook the garlic in the mixture for 2 to 3 minutes to flavour, then discard. Put in lobster, seasoning and parsley. Simmer under a lid for 20 minutes. Add Marsala, cook for 3 minutes and serve at once.

CHINESE DEEP FRIED LOBSTER

2–3 Servings

500 gr (1 lb) lobster
2 tablespoons cornflour
1 egg

1 tablespoon water
oil for deep frying
salt and pepper

Remove lobster flesh from shell and cut the meat into small pieces. Mix cornflour, egg and water to make Chinese batter. Heat the oil. Dip lobster into batter and drop the pieces one by one into smoking hot oil. Fry until golden.

Drain, sprinkle with salt and freshly grated pepper and serve.

LOBSTER, CEYLON STYLE

Yellow Face Hotel recipe.

4 Servings

90–100 gr (3 oz or 6 tablespoons)
  butter
2 chopped onions
2 chopped cloves garlic
½ teaspoon ground turmeric
pinch of salt

2 fresh chopped chillis
4 slices pickled ginger
2½ dcl (½ pint or 1 cup)
  coconut cream
1 shelled, sliced lobster

Heat butter and lightly fry onions and garlic. Add turmeric, salt, chillis and ginger. Stir the spices well, dilute with coconut cream, cover and simmer the sauce on the lowest possible heat for 10 to 12 minutes.

Add lobster, immerse completely in the sauce, spooning it over the lobster slices and cook uncovered on a low heat until the lobster is tender. Serve with rice.

ITALIAN BAKED LOBSTER

2 Servings

1 kg (2 lb) lobsters
2 tablespoons white wine
2 tablespoons water
3 tablespoons breadcrumbs
1 tablespoon chopped parsley
2 tablespoons grated Parmesan
  cheese

1 teaspoon chopped basil
1 clove chopped garlic
small pinch wild marjoram
salt and pepper
4 tablespoons olive oil

Split the lobster lengthwise, put in a pan, shell side down and pour in wine and water. Mix breadcrumbs with parsley, cheese, basil, garlic and marjoram. Sprinkle this mixture over the lobster.

Season to taste, baste with oil and bake for 20 minutes in a moderate oven 190°C (375°F or Gas Mark 4).

CANTONESE LOBSTER WITH RICE NOODLES

2 Servings

180 gr (6 oz or 2 cups) thick rice noodles
hot water
1 tablespoon oil
250 gr (½ lb or 1 cup) diced lobster meat
90 gr (3 oz or 1 cup) bean sprouts
30 gr (1 oz or 4 tablespoons) sliced mushrooms
60 gr (2 oz or ¼ cup) sliced cucumber

60 gr (2 oz or ¼ cup) sliced water chestnuts
60 gr (2 oz or ¼ cup) sliced bamboo shoots
30 gr (1 oz or 2 tablespoons) sliced celery
30 gr (1 oz or 4 tablespoons) sliced onion
½ teaspoon salt
1 teaspoon sugar
1 dessertspoon soya sauce
stock (any available)

Put the noodles in a bowl, cover with hot water and leave to stand for 30 minutes. Heat oil in pan and sauté the lobster for 1 minute. Add all the vegetables and cook together for 1 minute. Add salt, sugar, soya sauce and enough stock to cover. Cook for 1 minute, add drained noodles, cook for 2 minutes and serve.

LOBSTER À L'ARMORICAINE

8 Servings

4 chopped onions
1 chopped clove garlic
2½ kg (5 lb) fresh lobsters
75 gr (2½ oz or 5 tablespoons) butter
6 tablespoons oil
3 tablespoons brandy

2 tablespoons chopped parsley
1½ tablespoons tomatoe puree
½ litre (½ bottle) warmed dry white wine
salt and pepper
cayenne pepper

Boil the onion and garlic in a little water for 10 minutes. Drain thoroughly and rub through a fine sieve, or put through a blender.

Cut lobsters with a cleaver into large pieces (starting with the head). Heat butter and oil in a large pan, put in lobsters shell side down to prevent the meat turning brown. When the shells are red, transfer to a very large casserole placed over a low heat. Sprinkle with half the brandy and touch with a lighted match.

Add onion purée, parsley and tomato purée to the pan in which the lobsters were fried, blend well and pour over the lobsters. Add wine. Season with salt, pepper and cayenne. Cover and cook over low heat for 15 minutes. Add the rest of the brandy and simmer for another 10 minutes. Check seasoning.

LOBSTER, MACAO STYLE

Eugenio da Beça's recipe.

4 Servings

2 small lobsters
125 gr (4 oz or 1⅓ cups) shredded coconut
2 chopped onions
1 crushed clove garlic
125 ml (4 oz or ½ cup) single cream
1 teaspoon chilli powder

salt
1½ teaspoons paprika
½ teaspoon cinnamon
¼ teaspoon nutmeg
1 teaspoon powdered coriander
125 gr (4 oz or ½ cup) butter
2 tablespoons lime (or lemon) juice

Remove lobster flesh from shell and claws. Put in a deep dish. Mix coconut, onions, garlic, cream, chilli powder, salt, paprika, cinnamon, nutmeg and coriander, simmer carefully in a double saucepan or a bain-marie for 30 minutes. Allow to cool, spread over the lobster and leave in a refrigerator for 2 to 3 hours.

Take lobster out of its dressing, brush with melted butter, grill until done, basting frequently with butter, and the dressing it was steeped in. When done, arrange on a serving dish and keep hot.

Re-heat the rest of the coconut and cream mixture gently in a bain-marie, whisk melted butter into it little by little, heighten with lime juice and serve.

LOBSTER AND CHICKEN, COSTA BRAVA STYLE

This is a succulent dish, a speciality of Catalonia. The chicken should be a young roaster.

6 Servings

1 chicken
5 tablespoons olive oil
3–4 cloves garlic
1 tablespoon chopped parsley
250 gr (1 lb or 1 cup) peeled tomatoes

60 gr (2 oz or ½ cup) roasted almonds
1½ kg (3 lb) lobster
seasoning
small glass sherry

Joint the chicken. Heat oil and fry garlic with parsley. Add tomatoes and cook for 5 minutes. Add almonds, cook together for 1 minute, pass the mixture through a blender and put back in a pan large enough to take all ingredients.

Cut up lobster. Cook lobster and chicken in the prepared sauce, season, sprinkle in sherry, cover, simmer for 30 minutes and serve.

DEEP FRIED MOULDED CRAB CLAWS

This is a great South China speciality, called Hai Kim. The cooked crab claws have to be cracked with great care and skill so as to leave the nipper ends undamaged. The nipper both looks interesting and is useful for holding the claw as you eat it. The best oil to use for all Chinese frying is peanut oil. The Chinese never bother with special deep fryers. They use the same *wok* for all their cooking. Because of its shape and sloping sides, like an inverted dome, it uses very little oil.

6 Servings

6 cooked crab claws
4–5 cooked Pacific prawns
pinch salt and pepper
small pinch Ve-Tsin

beaten egg white
oil for deep frying
2 tablespoons
cornflour

Crack the shell and pick it off carefully, preserving the nipper ends and the claw meat attached to it in one piece. Peel prawns and remove digestive tract—the black intestinal line. Chop the prawns, season to taste with salt, pepper and Ve-Tsin. Mix with enough beaten egg white to bind the mixture.

Divide into 6 portions and cover the claw meat with the prawn mixture, sculpting it into its original but plumper shape and leave the nipper end free. Heat oil. Dip moulded crab claws lightly in cornflour, deep fry until uniformly golden. Drain and serve at once.

CATALAN CRAB IN BRANDY WITH TOMATOES

4 Servings

2 large cooked crabs
1 chopped onion
3 tablespoons oil
1 tablespoon flour
500 gr (1 lb or 3 cups) peeled,
    sliced tomatoes
salt and pepper

3 tablespoons brandy
60 gr (2 oz or $\frac{1}{2}$ cup) sifted
    breadcrumbs
1 tablespoon chopped parsley
30 gr (1 oz or 2 tablespoons)
    butter

Pick out the crab meat from the shells and claws and flake it. Keep the main shells. Heat oil and fry onion lightly. Add flour and blend in, add crab meat, whatever liquid comes from the crab, tomatoes, salt, pepper and brandy. Stir and simmer gently for ten minutes with a lid on.

Wash the crab shells, dry, fill with cooked crab and sauce. Sprinkle with breadcrumbs and parsley, dot with small pieces of butter, brown the tops under a grill and serve.

SOFT SHELL CRAB, HONG KONG STYLE

4 Servings

2 large, soft shell crabs
4 tablespoons oil
1 clove crushed garlic
125 gr (4 oz or ½ cup) fresh
   minced pork
1 teaspoon salt
2 tablespoons soya sauce
1 teaspoon sugar

½ teaspoon pepper
2½ dcl (½ pint or 1 cup) clear
   chicken stock
1 teaspoon cornflour
3 tablespoons cold water
1 lightly beaten egg
2–3 chopped spring onions

Cut the crabs into 6 to 8 pieces. Heat oil with the garlic, add pork and salt and brown lightly. Pour in soya sauce, stir, add sugar, pepper and boiling stock (or boiling water with a bouillon cube). Add crab, mix well, cover, simmer for 7 to 8 minutes.

Mix cornflour with cold water, stir into the pan until the sauce is smooth. Turn off heat, stir egg into mixture, sprinkle with spring onions and serve at once.

DEVILLED CRAB

4 Servings

2 medium-sized crabs
100 gr (3 oz or 1 cup) freshly
   grated soft breadcrumbs
salt
pinch cayenne pepper

1 teaspoon mixed mustard
few drops Worcestershire sauce
2 tablespoons butter
125 ml (4 oz or ½ cup) cream
   or coconut milk

Take crab meat out of shell and claws. Wash and dry the shell carefully. Chop crab flesh, add breadcrumbs, reserving two tablespoons. Season with salt and cayenne pepper to taste, add mustard, Worcestershire sauce and one tablespoon softened butter, blend in cream or coconut milk.

Put the mixture into the crab shells, sprinkle with the remaining breadcrumbs, scatter butter on top in tiny pieces, and brown in a hot oven 205°C (400°F or Gas Mark 5) for 12 to 15 minutes.

DRESSED CRAB MAYONNAISE

Arrange dressed crab on a bed of lettuce or chicory. Garnish with sliced cucumbers and hard-boiled eggs or tomatoes. Serve with watercress mayonnaise.

CHINESE CRAB AND BACON ROLLS

4 Servings

240 gr (8 oz or 1½ cups)
   crabmeat
2 egg yolks
240 gr (8 oz) bacon

2 egg whites
1 teaspoon soya sauce
oil for deep frying

163

Drain and flake crabmeat and mix with egg yolks. Cut bacon into 5 cm (2 in.) lengths. Beat egg whites with soya sauce. Wrap bacon round a portion of crabmeat, dip into egg white and soya sauce 'batter' and deep fry in hot oil for 30 seconds. Drain on absorbent paper and serve at once.

CRAYFISH TAILS IN DILL SAUCE, HUNGARIAN STYLE

4 Servings

1 kg (2 lb) crayfish tails	2 tablespoons butter
water	2 tablespoons flour
1 sliced onion	250 ml ($\frac{1}{2}$ pint or 1 cup) sour
4 slices lemon	cream
1 tablespoon salt	125 ml (4 oz or $\frac{1}{2}$ cup)
12 peppercorns	Madeira
1 teaspoon dill seed	3 tablespoons chopped fresh
3 sprigs fresh dill	dill
2 sprigs parsley	1 teaspoon paprika

Put the crayfish tails in a pan with enough water to cover. Add onion, lemon, salt, peppercorns, dill seed, fresh dill and parsley sprigs, bring to the boil, cover and simmer for 12 minutes. Remove crayfish tails, shell and dice. Strain the liquid in which the crayfish were cooked and keep 2$\frac{1}{2}$ dcl ($\frac{1}{2}$ pint or 1 cup) for sauce.

To make the sauce: melt butter, add flour and make a light roux. Dilute with the reserved liquid, stirring carefully and cooking gently until the mixture is smooth. Add sour cream, Madeira and chopped dill and blend well. Put in crayfish, heat through, sprinkle with paprika and serve at once.

Molluscs

OYSTERS ROCKEFELLER

6 Servings

12 oysters
1 tablespoon chopped parsley
1 tablespoon chopped raw
  spinach
½ teaspoon chopped tarragon
½ teaspoon chopped chervil

½ teaspoon chopped basil
1 teaspoon chopped chives
salt and pepper
breadcrumbs
butter

Open the oysters carefully to preserve as much of the liquor as possible. Put on the half shell on a baking sheet, sprinkle thickly with spinach and the chopped herbs, season to taste. Cover the top with breadcrumbs, dot with tiny pieces of butter and put in a hot oven 235°C (450°F or Gas Mark 7) for 5 minutes. Serve at once.

OYSTERS IN ASPIC

4–6 Servings

½ litre (1 pint or 2 cups) aspic
  jelly
juice of ½ lemon
2 tablespoons sherry

parsley
24 oysters
sliced lemon

Prepare aspic jelly as described, add to it lemon juice, sherry and a tablespoon of parsley and chill until half set. Open the oysters, de-beard, pour off their liquid into the aspic, and put the oysters into it for a while.

Wash and dry the deep shells, line with jelly, put an oyster in the middle and spoon over enough jelly to cover it properly. Decorate with thin slices of lemon cut into small sections and tiny pieces of parsley. Chill and keep cold until ready to serve.

GRILLED OYSTERS, VENETIAN STYLE

4 Servings

2 dozen oysters
1 tablespoon chopped parsley
1 shredded stalk celery
½ clove chopped garlic
pinch chopped fresh thyme

freshly ground black pepper
1 tablespoon toasted
  breadcrumbs
1 tablespoon olive oil
1 lemon

Open the oysters, loosen on the half shell. Combine all the other ingredients except oil and lemon, dress the oysters with the mixture. Sprinkle with olive oil and grill for 4 to 5 minutes. Serve garnished with lemon wedges.

OYSTERS IN PARMA HAM

Allow half a dozen oysters per portion, remove from shell, season with salt and a little cayenne pepper, wrap each oyster in a rasher-sized slice of Parma ham and fry in butter.

OYSTERS À LA RUSSE

Allow half a dozen oysters per portion.

Serve the oysters immediately after opening, in their own liquor, in the deep shell. Arrange in individual plates, with 'hinges' towards the centre. Put a small teaspoon of fresh caviar at the end of each shell. Garnish with wedges of lemon.

MUSSELS

Test each mussel to make sure it is alive. They should shut tightly and visibly if given a sharp tap. Discard all open ones. Scrub well and rinse in several waters.

Cook in white wine with sliced onions, parsley, thyme and bay leaf. Drain, remove shells and use the mussels as garnish. The liquor in which they are cooked should be strained, cooked down to reduce and added to the sauce. The only part of a mussel which needs to be removed is the 'beard', which is its breathing apparatus.

MOULES MARINIÈRES

4 Servings

2 litres (2 quarts) mussels
60 gr (2 oz or 4 tablespoons)
  butter
2 tablespoons chopped shallot
2 sprigs parsley

1 sprig thyme
¼ bay leaf
2½ dcl (½ pint or 1 cup) dry
  white wine
chopped parsley

Scrape and wash the mussels. Line a buttered saucepan with shallot, add parsley, thyme and bay leaf. Put in mussels, add 2 tablespoons butter in tiny pieces, moisten with wine, cover and cook over a very high flame. As soon as the mussels are fully open, lift them out, remove beards, return mussels to half shell, discarding the empty shell.

Arrange mussels in soup plates or serving dishes, and keep hot. Take parsley, thyme and bay leaf out of the saucepan, add rest of butter, blend in well. Boil rapidly to reduce pan juices by half, pour over the mussels, sprinkle with chopped parsley and serve.

An alternative method is to use onion instead of shallot and to add 3–4 tablespoons velouté sauce, based on fish stock, and a squeeze of lemon juice to the liquor in the pan.

MUSSELS À LA TARTARE

Prepare Moules Marinieres as above. Shell the mussels, arrange in an hors d'oeuvre dish, cover with Tartare sauce, surround with half slices of lemon cut with a fluted knife.

MUSSEL CHARLOTTE

4 Servings

½ litre (1 pint) plump mussels
1 tablespoon lemon juice
2½ dcl (½ pint or 1 cup) white wine
2 tablespoons butter
3 tablespoons flour
125 ml (4 oz or ½ cup) cream

pinch salt and pepper
¼ teaspoon nutmeg
180 gr (6 oz or ¾ cup) chopped, cooked prawns
sifted breadcrumbs
extra butter

Open the mussels and remove from shells as described above. Sprinkle them with lemon juice and poach in wine for 5 minutes.

In a saucepan melt butter, stir in flour, cook the roux without allowing it to colour, dilute gradually with the liquor in which the mussels were poached. Simmer, stirring all the time, until the sauce thickens. Add cream, season to taste with salt, pepper and nutmeg. Reserve 8 tablespoons of the sauce and mix the rest with the prawns. Butter a charlotte dish with breadcrumbs, fill with prawn mixture, surround with mussels and arrange some mussels on top.

Spoon over the reserved sauce, sprinkle lightly with breadcrumbs, scatter small pieces of butter on top, brown under the grill, or in the oven, and serve.

MUSSELS AU GRATIN

6–8 Servings

1½ litres (3 pints or 1½ quarts)
  mussels
3 tablespoons grated
  breadcrumbs

2 cloves chopped garlic
1 tablespoon chopped parsley
pinch salt
2 tablespoons olive oil

Scrape and clean the mussels as described, above, put in a wide pan, lay a folded damp cloth over them. Heat quickly, keep on a fairly high heat until the shells open (about 5 minutes), shaking the pan from time to time. Do not overcook as this makes the mussels tough. Remove shells and put the mussels in a gratin dish. Mix breadcrumbs with garlic and parsley and season with salt. Cover the mussels with this mixture, sprinkle with olive oil and brown under a hot grill or in the oven.

MUSSELS WITH PINE NUT SAUCE

4 Servings

2 dozen mussels
120 gr (4 oz or 1 cup) flour
salt
1 beaten egg
1 tablespoon olive oil
1 tablespoon lemon juice
120 ml (4 oz or ½ cup) milk

2 tablespoons peeled pine
  kernels
2 tablespoons washed currants
60 ml (2 oz or ¼ cup) wine
  vinegar
60 ml (2 oz or ¼ cup) water
1 tablespoon chopped parsley
hot fat for deep frying

Steam the mussels in their own juice to open, as described in the recipe for Mussels au Gratin above. Remove from shells, drain on a cloth and lightly dip in flour.

Put flour in a bowl, season with a small pinch of salt, make a well in the middle, add egg, olive oil and lemon juice. Gradually dilute with milk and beat the batter until smooth. Put the pine kernels, currants, vinegar, water and parsley into a small saucepan, season with salt and pepper to taste, bring to the boil, then simmer gently for 5 to 6 minutes and keep hot.

Dip the mussels in batter, allow surplus to drip off, deep fry until they acquire a delicate golden colour. Drain on kitchen paper, arrange on a heated serving dish, pour the sauce over them and serve.

MUSSELS À LA RAVIGOTE

Cook and drain large mussels. Put them in a dish. Sprinkle with vinaigrette sauce to which hard-boiled eggs, parsley, chervil, tarragon and chopped gherkins have been added.

MUSSELS IN ANCHOVY SAUCE

3 Servings

2 dozen de-bearded mussels
1 clove garlic
3 tablespoons olive oil
4 chopped anchovy fillets
125 ml (4 oz or ½ cup) dry
   white wine

125 ml (4 oz or ½ cup) wine
   vinegar
2 tablespoons chopped parsley
pinch black pepper

Drain the mussels. Fry garlic in oil in a pan large enough to take all the ingredients. Remove garlic before it gets a chance to brown. Add mussels and anchovies, simmer covered for 6–7 minutes. Add wine and vinegar and cook uncovered for 5 minutes to reduce liquid by half. Add parsley and pepper, allow to cool, decant into a glass dish, cover, chill for 24 hours and serve.

MUSSELS AU CITRON

4 Servings

2 dozen mussels
white wine court-bouillon
2 tablespoons olive oil
2 teaspoons lemon juice

1 teaspoon chopped dill
small pinch sugar
salt and pepper

Scrub mussels thoroughly and scrape off the beards. Put the mussels in a pan with court-bouillon and steam them covered for 8–10 minutes or until they open. Discard any that do not open. Remove the mussels from the shells, cool them and chill.

Reduce the liquor to 2½ dcl (½ pint or 1 cup), strain it and combine it with olive oil, lemon juice, dill, sugar, and salt and pepper to taste. Pour the sauce over the mussels and chill thoroughly.

SCALLOPS MORNAY

Scallops are usually sold opened and the fishmonger should be asked for the deep shells—these are useful not only for scallops but many other savoury dishes. To open scallops at home, put them rounded side down over a low heat. As soon as top shell shows signs of rising, take it off with a knife, remove scallops from shells, trim away beard and the black part. The flesh and the little coral tongue must be washed, drained and dried, then poached in court-bouillon made with white wine or cider, flavoured with onion, thyme and bay leaf and seasoned to taste.

Allow 1½–2 scallops per portion and poach them. Line the bottom of a well scrubbed scallop shell with Mornay sauce, arrange on this scallops sliced in rounds and the whole coral. Coat with mornay sauce, sprinkle with grated cheese and melted butter and brown in the oven or under a grill. If you are clever with a forcing bag, use a fluted nozzle and pipe a border of Duchesse potatoes (well mashed and seasoned, with extra butter added, spiced with a small pinch of nutmeg and bound with raw egg yolk) round the edge of the scallop shell. If the potato mixture is too thick, thin down with a little cream or milk and be sure it is hot before putting into the forcing bag.

SCALLOPS AND BACON BROCHETTES

4 Servings

4 scallops
salt and pepper
juice of ½ lemon

8 bacon rashers, without rind
chopped parsley

Cut each scallop in two round slices. Season, sprinkle with lemon juice. Wrap in rashers, put on skewers and grill. Sprinkle with chopped parsley and serve.

SCALLOPS À LA PARISIENNE

4 Servings

4 plump poached scallops (see
  Scallops Mornay)
180 ml (6 oz or ¾ cup)
  velouté sauce
60 gr (2 oz or ¾ cup) chopped
  mushrooms

1–2 chopped shallots
butter
2 tablespoons breadcrumbs
1 tablespoon chopped parsley
1½ tablespoons browned
  breadcrumbs

Make velouté sauce, incorporating in it the liquid in which the scallops were poached. Fry the mushrooms and shallots in butter, add breadcrumbs and parsley and enough velouté to bind. Spread some of this mixture on the bottom of the scallop shells, arrange scallops on top in slices, coat with sauce, sprinkle with browned breadcrumbs and a little melted butter, put in the oven to brown the top and serve.

PENANG CURRIED SCALLOPS

4 Servings

1 fresh coconut
½ litre (1 pint or 2 cups) warm
  water
8 scallops
45–60 gr (1½–2 oz or 3–4
  tablespoons) butter

2 medium-sized chopped onions
1 clove pounded garlic
1 finely sliced sweet pepper
salt
1 tablespoon curry powder
pinch allspice

Soak the coconut flesh in water and extract 125 ml (4 oz or ½ cup) coconut milk as described in the recipe for Lobster in Coconut (p. 157).

Wash, dry and slice the scallops into rounds. Heat butter, fry onions and garlic until they soften. Add pepper, cook for a few minutes, stirring all the time. Season with salt, blend in curry powder and sprinkle in allspice. Cover and simmer for 10 minutes.

Add scallops, stir, cook for 2 minutes, reduce heat, pour in coconut milk, simmer for 5 minutes and serve with rice.

SCALLOPS WITH PINEAPPLE IN SWEET AND SOUR SAUCE

4 Servings

1 dozen scallops	1 dessertspoon peanut oil
salt	2 tablespoons water
2 tablespoons sugar	2 tablespoons vinegar
2 teaspoons soya sauce	250 grs (½ lb) shredded fresh
½ litre (1 pint or 2 cups) oil	pineapple (or small tin of
for deep frying	pineapple cubes)
3 tablespoons plain flour	2 teaspoons cornflour
2 beaten eggs	

Soak the scallops in cold water for one hour to swell them. Drain, wipe and put in a shallow dish. Sprinkle with one teaspoon salt, one teaspoon sugar and the soya sauce and leave to macerate.

Heat the oil. While it is heating, roll the scallops lightly in flour, then dip in egg and drop them one by one into the boiling oil. Deep fry until golden and drain on kitchen paper. While the scallops are frying make the sweet and sour sauce as follows: heat the peanut oil, add water, vinegar, the rest of the sugar and one teaspoon salt. Bring to the boil, add pineapple with its juice and cornflour diluted with enough cold water to make a thin paste. Remove from heat, add scallops, quickly immerse them in the sauce to impregnate thoroughly and serve without further reheating.

SCALLOPS WITH BROCCOLI, CANTON STYLE

4 Servings

250 gr (½ lb) scallops	1 teaspoon finely minced green
250 gr (½ lb) broccoli	ginger
1 teaspoon cornflour	1 clove crushed garlic
125 ml (4 oz or ½ cup) water	½ teaspoon salt
2 teaspoons soya sauce	pinch finely ground pepper
1 tablespoon oil	1 dessertspoon brandy

Soak the scallops in cold water for half an hour, drain and wipe. If large, cut into convenient bite-size pieces. Cut broccoli into small chunks. Mix cornflour with water, add soya sauce and blend well. Heat oil in pan with ginger and garlic and fry the scallops for four minutes. Season with salt and pepper. Add broccoli and cook for three minutes. Pour in cornflour and soya mixture and bring to the boil. Light brandy in a large spoon and immediately sprinkle it into the pan. Stir and serve at once.

The same recipe for scallops is equally successful with courgettes, asparagus tips or brussel sprouts.

ORMERS

Ormers belong to a genus of univalve molluscs. About 60 species are known in the tropical waters and all are edible. The shells, which provide mother-of-pearls, are ear-shaped. The English name 'ormer' is a corruption of the French *oreille de mer,* or sea-ear.

They are better known as abalone and are very popular in Chinese cookery. The Chinese prefer the canned variety. This needs no cooking : you just drain it, slice and add to any dish—soups, salads, casseroles, etc. Abalone blends extremely well with all meat, poultry, vegetable and fish dishes. In the Pacific Islands fresh abalone is eaten raw, after pickling in lime juice, in the same way as scallops (see page 29).

In California and Japan abalone shells reach 10 in. in length. The mollusc is much appreciated and the shells are made into everything, from ash trays to buttons. Ormers are found in Europe. They are indigenous to the Channel Islands, but occur nowhere else in British waters.

ORMER CASSEROLE, JERSEY STYLE

Jacqueline Poux's recipe.

6 Servings

3 ormers	3 slices green bacon
seasoned flour	1–2 cloves crushed garlic
100 gr (3 oz or 6 tablespoons)	salt and pepper
butter	water

Remove ormers from shells, scrub, discard heads and clean the white 'foot' thoroughly. Beat with a rolling pin or a mallet, to ensure tenderness. Roll ormers in seasoned flour.

Heat butter and fry ormers until golden all over. Transfer to a casserole with all the pan juices. Add bacon slices and garlic, season to taste with salt and pepper and pour in enough water barely to cover the ormers. Cover and cook in the oven, pre-heated to 150°C (300°F or Gas Mark 2) for 4 hours.

SPANISH FRIED CLAMS

2 dozen clams	1 tablespoon lemon juice
4 tablespoons olive oil	120 ml (4 oz or ½ cup) water
2 cloves pounded garlic	salt
1 tablespoon chopped parsley	pepper

Wash the clams with care. Heat oil in a pan and put in clams. As soon as they open, add garlic, parsley and lemon juice. Fry lightly. Add water, season to taste, simmer for 15 minutes and serve.

RHODE ISLAND CLAM CAKES
4 Servings

4 eggs	500 gr (1 lb or 4 cups) flour
2 teaspoons salt	1½ tablespoons baking powder
¼ teaspoon pepper	½ litre (1 pint or 2 cups) milk
½ kg (1 lb) clams	fat for deep frying

Beat the eggs, season with salt and pepper. Put in clams, add flour and baking powder and dilute with milk. Heat the fat. Stir the batter lightly and deep fry in spoonfuls, scooping up one clam for each 'cake'. Drain on kitchen paper. Serve with aioli, bearnaise or Chinese seafood sauce.

WINKLES

Scrub and rinse the winkles well. Cook in court-bouillon or salted water for 15 minutes. Drain. Eat with a pin.

STUFFED SQUID À LA PROVENÇALE

This recipe is nearly a century old, from Reboul's collection, published in La Cuisinière provencale, 1895.

'Take 4 squid, remove the ink-bags and the cranial cartilage. Cut off the tentacles and wash the squids. Put the body bags flat on a cloth. Chop an onion finely, fry in a few tablespoons oil, add finely chopped tentacles, 2 to 3 finely chopped tomatoes, season and fry together. Soak a piece of French bread the size of a fist in milk, squeeze it out and add to the pan, together with 3 cloves of garlic, chopped with parsley. Blend well, moisten with 2 tablespoons hot water, add 3 yolks of egg and remove from heat. You should now have a stuffing of thick manageable consistency and agreeable flavour. Fill the squid up to three-quarters, sew them up to enclose the stuffing and put them, one by one into a sauté pan with some oil.

'Separately fry a finely chopped onion in oil. Add a bay leaf, crushed clove of garlic, and blend in a tablespoon of flour. Moisten with a glass of white wine and an equal amount of hot water. Season with salt and pepper and simmer for a quarter of an hour. Strain this sauce over the squid, sprinkle with breadcrumbs and oil and cook in a slow oven until the top acquires a golden crust. Serve at once. The squid can also be stuffed with chopped tentacles and spinach.'

SQUID, SPANISH STYLE

4 Servings

2 dozen small squid
3–4 tablespoons olive oil
2 chopped onions
1 clove chopped garlic
125 gr (4 oz or 1 cup) peeled, chopped tomatoes
½ tablespoon chopped parsley
1 tablespoon sherry

1–2 tablespoons water
60 gr (2 oz or ½ cup) grated breadcrumbs
salt and pepper
8 small slices bread
60 gr (1 oz or 2 tablespoons) butter

Wash the squid, carefully remove ink-bags and collect liquid in a small bowl. Heat the oil and lightly fry onion, garlic, tomatoes and parsley. Add squid, sherry and enough water to cover, bring to the boil, then simmer until tender. Add breadcrumbs to the ink in the bowl, season with salt and freshly ground pepper. Blend with 2 to 3 tablespoons cooking liquid, pour the ink mixture into the pan, stir, simmer for 2 minutes and serve. Cut the bread into heart-shaped or triangular pieces, fry in butter until golden and serve these croûtons with the squids.

SQUID, ITALIAN STYLE

6 Servings

1 kg (2 lb) squid
4 tablespoons olive oil
2 cloves crushed garlic
salt and pepper
pinch oregano (wild marjoram)

125 ml (4 oz or ½ cup) dry vermouth
500 gr (1 lb) ripe, small, peeled tomatoes
½ tablespoon chopped parsley
bread for croûtons

Clean the squid thoroughly, cut into pieces, rinse, drain and dry on a cloth. Heat oil in a deep sauté pan and cook the garlic for a few minutes to flavour the oil. Discard the garlic and fry the squids in the same oil for 7 to 8 minutes. Season with salt and freshly ground pepper and oregano, add vermouth, simmer for 10 minutes. Add tomatoes and parsley, cover, simmer for a further 15 minutes. Serve with small triangular croûtons fried in butter or oil.

CATALAN STUFFED SQUID

4 Servings

750 gr (1½ lb) squid
125 gr (4 oz or ½ cup) minced pork
2 cloves finely chopped garlic
1 tablespoon chopped parsley
1 egg
salt and pepper
3 tablespoons olive oil

1 chopped onion
125 gr (4 oz or 1 cup) peeled chopped tomatoes
250 gr (8 oz or 1¼ cups) thinly sliced carrots
125 ml (4 oz or ½ cup) water
8–12 mussels au gratin

Clean the squid, keeping the ink bags whole. Mince the head, tentacles and fins, add pork, garlic and parsley. Mix well, beat in egg, season with salt and pepper. Stuff the bags with this mixture and secure the opening with a couple of stitches.

Heat oil, fry the squid lightly, add onion and cook until it becomes transparent. Add tomatoes, carrots and water. Taste for seasoning, cover and simmer gently, until tender, shaking the pan from time to time. Transfer to a serving dish, remove stitches, garnish with mussels and serve.

OCTOPUS SPANISH STYLE, WITH SAFFRON SAUCE

4 Servings

750 gr (1½ lb) octopus
4 tablespoons olive oil
2 medium-sized, sliced onions
½ bay leaf
500 gr (1 lb or 2½ cups) sliced potatoes

salt and pepper
2 tablespoons sherry
1 clove garlic
2 sprigs parsley
pinch saffron

Choose small-size octopus. Wash and cut into pieces. Heat oil and fry the onions. Add octopus and bay leaf, cover and cook gently until the octopus begins to get soft. Add potatoes, seasoning and sherry, cover and simmer until the potatoes are done. Pound garlic in a mortar with parsley and saffron, or pass through a blender. Blend into a mooth paste with a little olive oil, add to the pan, stir and serve.

CALAMARETTI ALLA ROMANA

Cut off the head and tentacles, remove fins, taking great care not to break the bag. (In many countries—from Spain to Japan—the trimmed-off pieces are used for rice and other dishes.) Cut the bag into 1¼ cm (half-inch) rings, put in a bowl, sprinkle with olive oil and lemon juice and leave to stand for 45–50 minutes. Do not season with salt until ready to fry, to prevent toughness.

Just before frying salt the calamares, dip the rings in flour and beaten egg and fry until golden in smoking hot oil. Drain on kitchen paper to remove surplus oil, garnish with slices of lemon and serve at once.

CALAMARES EN SU TINTA A LA BILBAINA OR BILBAO SQUID IN THEIR INK

4 Servings

500 gr (1 lb) small squid
6 tablespoons olive oil
1 crushed clove garlic
2 chopped onions
salt and pepper

125 ml (1 gill or ½ cup) boiling water
1 tablespoon brandy
croûtons

Wash the squid, remove heads, slit open the bodies and clean inside, taking care to preserve the ink bags intact. Pour this ink into a cup and reserve. Chop squid into pieces. Heat oil, fry garlic, onion and squid, stirring, until the onion becomes soft. Season to taste.

Dilute ink with boiling water, stir into the pan. Add brandy, cover and simmer until the squid are tender. Serve with bread croûtons fried in butter or oil.

CALAMARETTI O SEPPIE ALLA VENEZIANA OR BABY INKFISH OR CUTTLEFISH, VENETIAN STYLE

4 Servings

1 kg (2 lb) tiny inkfish or
cuttlefish
6 tablespoons olive oil
2 crushed cloves garlic

125 ml (1 gill or ½ cup) dry
white wine
salt and pepper

Wash the inkfish or cuttlefish and drain. Heat oil and fry garlic until it browns lightly. Remove and discard garlic and put in fish. Cook uncovered over moderate heat, stirring from time to time. When most of the moisture evaporates, add wine, season to taste and continue to simmer for 10 minutes.

Serve with rice.

Frogs and Snails

SNAILS

Snails have been highly prized as food by the Romans. In France, the vine snail (*Helix pomatia*) and in the south of France the *petits-gris* (*Helix aspersa*) are the most popular varieties.

Unless you get your snails supplied ready for cooking, you have to perform a cleansing operation. As a preliminary to cooking clean the snails thoroughly by scouring and scrubbing them under running water, remove chalky deposits sealing them (only snails with shells sealed with such deposit are fit to eat). Put them in a large pot, cover with cold water and add salt. Rub some salt inside the rim of the pot, to prevent the snails coming out of the water, and leave for 12 hours. Rinse thoroughly, in many changes of water to remove every trace of slime; keep on rinsing until there is no sign of scum. Inspect each snail carefully—any snail which fails to pop its head out of the shell should be discarded. Put snails in a pan with lots of water, boil for 10 minutes, drain, rinse in a collander with cold water. They are now ready to be made into any of the dishes which follow.

Cook and serve the snails in an *escargotière*. *Escargotières*—special dishes for cooking and serving snails, as well as individual snail pots and snail forks and pincers, are available in shops specialising in catering equipment.

SNAILS IN CHABLIS

4–6 Servings

4 dozen snails	2 sprigs fennel
120 gr (½ lb or ½ cup) coarse salt	1 bay leaf
¾ litre (1½ pints or 3 cups) Chablis	1 small onion, studded with 2 cloves
2 sprigs thyme	3 tablespoons brandy
	escargot butter

Put the snails, treated as described above into a saucepan with

177

wine, thyme, fennel, bay leaf, clove-studded onion and brandy. Simmer for 3 hours. Allow to cool in the liquor. When cold, drain, take snails out of their shells, cut off tip of head and cloaca, the small black tip at the end of tail. Boil the empty shells in clear water for 15 minutes, rinse well and dry.

Make escargot butter (and this should be made fresh shortly before it is needed, for best results).

Put the snails back into their shells, packing them in with as much escargot butter as the shell will hold, pressing it in and spreading the butter to the edges. Arrange on an *escargotière* and, unless you are ready to serve within minutes, place in a refrigerator.

Pre-heat the oven to 220°C (425°F or Gas Mark 6). Cover the snails with buttered paper or foil and bake for 6 or 7 minutes, until the butter melts and the shells are very hot. Serve at once.

ESCARGOTS À LA CRÈME (SNAILS IN CREAM)

2–4 Servings

250 gr (8 oz) tin of escargots
60 gr (2 oz or ¼ cup) butter
1 finely chopped onion
2 crushed cloves of garlic
1 tablespoon chopped parsley
1 tablespoon chopped chives
salt and cayenne pepper
125 ml (4 oz or ½ cup) double cream

Drain, rinse and dry snails. In the butter fry onion, garlic, parsley and chives until onion goes transparent. Add salt and cayenne pepper to taste. Add snails to onion mixture and stir over a low heat for 5–10 minutes. Add cream and heat, stirring all the time for a further 2 minutes without allowing the sauce to boil after the cream is added. Serve on plain boiled rice.

SNAILS À LA BOURGUIGNONNE

Prepare the snails for cooking as described (p. 177). Drain, rinse, top and tail them and put in a saucepan. Moisten with equal parts of clear stock and white wine—there must be enough liquid to cover whatever amount of snails you decide to cook. (The number of snails you allow per portion depends on your guests' appetite and liking for snails and on whether you are serving snails as a starter, or as a course in its own right.) Add chopped carrot, onion, 2–3 chopped shallots, a bouquet garni (a little faggot consisting of parsley, thyme and bay leaf), season to taste and simmer gently for 3–3½ hours. Leave to cool in the liquor.

Proceed as described and replace snails in shells with escargot butter. First put a piece of butter into each shell, then the snail, then seal it with more butter. Put the filled shells into a lightly moistened *escargotière,* sprinkle the butter-sealed shells with freshly grated breadcrumbs, put in the oven to heat through the shells and soften the butter and serve at once.

SNAILS — SAN GIOVANNI

Snails cooked this way are traditionally served by the Romans to celebrate the Feast of San Giovanni (21st June), washed down with plenty of good dry white wine.

4–6 Servings

1 kg (2 lb) purged snails
1½ dcl (¼ pint or ½ cup) olive oil
2 cloves garlic
6 chopped anchovies
250 gr (½ lb or 1 cup) peeled, chopped tomatoes

½ litre (1 pint or 2 cups) water
1 sprig fresh mint
salt and pepper
½ teaspoon strong red pepper

Use cleaned snails, prepared as described (p. 177). Remove snails from shells, rinse, drain and trim off head and tail tips. Heat oil and fry the garlic in it to flavour. As soon as the garlic becomes brown, discard it. Add anchovies, tomatoes and water. Simmer for 15 minutes. Add mint, continue to simmer for another 15 minutes. Season with salt and pepper to taste, heighten with a small pinch of red pepper.

Put in snails, simmer on low heat for 40–45 minutes. Remove snails from pan, put them back into shells, reheat in the sauce again and serve.

SNAILS, SICILIAN STYLE

According to Pliny, the best snails of his day came from Sicily. Here is a Sicilian recipe.

6 Servings

1 kg (2 lb) snails cleaned and ready for cooking
5 tablespoons olive oil
1 clove crushed garlic
1 large chopped onion
pinch chopped fresh rosemary

1 tablespoon tomato purée
½ litre (1 pint or 2 cups) hot water
salt and pepper
1 tablespoon chopped parsley

Prepare the snails for cooking as described (p. 177). Heat oil in a saucepan big enough to take all ingredients. Add garlic and onion. Cook gently until they become soft. Add rosemary and tomato purée, simmer for 6–7 minutes, stirring all the time. Gradually incorporate water, bring to the boil. Put in snails, cook for 15 minutes, stirring at intervals. Season to taste, add parsley, cover, simmer for 25–30 minutes on low heat and serve the snails, with their juices in soup plates.

FROGS' LEGS

Frogs' legs are deservedly considered delicacies in such gastronomically-minded countries as China and our partners in the Common Market—France, Belgium and Italy.

They don't eat frogs because they have nothing else to eat. They often deliberately choose them from menus listing hundreds of dishes. We find that condemnation of frogs' legs as food almost invariably comes from people who have never tried them. People, who try frogs' legs for the first time, find the flavour similar to that of very tender chicken. It is, in fact, much more delicate. The flesh is also easily digestible. In France only green frogs with black markings are eaten and only the hind legs are used. These are normally sold in pairs, on skewers, skinned and ready for cooking.

Here, to begin with, are some French frogs' legs recipes. Until ready to cook, keep frogs' legs in cold water, changing it from time to time. This makes the flesh white and plump.

Allow about 10 minutes to cook the frogs' legs.

FROGS' LEGS À L'ANGLAISE

This is called 'à l'Anglaise', i.e. cooked the English way, only because 'à l'Anglaise' is the classical French cookery term for anything fried in egg and breadcrumbs. The name is also applied to vegetables, etc. boiled in water. In this recipe the frogs' legs are fried in egg and breadcrumbs and served with boiled potatoes. And very nice, too.

4 Servings

12 pairs frogs' legs	salt and pepper
2 beaten eggs	butter
breadcrumbs	maître d'hotel butter

Dip the frogs' legs in egg and breadcrumbs, season and sauté in hot butter for about 10 minutes, until golden brown. Drain, garnish with dollops of maître d'hotel butter and serve piping hot with boiled potatoes.

FROGS' LEGS MEUNIÈRE

4 Servings

12 pairs frogs' legs	butter
flour	chopped parsley
salt and pepper	lemon juice

Dip frogs' legs in flour, season and fry in butter. Drain, heap on a heated serving dish, sprinkle with chopped parsley and lemon juice. Keep hot.

Heat butter left in the frying pan, adding more butter if necessary, until it turns a light brown. Pour over frogs' legs and serve.

FROGS' LEGS IN GARLIC (COLONEL BLIMP'S DESPAIR)

4–5 Servings

20 pairs frogs' legs	2/3rds cup flour
salt	2 eggs, slightly beaten
1 cup butter or oil for frying	1 cup breadcrumbs
6 chopped cloves garlic	fried parsley

Wash frogs' legs and pat dry. Sprinkle with salt. Heat butter in a frying pan and add garlic. Stir until it turns the palest yellow. Dip frogs' legs in flour, egg and breadcrumbs. Fry in garlic butter until deep golden all over. Serve with fried parsley and good French bread to mop up the sauce.

FROGS' LEGS À LA NIÇOISE

4 Servings

salt and pepper	butter
12 pairs frogs' legs	4 tablespoons tomato fondue
flour	chopped parsley

Season frogs' legs, dip in flour and fry in hot butter until pale golden. Add tomato fondue, simmer for 2–3 minutes. Transfer to a heated serving dish, sprinkle with parsley and serve.

FROGS' LEGS À LA PARISIENNE

4 Servings

salt and pepper	2–3 tablespoons dry white wine
12 pairs frogs' legs	béchamel sauce
2–3 tablespoons butter	3 tablespoons fresh cream

Season the frogs' legs, cook for 10 minutes in 2 tablespoons butter and the wine over a lively heat. Mix béchamel sauce with cream, add to pan with frogs' legs, reduce heat, simmer for 2–3 minutes.

At the last moment add remaining tablespoon butter, blending it in in small pieces.

FROGS' LEGS, ITALIAN STYLE

4 Servings

12 pairs frogs' legs	oil for deep frying
salt and pepper	batter
butter	1 lemon, cut in wedges

Brush the frogs' legs with butter, season to taste, rubbing the salt and pepper well into the flesh. Heat oil for deep frying. Dip frogs' legs in batter, deep fry in oil, drain and serve with lemon wedges.

FROGS' LEGS, SPANISH STYLE

4 Servings

salt and pepper	tomato sauce
12 pairs frogs' legs	boiled rice or mashed potato
3 tablespoons oil	1 tablespoon chopped parsley

Season frogs' legs and fry in hot oil to brown lightly. Add tomato sauce, cover and simmer for 10 minutes. Transfer to a heated serving dish, surround with a border of rice or creamy mashed potatoes, sprinkle with parsley and serve.

CHINESE FROGS' LEGS WITH CHICKEN LIVERS

4 Servings

12–16 frogs' legs	125 gr (4 oz) shredded spring
1 tablespoon lard	greens
1 teaspoon fresh ginger, cut in shreds	pinch salt
	1 tablespoon soya sauce
6–7 spring onions, cut in 1½ cm (½ inch) pieces	1 teaspoon cornflour
	1 tablespoon Chinese wine or dry sherry
250 gr (8 oz) chicken livers, sliced	small pinch Ve-Tsin
50 gr (2 oz) fresh mushrooms, sliced	½ teaspoon sugar

Have the frogs' legs soaked and ready for cooking, as described. Drain and dry. Heat lard in a pan, add ginger, spring onions and frogs' legs. Cook for 2 minutes. Add chicken livers, mushrooms and spring greens and cook for 1 minute, stirring all the time. Add salt, soya sauce, cornflour diluted with wine or sherry, Ve-Tsin and sugar. Stir, simmer for 5 minutes and serve.

Fish Salads

SALADE NIÇOISE

4 Servings

1 crisp quartered lettuce
2–3 firm tomatoes, sliced and
seeded
125 gr (4 oz) cooked French
beans
8 diced anchovy fillets
1 dozen black olives
1 tablespoon capers

1 small tin tunny in oil
2–3 artichoke hearts (optional)
1 diced sweet green pepper
2 sliced hard-boiled eggs
French dressing
1 teaspoon chopped chervil and
tarragon

Put lettuce in a salad dish. Arrange tomatoes and French beans on top. Garnish with anchovy fillets, olives, capers, tunny, artichoke hearts and green pepper. Decorate with slices of hard-boiled egg. Just before serving, add French dressing. Sprinkle with chervil and tarragon.

COLD HAKE WITH PICKLED WALNUT SAUCE, CHILEAN STYLE

4 Servings

1 kg (2 lb) cold poached hake
lettuce
10 pickled walnuts
salt and pepper
pinch nutmeg

125 ml (4 oz or ½ cup) yoghourt
250 ml (½ pint or 1 cup)
mayonnaise
1 lemon

Arrange the hake on a bed of crisp lettuce leaves. Pound the walnuts in a mortar and rub through a fine sieve. Season to taste, add nutmeg, stir in yoghourt and blend in mayonnaise. Mask the fish with this sauce, garnish with lemon wedges and serve.

STEAMED HALIBUT WITH ORANGE AND WATERCRESS SALAD

4 Servings

500–750 gr (1–1½ lb) halibut
   cut in portions
seasoning
1 lettuce

mayonnaise
2 peeled, sliced oranges
1 bunch watercress

Season the fish and steam between two plates for 12 minutes. Leave to cool completely. Arrange on a bed of crisp lettuce, cover uniformly with home-made mayonnaise, garnish with orange slices and watercress.

HERRING AND CHICORY SALAD

4 Servings

2 heads chicory
1–2 medium-sized, cooked
   potatoes
1 medium-sized onion

1–2 herring fillets
oil and vinegar dressing
1 tablespoon chopped parsley
1 tablespoon chopped chervil

Cut chicory and potatoes into strips. Bake onion in its skin, cool, peel, chop and add to vegetables. Dice herring fillets, add to salad, dress with oil and vinegar. Sprinkle with chopped parsley and chervil.

NEAPOLITAN CHRISTMAS SALAD

4–6 Servings

1 large cauliflower
6 chopped anchovy fillets
1 dozen stoned, chopped black
   olives
1 tablespoon capers

6 tablespoons olive oil
3 tablespoons wine vinegar
salt and pepper
eels carpionata (p. 63)

Divide cauliflower into flowerets, cook in salted water for 6–7 minutes. Drain, put into cold salted water and leave for 20–30 minutes. Combine anchovies, olives, capers, oil and vinegar. Add drained cauliflower, season to taste, garnish with slices of eel.

SHRIMP OR PRAWN SALAD IN ORANGE SHELLS

4 Servings

4 oranges
½ kg (1 pint or 2 cups) shelled
   shrimps
4 tablespoons raw grated
   carrots

1 dcl (4 oz or ½ cup) French
   dressing
1 chopped hard-boiled egg

Cut tops off oranges, remove pulp, put in a bowl with shrimps and carrots. Sprinkle with dressing, mix well. Spoon into orange shells, garnish with egg, chill and serve.

INSTANT PRAWN CURRY SALAD

4 Servings

250 ml (½ pint or 1 cup) watercress mayonnaise
2 teaspoons garam-masala

360 gr (12 oz or 1½ cups) peeled cooked prawns

Mix mayonnaise with garam-masala to taste. Add prawns, stir and serve with a salad.

PRAWN AND BANANA SALAD WITH RICE, JAVA STYLE

6 Servings

180 gr (6 oz or 7/8 cup) Patna rice
clear stock
2 tablespoons olive oil
1 tablespoon lime (or lemon) juice
120 grs (4 oz or 8 tablespoons) chopped celery
seasoning
lettuce
½ litre (1 pint or 2 cups) peeled cooked prawns

4 tablespoons lemon and oil dressing
4 tablespoons coconut milk (optional)
4 bananas, halved lengthways
6 halves, hard-boiled eggs
250 gr (½ lb or 1 cup) sliced, ripe tomatoes
360 ml (¾ pint or 1½ cups) tomato mayonnaise

Cook the rice in stock, or water with a bouillon cube added to it, drain and while still hot add oil and lime juice, mix well and allow to cool completely. When cold, add celery, mix, check seasoning.

Line a serving dish with crisp lettuce leaves, heap the rice in a dome in the middle. Toss the prawns in lemon and oil dressing mixed with coconut milk, and sprinkle some of the dressing on bananas. Dispose the garnish of prawns, bananas and hard-boiled eggs around the rice. Make a border of tomato slices, overlapping slightly, round the outer edge of the dish. Put the pink mayonnaise in a Chinese rice bowl, imbed this in the centre of the slightly flattened rice dome and serve.

PRAWNS IN BEER

4 Servings

500 gr (1 lb or 2 cups) uncooked prawns
beer
salt and pepper

mayonnaise
1 tablespoon chopped dill
4 small heads lettuce

Shell the prawns, de-vein and cook in enough boiling beer to cover until they turn red. (A matter of a couple of minutes, so watch carefully.) Turn off heat and leave the prawns to cool in the liquor. Drain, chop coarsely, season to taste, mix with mayonnaise, sprinkle with dill and keep in a refrigerator until ready to serve.

Discard the inedible outside leaves but keep the lettuce heads whole. Wash well and leave upside down to drain thoroughly. Extract the heart with care so as to leave an undisturbed 'cup' in which the prawns are to be served. Keep in the crisper until needed.

Fill lettuce cups with prawns and serve. The dill imparts a very interesting fragrance to the mayonnaise.

PRAWN AND MUSHROOM SALAD

6 Servings

240 gr ($\frac{1}{2}$ lb or $1\frac{1}{2}$ cups) peeled prawns
240 gr ($\frac{1}{2}$ lb or $3\frac{1}{2}$ cups) sliced, fresh mushrooms

1 clove crushed garlic
French dressing
chopped parsley

Combine prawns and mushrooms in a salad bowl rubbed with garlic. Toss in dressing, sprinkle with parsley and serve at once.

MUSSEL SALAD

Prepare the mussels as for moules marinières (p. 116). Shell them, dress with oil, vinegar, pepper and chopped mixed herbs.

TOMATO AND TUNNY SALAD

Arrange alternate slices of tunny and tomato in a hors-d'oeuvre dish, interspersing each slice with a thin round of onion. Garnish the dish with a border of sliced, cooked potato, and sprinkle with salad dressing.

WHITEBAIT SALAD

Put a sprig of thyme, a bay leaf and some salt into a pan of water, bring to the boil, put in the fish and boil for 1 minute. Drain, arrange in a salad bowl and sprinkle with salad dressing.

TRUFFLED MUSSEL SALAD

4 Servings

4 small cooked, diced potatoes
8 poached, diced mussels (p. 116)
white wine dressing
lettuce

1 teaspoon each of chopped
  parsley, dill and chives
1 chopped hard-boiled egg
1 tinned truffle

Toss the potatoes and mussels in the dressing and arrange on lettuce leaves, sprinkle with parsley, dill and chives, garnish with egg and truffle cut in slivers.

HAKE IN ORANGE SAUCE

Israeli recipe.

4 Servings

500 gr (1 lb) hake
flour
salt and pepper
oil for frying

2½ dcl (½ pint or 1 cup) fresh
  orange juice
1 teaspoon cornflour, diluted in
  2 tablespoons cold water

Cut fish into portions. Mix flour with salt and pepper and coat fish pieces with it, then fry them in oil. Drain fish, put in a deep dish, and cool.

Bring orange juice to the boil, stir in cornflour, simmer until the sauce thickens, pour over fish, allow to cool. Chill and serve with Orange Salad with Poppy Seeds.

ORANGE SALAD WITH POPPY SEEDS

Israeli recipe.

4 Servings

4 oranges, peeled
1 tablespoon sugar
small pinch salt
¼ teaspoon dry mustard
3 tablespoons olive oil

1 tablespoon vinegar
¼ teaspoon finely grated onion
  (optional)
½ teaspoon poppy seeds

Cut oranges into very thin slices, remove seeds, arrange slices on a serving dish. Combine the rest of ingredients, except poppy seeds, in a jar and shake well. Pour over orange slices, chill. Just before serving, sprinkle with poppy seeds.

LOBSTER RAITA

4 Servings

250 gr (½ lb) diced cooked
  lobster
2 tablespoons diced cucumber
1 tablespoon finely chopped
  onion
1 crushed clove garlic

salt and pepper
2 teaspoons lemon juice
2 teaspoons mixed Dijon
  mustard
250 ml (½ pint) fresh yoghourt
1 bunch watercress

Combine lobster, cucumber, onion and garlic. Season to taste. Blend lemon juice and mustard into yoghourt and fold into lobster mixture. Serve on a bed of watercress.

CALIFORNIAN PRAWN AND PASTA SALAD

4 Servings

360 gr (12 oz or 3 cups) macaroni or pasta shells
salted water
360 gr (12 oz or 1½ cups) peeled, cooked prawns
2 sliced hard-boiled eggs
3 tablespoons chopped celery

1–2 onions, cut in very thin rings
2 teaspoons capers
mayonnaise
paprika
parsley, divided into small sprigs

Boil the pasta as described on the packet. Do not overcook. Drain, rinse with cold water and drain throughly again. Allow to cool.

Combine with prawns, eggs, celery, onion rings, capers and mayonnaise. Mix carefully, sprinkle with paprika and garnish with tiny bouquets of parsley.

SUMMER PICNIC SALAD

6 Servings

1 Webbs Wonder lettuce
1 bunch watercress
500 gr (1 lb) cooked, flaked fish (from salmon to cod, depending on whether your purse is at high or low tide)
60 gr (2 oz) de-salted anchovies (optional)

1 teaspoon chopped chives
1 tablespoon white wine vinegar
2 tablespoons olive oil
salt
pepper
2 tablespoons Dijon mustard

Discard as few outside leaves of the lettuce as possible (remember all those lovely vitamins in the greenest parts). Wash, dry and tear into manageable sized pieces into a pretty salad bowl. Wash and dry watercress and tear that into the bowl too. Add the flaked fish, anchovies and chives. Mix vinegar, oil, seasoning and mustard to make a dressing. Pour over the salad just before serving and toss once.

TROPICAL CRABMEAT SALAD

6 Servings

360 gr (12 oz or 1½ cups) cooked crabmeat (tinned crabmeat could be used, but it is worth saving for the real thing)

3 ripe grapefruit

1 small pineapple

1 small sliced onion

Dressing:

250 ml (½ pint or 1 cup) mayonnaise

125 ml (4 oz or ½ cup) tomato ketchup

1 teaspoon tabasco

1 tablespoon white rum

salt and pepper

Check that there are no hard membranes or bits of shell in the crabmeat. Halve the grapefruits and scoop out the fruit carefully, so as to get 250 gr (8 oz or 1 cup) of neat chunks. The rest of the fruit can be kept for a fruit salad or passed through the blender for juice.

Peel and core the pineapple, dice the pulp and add to the cup of grapefruit pieces. Add the onion and crabmeat.

Stir ketchup into mayonnaise. Add tabasco and rum. Season to taste. Fold into the crabmeat mixture. Serve in a pretty glass bowl, or on a bed of dark green lettuce leaves, or in the scooped-out grapefruit halves.

Egg and Fish Dishes

BAKED EGGS À LA NANTUA

Butter a dish, fill with crayfish tails, break in the eggs to nestle among the shellfish, and bake in the oven until set. Put a sliver of truffle on each yolk. Cover with Nantua sauce.

CHINESE STEAMED EGGS WITH PRAWNS

4 Servings

4–6 eggs
3 tablespoons water
1 dessertspoon soya sauce
½ teaspoon salt

3–4 chopped spring onions
120 gr (4 oz or ¾ cup) peeled prawns

Beat the eggs with water. Add the rest of the ingredients and mix well. Pour into large heatproof dish, or into individual ramekins, dividing the mixture into equal portions, and steam for 15 minutes.

DAUMONT EGGS

Arrange soft boiled or poached eggs on large mushrooms caps cooked in butter, lined with chopped crayfish tails à la Nantua Cover with Nantua sauce.

ANCHOVY EGGS

Arrange soft boiled or poached eggs on slices of bread fried in butter. Mask the eggs with anchovy sauce. De-salt anchovy fillets, shape them into rings and put one on each egg.

EGGS WITH SHRIMPS IN TARTLETS

Fill tartlet cases (p. 41) with shrimps blended with shrimp sauce. Arrange soft boiled or poached eggs on top, cover with more sauce, heat and serve.

CARDINAL EGGS

Fill small tartlet cases (p. 41) with sliced spiny lobster blended with a béchamel sauce. Put the eggs on top, cover with cardinal sauce.

BUCKLING WITH EGGS

4 Servings

4 smoked buckling	2 chopped hard-boiled eggs
360 ml (¾ pint or 1½ cups) béchamel sauce	2 tablespoons chopped chives

Skin the buckling, remove bones and flake the fish. Heat the sauce, taste for seasoning and adjust, if necessary. Add buckling, eggs and chives, stir until boiling is established and serve.

WHITEBAIT BAKED WITH EGGS

Roll in flour 4 tablespoons of whitebait and sauté in butter. When brown, add a tablespoon of Gruyère cheese, cut into very small dice, and a little crushed garlic. Break 4 eggs into the same pan, bake in the oven. Turn out on to a hot dish. Sprinkle with chopped parsley.

Fish Soufflés

FISH SOUFFLÉ

4–6 Servings

1 kg (2 lb) cooked (white) fish	seasoning
	3 raw egg yolks
2½ dcl (½ pint or 1 cup) thick béchamel sauce	3 whites of egg
	butter

Flake the fish, which has either been poached in court-bouillon or sweated gently in butter, and rub through a sieve, or pass through a blender. Mix with béchamel sauce, season well, remove from heat and beat in the yolks, one at a time. At the last moment—when you have done all essential jobs, and pre-heated the oven to 205°C (400°F or Gas Mark 5), putting in a baking sheet on which the soufflé will stand, and buttering a soufflé dish—beat the whites.

On this part of the operation depends the success of your soufflé. Make sure both the bowl and the egg whisk are clinically clean and dry. Any speck of grease, or the most minute bit of yolk mixed in with the whites, are about as helpful to a soufflé as a flat iron! Keep the whites cool, whisk them into a stiff foam. When they reach the stage of standing in little peaks, fold them carefully into the mixture, quickly but lightly turn them in with a wooden spoon to make sure they fuse with all the sauce and fish purée at the bottom of the bowl, but avoid beating.

This part of the soufflé making cannot be done in advance, though you can get everything up to this point ready hours before. Your oven and your soufflé dish *have* to be waiting before you start beating the whites.

Pour the mixture into a soufflé dish, filling it to within a finger's breadth of the top, smooth over the surface quickly, and immediately put it into the oven on a baking sheet and bake for 25 minutes.

FLORENTINE PRAWN AND CHEESE SOUFFLÉ

4–6 Servings

butter
250 ml (½ pint or 1 cup) thick
  white sauce
125 gr (4 oz or ½ cup) grated
  Parmesan cheese
salt and cayenne pepper

4 raw yolks
3 tablespoons prawn butter
4 tablespoons cream
6 stiffly beaten whites of egg
250 gr (8 oz or 1½ cups) peeled
  prawns

Pre-heat oven to 190°C (375°F or Gas Mark 4). Butter a soufflé mould. Add cheese to white sauce, season. One by one blend in yolks. Mix prawn butter with cream and stir into sauce. Fold in whites of egg.

Pour a layer of the mixture into the soufflé dish, scatter with prawns and continue in this manner until all are used up. Bake for 35 minutes.

COD SOUFFLÉ

4 Servings

500–750 gr (1–1½ lbs) filleted
  Cod (or other white fish)
1 finely chopped onion
2 tablespoons butter
2 tablespoons flour

salt and pepper
pinch nutmeg
2½ dcl (½ pint or 1 cup) milk
3 eggs

Mince or chop the fish finely. Chop the onion and fry lightly in butter without allowing it to get brown. Add flour, blend in, add cod, season with salt, freshly ground pepper and nutmeg. Gradually add milk, stirring constantly. Simmer until the sauce thickens. Remove from heat, let the mixture cool, taste for seasoning and correct, if necessary. Put in 3 yolks of egg and stir.

Beat the whites until stiff, fold gently into the cod mixture, pour into a lightly-buttered soufflé dish, dot with tiny pieces of butter, bake in the oven preheated to 910°C (375°F or Gas Mark 4) for 25 minutes and serve at once.

There is nothing extraordinary about this recipe, but it is a splendid way of stretching a piece of fish (haddock or hake will do equally well) to make an extra portion or two for unexpected guests. We remember it being whipped up by an Icelandic friend who catered for two and was faced with having to provide dinner for four.

PRAWN AND RICE SOUFFLÉ

4 Servings

250 gr (8oz) rice
1 litre (1 quart) fish fumet
125 gr (4 oz) butter
250 gr (8 oz) peeled cooked
    prawns
3 tablespoons Marsala

6 tablespoons grated **Parmesan**
    cheese
salt and pepper
4 egg yolks
4 beaten whites of egg

Cook the rice as described before using fish stock or fumet instead of water, for 20 minutes. Heat 30 gr (1 oz) of butter, lightly toss the prawns in it. Sprinkle with Marsala, cook for 3 minutes. Stir in remaining butter, Parmesan cheese and prawns with their residue into the rice. Allow to cool, taste, season as required. One by one beat in the yolks and mix well.

Fold in the whites, pour the rice and prawn mixture into a buttered soufflé dish, bake in a pre-heated moderate oven 190C° (375°F or Gas Mark 4) for 15 minutes and serve.

SMOKED HADDOCK SOUFFLÉ

4 Servings

¼ kg (8 oz) smoked haddock
45 gr (1½ oz) butter
30 gr (1 oz) flour
¼ litre (½ pint or 1 cup) milk

½ teaspoon grated lemon rind
salt and pepper
3 raw yolks
3 egg whites

Steam the haddock in a little milk between two plates over boiling water. As soon as it is done, strain and keep the liquid. Discard any bones or skin.

Put the fish through a mincer (or purée in a blender). Pre-heat oven to 175°C (350°F or Gas Mark 3). Heat 30 grs (1 oz) butter, stir in flour, cook for a few minutes to amalgamate, without browning. Dilute gradually with warmed milk, add liquid in which the haddock was steamed, lemon rind and seasoning. Simmer, stirring until the sauce thickens. Remove from heat, add fish and stir in yolks.

Whisk the whites into a stiff foam, fold into haddock mixture and pour into lightly buttered 17 cm–19½ cm (8–9 in.) soufflé dish. Dot with tiny pieces of butter and bake for 18–20 minutes. Serve with anchovy sauce.

To make anchovy sauce, put béchamel sauce through a blender with 5–6 anchovy fillets until smooth.

Fish Omelettes

SEA-FOOD OMELETTE

4 Servings

4 eggs
1 teaspoon parsley
1 teaspoon chervil
salt and pepper
butter
12 cooked, shelled mussels
4-5 sliced scallops

125 ml (4 oz or half cup)
  shrimp sauce
125 ml (4 oz or half cup)
  cream sauce
1 tablespoon anchovy butter

Heat oven to 220°C (425°F or Gas Mark 6). Beat the eggs with chopped parsley and chervil, season with salt and pepper and make two flat omelettes, using butter to fry them.

Put one of the omelettes on a round buttered ovenproof dish and cover it with mussels and scallops bound with shrimp sauce. Cover with the second omelette, pour over some cream sauce flavoured with anchovy butter and glaze quickly in the oven.

CRAB FOO YUNG

4 Servings

125 gr (4 oz) crab meat
3 tablespoons bamboo shoots
2-3 tablespoons peanut or other
  vegetable oil
1 small chopped onion
1 crushed clove garlic
3 tablespoons bean sprouts
1-2 finely shredded slices green
  ginger

pinch salt
pinch sugar
pinch Ve-Tsin
1 tablespoon dry sherry
½ teaspoon sesame oil
1 tablespoon chicken stock or
  water
4 beaten eggs
2-3 peeled sliced tomatoes

Flake the crab meat. Finely slice bamboo shoots. Heat oil and 'stir-fry', or scramble, onion and garlic for about 1 minute. Add crab meat, bamboo shoots, bean sprouts and ginger. Cook stirring for half a minute. Add salt, sugar, Ve-Tsin, sherry and sesame oil. Cook stirring for half a minute.

Blend cornflour with stock, stir into the frying pan, cook for about 1 minute. Add beaten eggs, scramble for half a minute and serve garnished with tomato slices.

OYSTER AND BAMBOO SHOOT OMELETTE

4 Servings

1 dessertspoon oil
1½ dozen plump oysters
2 tablespoons finely sliced
   bamboo shoots
1 tablespoon chives

salt and pepper
120 ml (4 oz or ½ cup) milk
¼ teaspoon Ve-Tsin
4 eggs

Heat oil in pan and fry the oysters for 2–3 minutes. Add bamboo shoot, chives and salt and pepper to taste. Add milk and Ve-Tsin to eggs, beat and pour mixture into the pan. Cook for one minute and serve with sauce, prepared just before you fry the omelette.

Combine :

1 dessertspoon oyster sauce
1 teaspoon soya sauce
1 teaspoon cornflour diluted
   with

6 tablespoons water

Cook together until the sauce thickens, pour over omelette and serve.

SHRIMP SANDWICH OMELETTE

4 Servings

8 eggs
1 tablespoon chopped parsley
1 tablespoon chopped chervil
salt and pepper
butter

250 gr. (8oz or 1 cup) shrimps or
   prawn tails
shrimp sauce
cream sauce
shrimp butter

Heat oven to 220°C (425°F or Gas Mark 6). Beat the eggs with chopped parsley and chervil, season with salt and pepper and make two flat omelettes, using butter to fry them. Put one of the omelettes on a round buttered ovenproof dish and cover it with shrimps or prawn tails, bound with shrimp sauce. Cover with the second omelette, pour over some cream sauce flavoured with shrimp butter and glaze quickly in the oven.

OMELETTE CARDINAL

3–4 Servings

4 eggs
salt and pepper
30 gr (1 oz or 2 tablespoons)
　butter
shredded zest of 1 orange
120 gr (4 oz or ¾ cup) cooked,
　peeled prawns

1 tablespoon single cream
120 ml (4 oz or ½ cup) hot
　béchamel sauce
1 peeled, thinly sliced orange

Beat eggs with seasoning. Heat the butter in a pan, pour in eggs and cook omelette in the usual way. Mix half the orange zest and half the prawns with the cream. Fill the omelette with this mixture. Fold it, transfer to a hot serving dish, make a lengthwise incision and spoon remaining prawns into it. Pour béchamel sauce over the ends of the omelette. Garnish with orange slices, sprinkle with remaining zest and serve.

LOBSTER OMELETTE

As above, using as filling diced lobster meat bound with lobster sauce.

SHRIMP OMELETTE

Make the omelette in the usual way. Fill with peeled shrimp tails dressed with shrimp sauce.

OMELETTE DE SAVARIN

The original recipe was the source of memorable discussions between the *Directeur de la table* of the Archbishop (a master of gastronomy) and the *Chef de cuisine,* at which Frédéric (p. 198) declared himself against the massacre of the soft roes and emphatically repudiated the use of the shallot. The Monseigneur, who acted as arbiter, declared his wish to preserve neutrality, on condition that Frédéric's omelette, a Lenten mortification dish, left nothing to be desired. The principle had to be respected.

Frédéric absolutely refused to use more than eight eggs in an omelette, and those who have to hold the handle of the frying pan cannot but approve of this.

His method of procedure was as follows: the roes instead of being chopped, were cut into thin slices and done 'à la meunière'. The tunny (he normally used tunny in oil) was dried on a cloth, cut into a fairly coarse salpicon, seasoned and simmered in butter. The eggs, beaten simply to assure the blending of the whites and the yolks, were mixed with two spoonfuls of very thick fresh cream.

At the precise moment, when the butter was singing in the omelette pan, the sliced roes and the diced tunny were married in a shrimp sauce, discreetly seasoned and amply enriched with cream. And the centre of omelette, cooked to just the right consistency and folded twice, received this 'cardinalized' ragoût.

Arranged on its serving dish, the omelette (or omelettes, depending on the number of guests present) was frugally masked with the same sauce, decorated with some large slices of truffles, to provide a sober note of mourning, and served at once, as Frédéric, whose tyranny was dreaded by the servants, always insisted that the house steward be present during the preparation so that the omelette would not be kept waiting even for a second.

Sometimes for a change, the omelette, prepared as described, was girdled with fried frog's legs (Philéas Gilbert).

BRILLAT-SAVARIN'S TUNNY OMELETTE

Recipe invented for Monseigneur de la T., by his chef Frédéric.

'Preparation of tunny omelette : For 6 persons, take two well washed soft carp roes, which you will blanch by plunging them into slightly salted, boiling water for 5 minutes. Have a piece of tunny, the size of a chicken's egg ready for use. Add to it a small shallot chopped into minute particles.

Chop together the soft roes and the tunny in such a way as to blend them thoroughly. Put the mixture into a saucepan with a sufficient amount of the best butter to sauté until the butter is melted. This constitutes the speciality of the omelette.

'Take a second piece of butter (the size being left to your discretion), blend it with parsley and spring onions, put into a pisciform dish intended for the omelette. Sprinkle with a dash of lemon juice and put on hot coals. Proceed to beat a dozen egg (the fresher the better), add the tunny and roe mixture to them and stir to blend well. Fry the omelette in the usual manner; try to make it longish, thick and fluffy. Transfer it adroitly to a dish which you have ready to receive it and serve at once.

'These dishes should be reserved specially for elegant luncheons, for connoisseurs, where people know what's what and where they eat in a leisurely manner; above all, these dishes should be washed down with some good wine and you will see wonders.

'Notes on the preparation : The soft roes and the tunny should be sautéed without allowing them to boil, to stop them going hard, which would prevent their blending with the eggs smoothly. The dish should be deep enough to collect the sauce which should be served with a spoon. The dish itself should be warmed slightly, for if it is cold the porcelain will extract all the heat from the omelette and there will not be enough heat left to melt the maître d'hôtel butter on which it is laid.'

SMOKED SALMON OMELETTE, RUSSIAN STYLE

2 Servings

3 eggs
1 tablespoon milk
60 gr (2 oz or 2 tablespoons)
  diced smoked salmon

½ tablespoon butter

Beat the eggs with the milk, add salmon, fry the omelette in buter and serve at once.

AMERICAN OYSTER OMELETTE

4–5 Servings

8 yolks
4 egg whites
12 small chopped oysters
2 drops Tabasco

pinch freshly ground black
  pepper
butter

Beat yolks and whites until the mixture is very light. Mix in oysters and add Tabasco and pepper. Melt a lump of butter in a pan and, when the butter foams, skim it and add the omelette mixure. Cook until the eggs set on the bottom, lift the edges, and let the uncooked egg run underneath. Continue to cook until the omelette is almost set. Slide it on to a warm heatproof dish, brown the top under the grill and serve.

CHINESE LOBSTER OMELETTE

6 Servings

240 gr (8 oz or 1½ cups)
  lobster meat
1 tablespoon oil
1 tablespoon chopped onion

salt
6 beaten eggs
pinch freshly ground pepper

Dice the lobster meat. Heat oil, put in onion and cook gently for 30 seconds. Add lobster, cook for 2 minutes, season with salt to taste. Pour on eggs, mix quickly, cook for one minute, sprinkle with pepper. Shake the pan carefully to ensure even cooking, cook for one minute and serve at once.

Compound Butters and Creams

CLARIFIED BUTTER (GHEE)

Melt the butter on a very low heat until it begins to look like olive oil and a whitish deposit forms on the bottom of the pan. Strain into a clean container and use as directed.

ANCHOVY BUTTER

60 gr (2 oz or ¼ cup) anchovy
  fillets

150 gr (5 oz or 10 tablespoons)
  butter

De-salt the anchovy fillets (i.e. rinse with cold water), pound them in a mortar with the butter and rub through a fine sieve. Store in a refrigerator in a jar with a well-fitting lid.

ANCHOVY BUTTER II

Mix 2 tablespoons butter with 1 teaspoon anchovy paste.

BERCY BUTTER

1 tablespoon finely chopped
  shallots
1 dcl (4 oz or ½ cup) white wine
250 gr (½ lb) bone marrow

125 gr (4 oz or ½ cup) butter
1 tablespoon chopped parsley
salt and pepper
juice of ½ lemon

Cook the shallots in wine until the liquid is reduced by half and allow to cool. Dice the bone marrow, poach in salted water, and drain. Blend shallots with butter, parsley, seasoning, and lemon juice, add marrow, and serve on grilled fish, or as indicated.

ESCARGOT BUTTER

2 cloves garlic
250 gr (8 oz or 1 cup) best
  unsalted butter
30 gr (1 oz or 3 tablespoons)
  chopped shallot

1 tablespoon washed, dried
  chopped parsley
¼ teaspoon salt
freshly ground pepper
¼ teaspoon nutmeg

Pound the garlic in a mortar to a paste, discarding all unpulpable shreds. Add butter and the other ingredients, blend well and use as described. The above amount is sufficient for 4 dozen snails.

HORSERADISH BUTTER

Put 75 gr (2½ ounces or 1/3rd cup) grated horseradish and 240 gr (8 ounces or 1 cup) butter through a blender or rub through a sieve.

LOBSTER BUTTER

This can easily be made at home whenever lobster, crayfish, prawns or shrimps are cooked in court-bouillon. It is both delicious as a flavouring and useful as a colouring butter, whenever a sauce requires pink tinting. It can be stored in small jars when it solidifies.

Pound the coral or eggs of the lobster (or other crustaceans) in a mortar, or pass through a blender, with an equal quantity of butter.

MAITRE d'HOTEL BUTTER

125 gr (4 oz or ½ cup) butter
1 teaspoon salt
pinch black pepper

1½ tablespoons chopped parsley
1 tablespoon lemon juice

Cream the butter in a bowl, add salt, pepper and parsley, mix well, blend in lemon juice little by little and use as directed.

PRAWN BUTTER

185 gr (6 oz or ¾ cup) prawns   125 gr (5 oz or ½ cup) butter

Cook the prawns in a court-bouillon à la mirepoix. Drain, pound in a mortar, shells and all. Put butter in a double saucepan, add prawns and let the butter melt slowly. Stir to blend well, strain through a cloth and store in a jar with a well-fitting lid. It will keep like ordinary butter.

SARDINE BUTTER

Using fillets of sardines in oil, follow recipe for anchovy butter (p. 200).

TARRAGON BUTTER

125 gr (4 tablespoons) fresh   180 gr (6 oz or ¾ cup) butter
  tarragon leaves

Blanch tarragon leaves for 2 minutes in salted boiling water, drain, dip in cold water, dry, pound in a mortar with butter and rub through a fine sieve.

SMOKED SALMON CREAM

60 gr (2 oz or 6 tablespoons) smoked salmon, finely pounded, diluted little by little with 3 tablespoons of fresh cream, blended with 60 gr (2 ounces or ¼ cup) of softened butter, then rubbed through a sieve and finished off with 2 tablespoons whipped cream. This makes a delicious filling for savoury tartlets or éclairs.

CAVIAR CREAM

30 gr (1 oz) caviar   softened butter
2 tablespoons fresh cream   2 tablespoons whipped cream
60 gr (2 oz or 4 tablespoons)

Blend caviar with fresh cream and butter. Rub through a sieve, incorporate whipped cream.

HORSERADISH CREAM

30 gr (1 oz or 1 tablespoon)   1½ dcl (¼ pint or ½ cup)
  freshly grated horseradish   whipped cream
½ teaspoon lemon juice   pinch sugar

Sprinkle horseradish with lemon juice, fold into whipped cream sweetened with sugar.

Sauces and Dressings

AIOLI OR AILLOLI

This famous dish, consisting of garlic mayonnaise and an assortment of cooked fish and vegetables—hot or cold—makes a splendid meal. It has a marvellously smooth texture and an exciting flavour. It is a great favourite in Provence, in addition to being a traditional Christmas Eve dish, and can be composed of boiled fish of all kinds, shellfish, snails, carrots, French beans, artichokes, hardboiled eggs, and last, but by no means least, potatoes boiled in their skins. The ingredients can be varied according to availability and taste.

To make aioli:

4 large juicy cloves of garlic
pinch salt
1 fresh egg yolk

250 ml (½ pint or 1 cup) olive oil

Peel the garlic, crush and pound into a paste in the mayonnaise mixing bowl. Season, add yolk, stir with a wooden spoon to blend yolk and garlic completely. When they are fused, start adding oil drop by drop until the aioli begins to thicken, exactly as you would for mayonnaise, and don't be alarmed if it appears to take longer than it should. That is because the garlic juice thins down the fat content of the yolk. When about half the oil has been incorporated the aioli should be quite thick.

Continue to blend in the rest of the oil, now adding it in a thin trickle. The finished aioli should be quite solid. If you attempt to take any short cuts, the aioli will most likely separate. To resuscitate curdled aioli, take a fresh yolk and proceed to rescue it as described in the recipe for mayonnaise.

AVGOLEMONO SAUCE

2 tablespoons butter
2 tablespoons flour
2 dcl (½ pint or 1 cup) hot
  stock
3 eggs

juice of 2 lemons
2 tablespoons cold water
salt
pinch cayenne pepper

Melt butter, add flour, and stir well. Cook for a few minutes, stirring all the time, gradually add stock, stirring to prevent the formation of lumps. Keep hot in a bain-marie or a pan of hot water. Beat the eggs, little by little, whisk lemon juice and water into them. Very gradually, add hot sauce, stirring all the time to prevent the eggs curdling. Season with salt and cayenne pepper. Re-heat, but on no account allow to come to boil.

AVOCADO SAUCE

For cold fish and shell fish.

This sauce is delicious with fish generally and lends subtlety to an ordinary cold plaice fillet. Use lime whenever available instead of lemon. The difference fresh lime makes as a garnish to fish has to be tasted to be believed.

2 medium-sized avocado pears
1 teaspoon onion juice
3 tablespoons lime (or lemon)
  juice

small pinch cayenne pepper
pinch salt
2 tablespoons olive oil

Mash the avocado pears, sprinkle with onion and lime juice, season with salt and pepper to taste and amalgamate the oil.

BANANA MAYONNAISE

2 ripe bananas
90 gr (3 oz or 6 tablespoons)
  mayonnaise
4 tablespoons sour cream

1–2 tablespoons lemon juice
pinch salt
pinch sugar
1–2 teaspoons grated horseradish

Mash the bananas, mix with the rest of the ingredients, blend in a mixer or rub through a sieve. Chill until required. Excellent with boiled prawns.

BÉARNAISE SAUCE

1 tablespoon chopped shallot
2 tablespoons chopped tarragon
2 tablespoons chopped chervil
1 sprig thyme
¼ bay leaf
¼ dcl (4 oz or 2 tablespoons) vinegar
¼ dcl (4 oz or 2 tablespoons) white wine

pinch of salt
pinch of mignonette pepper
2 raw egg yolks
water
125 gr (4 oz or ½ cup) butter
a few drops lemon juice
pinch cayenne pepper

Put shallot, half the tarragon and half the chervil into a saucepan, add thyme, bay leaf, vinegar, wine, salt and pepper, bring to the boil and reduce by two-thirds. Allow to cool.

Dilute egg yolks with one tablespoon water, add to pan, put on very low heat, heat until the yolks begin to thicken. Little by little incorporate butter, whisking all the time. Taste, adjust seasoning, heighten with lemon juice and cayenne pepper, strain, add remaining tarragon and chervil and use. If béarnaise sauce has to wait, keep in a bain-marie.

BÉCHAMEL SAUCE

60 gr (2 oz or ¼ cup) butter
60 gr (2 oz or ½ cup) flour
2 dcl (½ pint or 1 cup) hot milk

salt and pepper

Melt the butter, add flour gradually and cook this roux on a fairly low heat until it begins to come away from the pan, but on no account allow it to colour. Little by little add milk and season, simmer, stirring constantly until smooth and creamy.

CAROLINE'S MUSTARD SAUCE FOR FISH

180 gr (6 oz or ¾ cup) butter
4 teaspoons mixed Dijon mustard

2 tablespoons chopped parsley
pinch of salt
3 teaspoons lemon juice

Warm butter over a low flame. When soft, but not runny, add mustard, parsley and salt. Blend into a smooth paste, add lemon juice and serve over plain fish.

CAPER SAUCE

180 gr (6 oz or ¾ cup) butter

5–6 tablespoons capers

Melt the butter over hot water. Chop the capers finely, add to butter, stir and serve.

CARDINAL SAUCE

2 tablespoons lobster butter
2½ dcl (½ pint or 1 cup) hot
 velouté or béchamel sauce

2–3 tablespoons milk (if
 needed)
a little truffle juice (optional)

Add lobster butter to the hot velouté or béchamel. If sauce is too thick, thin down with milk. Add truffle juice, if used.

CHINESE SEA-FOOD SAUCE

This is a delicious Chinese sauce and can be served with all kinds of shell fish.

2 spring onions
1 tablespoon soya sauce
1 tablespoon sesame oil

1 teaspoon brown sugar
¼ teaspoon chilli powder
½ tablespoon wine vinegar

Chop the spring onions finely, using both white and green parts. Combine with rest of ingredients, mix well and serve in a small shallow dish.

CHORON SAUCE

2 dcl (½ pint or 1 cup)
 béarnaise sauce

2 tablespoons tomato purée

Blend concentrated tomato purée into béarnaise sauce.

CLAM SAUCE

2 litres (2 quarts) fresh
 cockles (or 2 dozen shelled
 little-neck clams)
4 tablespoons olive oil
1 small chopped onion
2 chopped cloves garlic

750 gr (1½ lb) peeled, chopped
 tomatoes (or 1 large tin
 Italian peeled tomatoes)
2 tablespoons chopped parsley
salt and pepper

Scrub the cockles, rinse thoroughly until no trace of grit remains. Toss in a large pan over a high flame, until they open, remove and discard shells, but strain and keep their juices. Cut into pieces, unless they are very small, in which case leave whole.

Heat oil, lightly fry onion and garlic, add clam juice, tomatoes, parsley, and salt and pepper to taste. Simmer on very low heat for half an hour. Add the shellfish to the sauce when your spaghetti is nearly ready. They only need 1 minute—2 at most—to heat through. If you keep them cooking longer than that, they will become rubbery.

Clams or cockles pickled in vinegar are too acid and not suitable for this sauce.

DEMI-GLACE SAUCE

Cook down Espagnole sauce by two-thirds of its volume, dilute to desired consistency with good, clean brown stock and, just before serving, add a tablespoonful or two of Madeira.

DUXELLES SAUCE

120 ml (4 oz ¼ cup) white wine
2 tablespoons chopped
mushrooms, prepared as
duxelles p. 214
180 ml (6 oz or ¾ cup)
demi-glace sauce

120 ml (4 oz or ½ cup)
tomato purée
1 tablespoon chopped parsley

Stir white wine into duxelles, reduce, stir in demi-glace sauce and tomato purée, simmer for a few moments, add chopped parsley.

FRENCH DRESSING

2 tablespoons tarragon vinegar
or lemon juice
6 tablespoons salad oil
salt
freshly ground black pepper

½ clove garlic, finely crushed
½ teaspoon french mustard
small slice onion or spring
onion (optional)

Put all the ingredients into the liquidizer, cover and switch on for about 30 seconds until blended together.

GREEN MAYONNAISE

In a blender mix 45 gr (1½ oz or 1 cup) watercress leaves, 30 gr (1 oz or ¾ cup) parsley, 4 peeled chopped shallots, 1 egg yolk, 2 tablespoons each of tarragon vinegar and lemon juice, 1 teaspoon French mustard, ¼ teaspoon sugar and a pinch of salt. Add 2½ dcl (½ pint or 1 cup) mayonnaise and an equal amount of sour cream, blend until smooth.

HOLLANDAISE SAUCE

2 dessertspoons water
pinch salt
pinch coarse ground
fresh black pepper

3 raw egg yolks
250 gr (8 oz or 1 cup)
clarified butter
few drops lemon juice

Boil down water with salt and pepper to reduce by half. Remove from direct heat, let the bottom of the pan cool and proceed to cook the sauce in a bain-marie (or in a bowl over a pan of boiling water).

Beat the yolks with a teaspoon of water and add to seasoned water. Keep the heat very low and whisk the sauce until the yolks thicken to a creamy consistency. Little by little, almost as you would oil for a mayonnaise, incorporate clarified melted butter, whisking all the time, until all has been absorbed and the sauce thickens. Remove from heat at once, sharpen with lemon juice and serve hot or cold. If the sauce has to be kept hot, let it stand in a bain-marie; on no account attempt to reheat it, or it will break up on you.

'Curdled' hollandaise sauce (which occurs in case of overcooking) can be reconstituted on the same principle as mayonnaise. The rescue operation is similiar; start afresh, with a spoonful of water and a clean bowl (or double saucepan), whisking the separated hollandaise in little by little.

HORSERADISH AND WALNUT SAUCE

60 gr (2 oz or 3 tablespoons) grated horseradish
60 gr (2 oz or ½ cup) finely chopped peeled walnuts
pinch salt
pinch castor sugar

½ tablespoon white breadcrumbs
125 ml (4 oz or ½ cup) fresh cream
dash lemon juice

Combine all ingredients and blend well.

HORSERADISH SAUCE

1 root horseradish
½ teaspoon sugar

1 teaspoon vinegar
1 dcl (4 oz or ½ cup) cream

Grate horseradish finely, add sugar and vinegar, mix in cream— and the sauce is ready, and will be far superior in texture and flavour to any commercially manufactured article. Well worth the tears! And marvellous for clearing the head.

ITALIAN TOMATO SAUCE

4 tablespoons olive oil
1 finely chopped onion
500 gr (1 lb or 2 cups) peeled, chopped tomatoes
pinch pounded garlic

1 teaspoon chopped basil
½ teaspoon sugar
pinch salt
freshly ground black pepper

Heat oil, fry onion until it becomes soft, add tomatoes, garlic and basil, simmer slowly for half an hour, stirring from time to time. Add sugar, season with salt and pepper to taste, continue to simmer for 10 minutes.

LOBSTER SAUCE

Excellent with boiled or poached hake, halibut, cod, etc.

2½ dcl (½ pint or 1 cup)
  béchamel sauce
4 tablespoons double cream
4 tablespoons lobster butter

60 gr (2 oz or ½ cup) diced
  cooked lobster meat
few drops anchovy essence
pinch paprika

Combine béchamel sauce, cream and lobster butter, blend well, add diced lobster, flavour with anchovy essence, heighten with a little paprika.

MAYONNAISE (made in a mixer or blender)

2 raw egg yolks
salt and pepper
pinch dry mustard
3–4 tablespoons lemon juice
  (or vinegar)

2½ dcl (½ pint or 1 cup) olive
  oil

Make sure your mixer is dry and cool. Put in yolks, salt, pepper, mustard and half the lemon juice. Start whisking on low speed. Drip in oil gradually, keeping the speed slow, until the mayonnaise thickens. Whisk in the remainder of the lemon juice.

Mayonnaise can also, of course, easily be made in the blender. Follow the same recipe and the manufacturers' instructions.

MORNAY SAUCE

2½ dcl (½ pint or 1 cup)
  béchamel sauce
1 dcl (4 oz or ½ cup) fresh
  cream

60 grs (2 oz or ½ cup) grated
  Gruyère or Parmesan cheese
30 gr (1 oz or 2 tablespoons)
  butter

Add cream to béchamel sauce, boiled down to reduce by one-third, stir in cheese and incorporate butter, stirring it in in small pieces.

MOUSSELINE SAUCE

Excellent with all grilled fish.

Combine 2½ dcl (½ pint or 1 cup) hollandaise sauce with 1 dcl (4 oz or ½ cup) whipped cream.

MUSHROOM SAUCE FOR FISH

125 gr (4 oz or ½ cup) sliced
  mushrooms
3 tablespoons butter
2 tablespoons flour
2 dcl (½ pint or 1 cup) fish
  stock

1 dcl (4 oz or ½ cup) cream
2 tablespoons dry white wine
salt and pepper
1 teaspoon chopped dill (or
  parsley)

Toss the mushrooms in 1 tablespoon butter. Melt the rest of the butter, blend in flour, fry this roux lightly, without allowing it to colour. Dilute gradually with fish stock, stirring constantly to ensure smoothness. Simmer for 7 to 8 minutes. Add mushrooms with their pan juices, stir, add cream, heat almost to boiling point, pour in wine, season to taste, sprinkle with dill, simmer without boiling for 2 minutes and serve.

NANTUA SAUCE WITH BÉCHAMEL

1½ dcl (4 oz or ½ cup) béchamel sauce
prawn (or crayfish) cooking liquor
1½ dcl (4 oz or ½ cup) cream

3 tablespoons prawn (or crayfish) butter
½ teaspoon brandy
pinch cayenne pepper

Boil down béchamel sauce with the strained liquid left from cooking prawns (or any other crustacean) to reduce by half. Add cream, finish off with prawn butter, brandy and cayenne pepper.

NANTUA SAUCE WITH BUTTER AND CREAM

180 ml (6 oz or ¾ cup) prawn or crayfish purée
4 tablespoons butter

cream
salt
cayenne pepper

This sauce is easy to make in a blender. (If you haven't got a blender, you will have to pound the peeled prawns or crayfish tails into a paste.) Pass the prawns through a blender, add butter in small pieces and whisk it in. Little by little, add enough cream to give you the consistency you want. Season to taste with salt and cayenne pepper.

OIL AND LEMON DRESSING

4 tablespoons olive oil
pinch salt and pepper

pinch paprika
2 tablespoons lemon juice

Mix oil and seasoning, drip in lemon juice gradually, stirring all the time to form an emulsion.

PARSLEY SAUCE (to make in a blender)

white sauce

chopped parsley to taste

Make the white sauce as described. As soon as it thickens, add parsley, cook for a couple of minutes and remove from heat. Warm the blender goblet, put the sauce into it, switch on to high speed and blend until the sauce is emulsified.

PINK OR TOMATO MAYONNAISE

Mix ¼ litre (½ pint or 1 cup) mayonnaise with ½ dcl (2 oz or 4 tablespoons) tomato purée, juice of 1 lemon, 1 teaspoon grated lemon rind, and salt and pepper to taste.

SAUCE ESPAGNOLE

45 gr (1½ oz or 3 tablespoons) butter
2–3 rashers diced bacon
1 small onion
1 medium-sized carrot
small piece bay leaf
small sprig thyme
salt and pepper

120 ml (4 oz or ½ cup) dry white wine
45 gr (1½ oz or 6 tablespoons) flour
½ litre (1 pint or 2 cups) stock
250 gr (½ lb or 1¾ cups) peeled, chopped tomatoes

Heat one tablespoon butter and gently sweat the bacon to make it yield up its fat and flavour. Chop onion and carrot and add to bacon, together with bay leaf, thyme, salt and pepper to taste. Cook, stirring until the ingredients acquire a pale golden colour, gradually add wine, and simmer to reduce by half.

Separately, heat the rest of the butter, blend in flour, cook until the mixture browns. Dilute with stock, adding the liquid gradually and stirring to prevent formation of lumps. Add contents of the other pan, simmer for at least an hour. Add tomatoes, simmer for a further 45 minutes, to make sure the sauce is sufficiently reduced to give the right consistency, and strain.

SOFT ROE SAUCE

4 soft herring roes
1 tablespoon lemon juice
2 tablespoons mayonnaise
1 teaspoon each finely chopped onion, parsley, chervil, chives tarragon

pinch salt
pinch cayenne pepper

Rub the roes through a sieve, or reduce them to a purée in a blender. Add chopped ingredients, season to taste, and use as required.

SOUBISE SAUCE

250 gr (8 oz or 2 cups) sliced onions
2 tablespoons butter
2 tablespoons flour
2½ dcl (½ pint or 1 cup) milk

120 ml (4 oz or ½ cup) cream
salt and pepper
pinch nutmeg
¼ teaspoon sugar
1 egg yolk

Scald the onions with boiling water and shake well in a collander to drain thoroughly. Melt butter and soften the onions in it. Blend in flour, cook for 30 to 40 seconds, without allowing the mixture to colour. Gradually add milk and cream. Stir until smooth and add all the seasoning and sugar. Simmer for 15 minutes, stirring from time to time. Rub through a sieve or reduce to a fine purée in a blender. Put the soubise purée back into the saucepan and start reheating gently. Dilute the egg yolk with a little of the sauce, pour into the saucepan, simmer over very low heat, stirring to amalgamate the mixture, for one or two minutes. The sauce should have a velvety, creamy texture.

SOUR CREAM SAUCE

2 tablespoons butter
1 tablespoon flour
120 ml (4 oz or 1 cup) hot stock

120 ml (4 oz or ½ cup) sour cream
1 chopped onion
salt and pepper

Melt 1½ tablespoons butter sprinkle in flour and fry until it acquires a pale golden colour. Gradually dilute with hot stock, stirring constantly till smooth and creamy. Add sour cream and simmer gently for 6 to 7 minutes. Fry onion in half a tablespoon of butter, add to sauce, season, stir and serve.

SWEET AND SOUR SAUCE

½ green and ½ red sweet pepper, deseeded and chopped
½ medium-sized onion, peeled and chopped
oil
pinch ground green ginger
2 tablespoons vinegar

4 teaspoons sugar
2 teaspoons tomato sauce
2 teaspoons cornflour
1½ teaspoons soya sauce
1 teaspoon Chinese wine or brandy
2½ dcl (½ pint or 1¼ cups) water

Fry peppers and onion in very little oil sprinkled with ginger. Mix together vinegar, sugar, tomato sauce, cornflour, soya sauce and brandy. Stir well, blend in water and add mixture to fried vegetables. Simmer gently for 5 minutes, stirring all the time. If the sauce becomes too thick, add a little more water to thin down.

TARTARE SAUCE I

½ teaspoon French mustard
1 teaspoon wine vinegar
1 tablespoon dry white wine
1 teaspoon chopped chives
1 teaspoon chopped capers

1 teaspoon chopped parsley
1 teaspoon chopped gherkin
1 teaspoon chopped olives
2½ dcl (½ pint or 1 cup) mayonnaise

Blend mustard with vinegar and wine, add chives, capers,

parsley, gherkin and olives. Mix, add all these ingredients to the mayonnaise and blend well.

TARTARE SAUCE II

2½ dcl (½ pint or 1 cup)
  mayonnaise
2–3 chopped shallots
1 teaspoon chopped parsley
1 teaspoon chopped chives

1 teaspoon chopped chervil
1 teaspoon chopped tarragon
1 teaspoon chopped watercress
½ teaspoon French mustard
dry white wine

Add the finely chopped ingredients and mustard to mayonnaise, stir well to mix, thin down to desired consistency with wine.

TEMPURA SAUCE

2½ dcl (½ pint or 1 cup) dashi
4 tablespoons soya sauce
4 tablespoons sake (or dry
  sherry)

pinch Aji-no-Moto

Bring dashi, soya sauce and sake to the boil, season with Aji-no-Moto to taste and serve.

VELOUTÉ SAUCE

This is a great basic sauce used in many dishes in European cooking. It needs care and time, but it can be prepared in advance. When fish is cooked with just enough liquid to cover, use this as a basis for sauce.

60 gr (2 oz or ¼ cup) butter
30 gr (1 oz or 4 tablespoons)
  mushrooms
3–4 sprigs parsley
10 peppercorns

60 gr (2 oz or ½ cup) flour
½ litre (1 pint or 2 cups) fish
  stock
½ dcl (4 oz or ½ cup) cream

Heat butter and cook the mushrooms, unpeeled and with stalks, for 5 minutes. Add parsley and peppercorns and cook for another 3 to 4 minutes on low heat. Blend in flour and cook the roux without allowing it to colour. Stir in stock, bring to the boil, stirring with a wooden spoon until the first bubble appears, then reduce to simmering point and cook gently—tenderly—for 1½ hours, skimming from time to time. Strain through damp muslin bag and continue to stir until the sauce is quite cold.

Rinse the mushrooms and use as part of the garnish. A little while before the velouté is required, reheat, taste for seasoning, incorporate cream and remove from heat without allowing the sauce to boil. The amount of seasoning you will need will depend on how well seasoned the stock was; it is better, therefore to taste and adjust.

VINAIGRETTE SAUCE

Mix three parts oil to one part vinegar, with salt and pepper. Lemon juice may be used instead of vinegar. This is such a useful dressing that we feel it is worth while making 500 ml—1 litre (1–2 pints) at a time. Keep well corked in a bottle and shake before use.

WHITE SAUCE

60 gr (2 oz or ¼ cup) butter   salt and pepper
60 gr (2 oz or ½ cup) flour
½ litre (1 pint or 2 cups) milk
  or fish stock (or a mixture
  of milk and fish stock)

Choose a saucepan which will hold all the ingredients comfortably. Melt the butter over low heat, stir in flour and cook gently for 3 minutes, stirring all the time and without allowing the roux to colour, if you want your white sauce to be white. Remove from heat, blend in half the liquid, return to heat and cook, stirring vigorously. When the sauce thickens, add the rest of the liquid. (The amount of milk or stock will, of course, have to be correspondingly reduced if you add, say, the liquid left from cooking the fish, or natural liquid from oysters, clams, lobsters, etc.) Continue to simmer and beat the sauce until the desired consistency is reached. Season, stir and use at once.

WHITE WINE DRESSING

4 tablespoons olive oil   1 teaspoon lemon juice
4 tablespoons white wine   salt and pepper

Blend oil and wine, stir in lemon juice and season to taste.

Dough, Pastry, Batter

PLAIN LINING PASTE

4 Servings

125 gr (4 oz or 1 cup) flour
salt
125 gr (4 oz or 8 tablespoons)
   butter

iced water

Mix flour with a pinch of salt, cut in butter with a knife. Add enough iced water to bind the pastry, sprinkling the water in a tablespoon at a time, and blending it in evenly. Roll out and proceed as indicated in individual recipes.

SHORT CRUST PASTRY (made in a mixer)

Use the mixer for all short crust pastry, i.e., when the fat has to be rubbed into the flour. Here is a general short crust pastry recipe for savoury dishes.

240 gr (8 oz or 2 cups) plain
   flour
pinch salt
120 gr (4 oz or 8 tablespoons)
   butter or other fat, cut in
   small pieces

iced water

Put flour, salt and butter into mixer bowl. Set to lowest possible speed and mix until the fat and the flour have been thoroughly amalgamated. Switch off, stir in enough water to bind and using a knife mix to a stiff paste.

FINE CHOU PASTE

1/2 litre (1 pint or 2¼ cups)
   water
pinch salt
1 tablespoon sugar
250 gr (8 oz or 1 cup) butter

220 gr (7½ oz or 2 cups) sifted
   flour
7–8 eggs (or 6–7 eggs and 4
   tablespoons milk or cream)

215

Pour the water into a large saucepan with a thick bottom. Add salt, sugar and butter in small pieces, bring to the boil. Remove from heat and add flour, pouring it in all at once. Mix well. Cook, stirring with a wooden spoon, until paste comes away from the sides of the pan. Remove from heat and, stirring constantly, put in eggs one by one, then the milk or cream, if used. (The number of eggs used depends on their size.) The amount of milk indicated would replace one egg and make a smother mixture.

Beat the mixture vigorously until it is very light.

If you have a portable mixer, the work will be simplified if you do the beating with a whisk.

PUFF PASTRY

240 gr (½ lb or 2 cups) sifted flour
½ teaspoon salt
7 tablespoons cold water
1 tablespoon lemon juice
240 gr (½ lb or 1 cup) butter

Put the flour on a board in a circle, make a well in the middle, put in salt. Combine water and lemon juice, moisten the flour with it and work the paste with your fingers very quickly to form a ball of fairly firm dough. Leave for 20 minutes. To make sure your butter is exactly the same consistency as the dough, knead it (either on a pastry slab or in a lightly floured cloth) to soften to the correct degree.

Roll out the paste into a sheet to a thickness of 6 mm (¼ in.), which should give you a strip of 15 cm by 45 cm (6 in. by 18 in.). Put the butter in the middle, fold the ends of the paste so as to enclose it completely and leave for 10 minutes in a cold place.

Roll out the pastry on a lightly floured board, refold the strip in three, i.e. fold each end towards the middle. Leave for 10 minutes. This is called giving the pastry a turn (*tourage*)—the second turn is done by rolling out the folded paste in the opposite direction, and so forth. Give four more turns to the paste, rolling out and turning the strip each time and leaving it to rest in a cold place for 10 minutes between each turn.

The purpose of all this turning and rolling is to spread the butter evenly in the paste. In between turns, keep in a cold place but do not allow the butter to freeze and harden, otherwise you will have trouble in getting the two elements—flour and water paste and butter—to amalgamate. Do not use a lot of flour either on the table or the rolling pin, a mere dusting is enough.

Use this puff pastry for vol-au-vents and bouchées. Trimmings

which are cut off and rolled out again are suitable for barquettes
and other tartlets.

QUICK PUFF PASTRY

120 gr (4 oz or ½ cup) butter	4 raw egg yolks
240 gr (8 oz or 2 cups) flour	7 tablespoons cold water
½ teaspoon salt	1 tablespoon lemon juice

Work in a cool place and keep all ingredients cool. Soften
butter as described in recipe for puff pastry. Using a palette knife,
cut butter into the flour, add salt, continue to mix, incorporate
yolks, water and lemon juice, work with the knife until the paste
is smooth, then put on a lightly floured board. Roll out to a thickness of 6 mm (¼ in.), fold and leave to rest for 10 minutes—as
described in the recipe for puff pastry. Repeat the rolling and
folding process three times.

DOUGH FOR PIROZHKI

240 gr (8 oz or 2 cups) self-raising flour	2 eggs
¼ teaspoon salt	100 ml (4 fl oz or ½ cup) oil
	2–3 tablespoons water

Sift flour into a mixing bowl, sprinkle in salt. Make a well in the
middle, add eggs, oil and water. Mix well then knead and roll
out as required.

QUICK BRIOCHE DOUGH

7½ gr (¼ oz or ½ cake) fresh dry yeast	2 eggs
120 ml (4 oz or ½ cup) lukewarm water	1 teaspoon sugar
375 gr (12 oz or 3 cups) sifted flour	pinch salt
	125 gr (4 oz or 8 tablespoons) softened butter

Dissolve the yeast in water and mix with one cup flour to make
a soft dough. Put remaining flour in a bowl, make a well in the
middle, put in eggs, sugar, salt and the yeast mixture. Mix and add
butter. Beat the dough until smooth and soft.

Cover and leave to stand in a warm place for 1–1½ hours. Then
use as directed.

PANCAKE BATTER

90 gr (3 oz or ¾ cup) flour	2 tablespoons cold water
pinch salt	2½ dcl (½ pint or 1 cup) milk
2 eggs	2 teaspoons melted butter

Beat flour, salt and eggs together, mix well, gradually dilute with water and milk, incorporate melted butter, stir until the batter is smooth and creamy and chill until needed. Stir well before using.

BEER BATTER

250 ml (½ pint or 1 cup) beer
150 gr (5 oz or ⅓rd cup) flour
2 egg yolks

pinch of salt
1 tablespoon olive oil
2 stiffly beaten egg whites

Blend beer, flour, egg yolks, salt and olive oil. Leave to stand for half an hour. Fold in egg whites.

PANCAKE BATTER MADE IN A BLENDER

240 ml (½ pint or 1 cup) milk
1 egg
pinch salt

120 gr (4 oz or 1 cup) plain flour

Put milk and egg into blender goblet. Sprinkle in salt, then add flour. Switch on at low speed, little by little increase to high and blend until the batter is smooth.

Miscellaneous: Fondues, Forcemeats, Garnishes, etc.

CHINESE PLAIN BOILED RICE I

6–8 Servings
500 gr (1 lb or 2 cups) rice

¾ litre (1½ pints or 3 cups) water

Wash the rice thoroughly until the water is clear. The amount of water required varies with the quality of the rice. The thing to remember is that the better the quality of rice, the less water it needs. Put rice and water in a thick saucepan, cover as soon as boiling is established, then leave undisturbed to simmer for 20 minutes.

CHINESE BOILED RICE II

4 Servings
250 gr (½ lb or 1 cup) rice   water

Put the rice into a fairly broad saucepan and cover with water, allowing 'two fingers', i.e. 2½ cm (1 in.) of water above the level of the rice. Bring to the boil and allow to boil fast until the water is absorbed. Cover with a lid, reduce heat to the minimum and leave to simmer for 12 minutes, without disturbing or uncovering.

JAPANESE BOILED RICE

Wash the rice an hour before cooking and leave to drain. Put in a deep saucepan, add water (allowing 1¼ cups water for 1 cup rice), cover, put on a high flame, bring to the boil, reduce heat, simmer for 10 minutes, bring heat down to its lowest, simmer for another 10 minutes, turn off the heat completely, but leave the pan to stand for a further 10 minutes before removing the cover.

Never take the lid off during cooking because the loss of steam affects the cooking process. You can check how far evaporation has gone (and the rice is ready when all the water has been absorbed, so complete evaporation signifies the end of cooking) by feeling the knob or handle of the saucepan lid. The bubbling of the water produces a vibration; if you can't feel any bubbling, the rice is done. It is also important to let the rice 'rest' for 10 minutes after cooking before uncovering. This prevents the rice going gummy and gives it an attractive 'risen' look.

BAKED KASHA (BUCKWHEAT)

Buckwheat, or burghul, a variety of Saracen corn, is delicious; possesses excellent nutritive qualities, an agreeable texture, an interesting nutty flavour and has been a popular cereal for a long time in many countries—it is mentioned in the Bible as arisah. In Russia is is called kasha and is traditionally served as an accompaniment to many dishes.

500 gr (1 lb) buckwheat water
1 teaspoon salt
60 gr (2 oz or 4 tablespoons)
   butter

Sort the buckwheat and pick out any black grains—these are perfectly wholesome but are unsightly, because they still retain their husks. Roast the buckwheat in an ungreased frying pan, stirring and taking care not to burn, until the grains acquire a pale golden colour.

Put in an ovenproof dish, season with salt, stir in butter and pour in enough boiling water to cover. Bake in a slow oven 135°C (275°F or Gas Mark 2) for 2½ to 3 hours. The amount of butter may be increased ad lib. The grains absorb it, and the Russian equivalent of 'you can't have too much of a good thing' is 'you can't spoil kasha with too much butter'.

FISH FORCEMEAT

250 gr (½ lb) skinned and   2 whites of egg
   boned fish   2½ dcl (½ pint or 1 cup) fresh
pinch salt and pepper   cream
pinch nutmeg

Chop and pound the fish in a mortar, or purée in a blender,

season and add the whites of egg, a little at a time. Blend until very smooth, chill for 2 hours. Whisk in cream a little at a time, season to taste and use as directed.

For prawn, shrimp and other shellfish forcemeat, follow this recipe, substituting equivalent amounts of prawns, etc., for fish.

TOMATO FONDUE

This is used in the preparation, as well as a garnish, for many hot and cold dishes.

1 medium-sized onion	1 grated clove garlic
1½ tablespoons butter (or oil)	salt and pepper
250 gr (½ lb) tomatoes	½ tablespoon chopped parsley

Chop the onion and cook until it becomes soft and transparent in butter (or oil depending on whether the dish for which it is intended is cooked with butter or oil). Peel, seed and chop the tomatoes and add to pan. Add garlic, season to taste, simmer gently until all the liquid yielded by the tomatoes evaporates. At the last moment sprinkle with chopped parsley.

FONDUE NIÇOISE

1 medium-sized onion	salt and pepper
1½ tablespoons butter (or oil)	½ tablespoon chopped parsley
250 gr (½ lb) tomatoes	1 teaspoon chopped tarragon
1 grated clove garlic	1 teaspoon chopped chervil

Chop the onion and cook, until it becomes soft and transparent, in butter (or oil depending on whether the dish for which it is intended is cooked with butter or oil). Peel, seed, and chop the tomatoes and add to pan. Add garlic, season to taste, simmer gently until all the liquid yielded by the tomatoes evaporates. At the last moment, sprinkle with chopped parsley, tarragon and chervil.

TEHINA

Tehina, a preparation which can best be described as a sesame seed butter, is used in Arab countries as a dip for bread. In Greece it is used as a lenten soup and in Israel it is a favourite hors-d'oeuvre. It is also a vital ingredient for making humous.

4 Servings

120 gr (4 oz or ¾ cup) sesame
  seeds
1–2 cloves crushed garlic
salt
150 ml (6 fl oz or ¾ cup) cold
  water
juice of 1–1½ lemons
pinch cayenne pepper or zhug
  (see below)

2 chopped hard-boiled eggs
  (optional)
2 tablespoons olive oil
pinch paprika
1 tablespoon chopped parsley
2 tablespoons black or green
  olives for garnish

Reduce the sesame seeds with garlic, salt and water to a paste in a blender. (If you don't possess a blender, then do as 99% of Middle Eastern housewives do—pound the sesame seeds and garlic in a mortar, adding water gradually to obtain a thick butter-like paste.)

Transfer to a bowl and, little by little, as for mayonnaise, stir in lemon juice. Season with cayenne pepper or zhug and the tehina is ready if you are going to use it as an ingredient for another dish.

If served as an independent hors d'oeuvre, add chopped egg, arrange on a serving dish, flattening the surface evenly, then make a few shallow channels with the back of a spoon. Trickle olive oil into these channels, sprinkle the surface with a small pinch of paprika, decorate with parsley, garnish with olives and serve.

ZHUG

This is one of a series of Yemeni bread dips. There are many others including, in order of popularity, hawayij, hilbeh, samneh.

These blends of spices, reminiscent of the Indian garam-masala are splendid for giving flavour to a simple meal. The Yemenites further claim that their immunity to coronary diseases, as well as to high blood pressure and the digestive troubles which afflict the Western world, is due to their use of these spice dips from time immemorial to the present day.

2 teaspoons black pepper
2 teaspoons caraway seeds
6–7 cardamom peeled seeds
3–4 dried red chillis

1 head garlic
a few coriander leaves
1 teaspoon salt

Grind all ingredients, blend well. Transfer to a jar with a tightly fitting lid and store until required.

VINDALOO PASTE

5–6 seeded fresh red chillis
1¾ cm (½ inch) slice of fresh
  green ginger
1½ teaspoons coriander

1 teaspoon cumin
1–2 cloves garlic
¼ teaspoon powdered turmeric

Combine all ingredients and pound in a mortar or blend in a liquidizer to make a smooth paste. Use as directed.

GARAM-MASALA

60 gr (2 oz or ½ cup) coriander
  seeds
60 gr (2 oz or ½ cup) black
  peppercorns
45 gr (1½ oz or 6 tablespoons)
  caraway seeds

15 gr (½ oz or 6 teaspoons)
  cloves
20 peeled cardamon seeds
15 gr (½ oz or 2 tablespoons)
  ground cinnamon

Mix all ingredients and grind. A coffee grinder does this job very well and the final product should be fine but not reduced to dust. Store in a jar with a well-fitting lid. Garam-masala is an essential ingredient in most curry dishes.

COCONUT MILK

Fresh or desiccated coconut can yield both cream and milk and this can be used for enriching many preparations, including meat dishes. It lends a velvety smoothness and mellowness to sauces.

To make coconut cream:

1 fresh coconut
100 ml (4 fl oz or ½–1 cup)
  boiling water

Ask the greengrocer to saw the coconut in half, pour out the liquid. (The natural, and drinkable, liquid inside the coconut is not coconut milk.) Extract the flesh by scraping it out. Pour boiling water over it and let it stand for twenty minutes. Squeeze out in a muslin bag or pass through a fine strainer. (An Indian restaurateur advocates the use of a potato presser for extracting coconut milk.) The first pressing produces coconut cream, which after several hours' refrigeration acquires the density of double cream.

To make coconut milk:

Put the husks of the coconut which has been pressed to extract cream into a pan, add the same amount of water as for the first pressing, bring to the boil, and press out again.

Both coconut cream and milk can be made in a liquidizer. Observe the indicated proportions, and blend a couple of tablespoonfuls of grated or shredded coconut and water at a time. Then squeeze through a muslin bag as described. If fresh coconut is not available good quality desiccated coconut may be used.

HORSERADISH JELLY

240 gr (½ lb or 1 cup) sugar
120 ml (4 oz or ½ cup) white vinegar
75 gr (2½ oz or ½ cup) freshly grated horseradish

juice of ½ lemon (or ¼ teaspoon) tartaric acid
1 sweet red pepper

Put sugar and vinegar into a pan, bring to the boil, simmer for 5 minutes. Add horseradish, bring to the boil and add lemon juice. Stir with a wooden spoon, boil fast for 1 minute, remove from heat, skim with a perforated spoon and leave to stand for a few minutes.

Cut the pepper, discard seeds, shred into very thin strips and stir into horseradish. Pour into a hot, dry jar, cover with a circle of waxed paper and seal with a well-fitting cap.

FRIED PARSLEY

30–60 gr (1–2 oz) parsley
1 tablespoon melted butter or margarine

Wash the parsley, cut off the long stalks, dip lightly in melted butter or margarine and put in a hot oven to dry off. Be careful not to burn.

Alternative method: Heat a large cup of olive oil until it begins to smoke. Trim, wash and dry the parsley on a cloth, drop into sizzling oil for two minutes, stir, take out with a perforated spoon, drain on a piece of kitchen paper, sprinkle with salt and use for garnishing.

CROÛTONS

Bread cut in dice or sliced in any shape or size, fried in oil, butter or any other fat. Croûtons can also be toasted under the grill or dried in the oven.

GLOSSARY

AJI-NO-MOTO. Japanese variant of monosodium glutamate, seasoning powder, known as Ve-Tsin in Chinese cookery. Tasteless in itself but excellent for bringing out flavours.

BAIN-MARIE. Vessel containing hot water in which foods can be poached and various dishes and sauces can be kept hot without coming into contact with direct source of heat.

BARDING. To bard is to cover a piece of meat, poultry, game or large fish with thin slices of salt or fresh pork or rashers of bacon, to protect delicate flesh of all kinds and it is normally removed after cooking.

BLANCHING. Boiling various ingredients for 1–2 minutes. Some foods, previously soaked in cold water (such as calf's head, kidneys, sweetbreads, certain vegetables, etc.) are blanched in water gradually brought to the boil, both to cleanse and harden them, and to remove a strong taste.

BLEU (AU BLEU). Method of poaching fish (mainly trout) in water and vinegar, which gives the fish a beautiful bluish colour.

BLIND (BAKED). Method of baking a flan, or pie shell, or any other pastry case 'blind', i.e. empty.

BLINI. Russian pancakes, made of yeast batter.

BOUCHÉE. A small puff-pastry pattie.

BOUILLON. Stock.

BOUQUET GARNI. A faggot or bunch of herbs, normally containing three sprigs of parsley, one sprig of thyme and small bay leaf. To facilitate extraction from soups, sauces, stews, etc., tie together in a piece of muslin.

BRANDADE. A salt cod dish, speciality of Languedoc and Provence.

BROCHETTE, EN. On skewers.

BRUNOISE. Finely shredded or diced vegetables, cooked in butter or other fat.

BUCKWHEAT. Blé noir, a variety of Saracen corn.

CHORIZO. Hard, Spanish, paprika-spiced sausage. Used in paella.

COULIBIAC. A Russian pie, usually hot and often made of brioche dough or puff pastry with a filling of salmon, veziga, etc.

COURT-BOUILLON. Aromatized liquid for cooking meat, fish, vegetables. See recipes.

CROUTONS. Bread cut in dice or sliced any shape or size, fried in

225

oil, butter or any other fat; toasted under the grill or dried in the oven.

DASHI. Japanese stock, based on dried bonito shavings and konbu seaweed.

FINES HERBES. Equal parts of finely chopped chervil, chives, parsley and tarragon.

FUMET. Liquid used to give flavour and body to stocks and sauces, made by boiling down almost to nothing foodstuffs of various kinds, either in stock or wine. Also concentrated fish stock.

JULIENNE. Food cut to match-like shreds.

KASHA. See Buckwheat.

MACERATE. To steep food.

MARINADE. A seasoned liquid, cooked or uncooked, in which fish is steeped before cooking. The purpose is to impregnate the fish with the flavour of the marinade. It also tenderises the flesh and increases its keeping qualities.

PAPILLOTES, EN. Cooked in greased paper.

PARCH, TO. Operation applied to sesame seeds, consisting of dry-frying them in a pan until they begin to 'jump'.

ROUX. A mixture of butter (or other fats) and flour, cooked for varying periods of time, used for thickening sauces and soups.

TABASCO. A bottled sauce, made of capsicums matured in sherry, hot and spicy and to be used very sparingly.

TEMPURA. A great Japanese speciality consisting of ingredients dipped in batter and deep fried.

VOL-AU-VENT. Puff pastry case filled with fish, shellfish and various other mixtures.

Index

237